Startup.com

Sebastian Nokes

FINANCIAL TIMES
Prentice Hall

An imprint of Pearson Education

London • New York • San Francisco • Toronto • Sydney • Tokyo • Singapore
Hong Kong • Cape Town • Madrid • Paris • Milan • Munich • Amsterdam

PEARSON EDUCATION LIMITED

Head Office:
Edinburgh Gate
Harlow CM20 2JE
Tel: +44 (0)1279 623623
Fax: +44 (0)1279 431059

London Office:
128 Long Acre
London WC2E 9AN
Tel: +44 (0)20 7447 2000
Fax: +44(0)20 7240 5771

Website www.business-minds.com

First published in Great Britain 2000 © Sebastian Nokes 2000
Email: Nokes@ITVA.Net   URL: *http://www.ITVA.net*
ITVA is a trademark of Sebastian Nokes.

The right of Sebastian Nokes to be identified as author of this work has been asserted by him in accordance with the Copyright, Designs and Patents Act 1988. The rights of Keith Young, KPMG, Iqbal S. Bassi, Charles E. Bruin, Mannie Gill, Alastair Shaw, Michael Cover, Andrew Millet, and Edmond Jackson to be identified as authors of their respective sections of this work have been asserted by them in accordance with the copyright, Designs and Patents Act 1988.

ISBN 0-273-65091-2

British Library Cataloguing in Publication Data
A catalogue record for this book is available from the British Library.

This publication is designed to provide accurate and authoritative information in regard to the subject matter covered. It is sold with the understanding that neither the authors nor the publisher is engaged in rendering legal, investing, or any other professional service. If legal advice or other expert assistance is required, the service of a competent professional person should be sought.

The publisher and contributors make no representation, express or implied, with regard to the accuracy of the information contained in this book and cannot accept any responsibility or liability for any errors or omissions that it may contain.

Many of the designations used by manufacturers and sellers to distinguish their products are claimed as trademarks. Pearson Education Limited has made every attempt to supply trademark information about manufacturers and their products mentioned in this book.

10 9 8 7 6 5 4 3 2 1

Typeset by M Rules.
Printed and bound in the United Kingdom by Biddles of Guildford Ltd.

The publishers' policy is to use paper manufactured from sustainable forests.

Acknowledgements

The publishers wish to thank *The Economist* for permission to reproduce 'Internet Economics, A Thinker's Guide' in Chapter 1; Tornado-Insider.com for permission to reproduce 'Michael Jackson – Taking Sweet Equity' in Chapter 2 and 'Of Grassroots and Revolutions' and 'Guy Kawasaki – A Master of High-Tech Theatre' in Chapter 4; and Moody's for permission to reproduce Table 1 in the Appendix.

Contents

Introduction

Keith Young

Executive Chairman, NetB2B2

You can be a successful entrepreneur. You can change the world. You can be anything you want to be. You are lucky. Five years ago this was not possible for most people. In the UK and in Europe generally, we did not think ourselves a nation of entrepreneurs. That was something in our past. Our ancestors had done that, but to build a big business these days – most of us thought five years ago – meant either being a complete maverick or being well connected and probably fairly old. But innovation is back. Entrepreneurship is accessible. The Internet means that anyone with a great idea can start a business; and look how many people have. So many people started Internet businesses in 2000 that the trade mark offices and stock exchanges of the world can barely cope with the increase in workload. What's happening is that there is a fundamental shift of power away from the large corporations of the last century towards new kinds of organizations where individual talent and individual values are recognized and rewarded. Large corporations will still survive, but they must change. The Internet is the most liberating force that the business world has seen for a century.

This book has been written by people who are working in Internet businesses and have succeeded in creating new kinds of organizations and new kinds of business. We hope that it will be useful for others who wish to join the Internet economy and share in the excitement, the reward for delivering value, and the challenges of building a new world. It's hard work, and it is risky work. There are many general guides to setting up a traditional new business, that show how to form a company, how to draw up reports and accounts, and so on. Those guides are useful, but this is not one of those guides. This book assumes that you have all that general business start-up knowledge already. The contributors to this book have been asked to focus on issues that are of immediate practical relevance to the entrepreneur who is setting up or running an Internet business. It will also be useful to the investors and the advisers, managers, suppliers and customers of that entrepreneur.

Some of the most valuable property in the world is in Manhattan. It was once almost worthless bush. The Internet is like a new (uninhabited) country. It is still relatively easy to turn up and claim a piece of property in the new Internet economy that will become valuable. And it *will* become valuable if it is useful to others, but speed is vital. Your idea must be evaluated and implemented fast, today. Next week six other people who are better or brighter or faster or luckier than you could turn up on the same patch of idea and start work. The headstart that you have is your best protection in the new Internet economy against someone else with the same new idea. Use your headstart – this is Internet time! We see many Internet entrepreneurs in Europe who are trying to reinvent what was done six months ago in the USA. There is no need to take on such an unequal struggle, because there is plenty of new space to plant your entrepreneurial venture. The Wireless Application Protocol (WAP) is the new Internet for mobile phones, and many European entrepreneurs have stolen a march on their US competitors in WAP and similarly in cryptography. You must find out who in the USA may have been developing your idea already.

The book you are reading starts with Chapter 1 by Sebastian Nokes, who is one of our managers at NetB2B2. Chapter 1 shows some of the ways that the Internet environment is different from the traditional business environment. Most big and great ideas start with a plan of some kind. They don't just happen. KPMG have written Chapter 2 on how to plan your Internet business. Plans don't get implemented without people. Good people are rare anyway, and one of the problems you are likely to have as an Internet entrepreneur is to find and retain the right people. The Internet has enabled good people to set themselves up in a business with good prospects more easily than ever before. Renaissance Search & Selection are uniquely well positioned to write about how to hire the right people, and have done so here in Chapter 3. But having looked at the problems of finding your team, are you the right person to run the business? Do you have what it takes? Most people, at least until now, would rather take the considerable comforts of a corporate position than tread the hard path of entrepreneurship, and perhaps they are right. Are you different? Have you got what it takes? Alastair Shaw asks you these questions in Chapter 4. Once you have decided that you are the right person for the job, you have assembled your team according to your plan and you are at last in business, what is to stop someone from copying you and cheating you of the success that we all hope you deserve? Intellectual property rights (IPR) exist precisely to do this. Michael Cover, of Mishcon de Reya, a law firm with considerable Internet expertise, describes the possible approaches to securing your IPR in an Internet business, in Chapter 5. Even if a patent is likely to be contended, it is usually preferable to be arguing as the party that owns the patent instead of being the party arguing that someone else's patent should be voided. (Just think of the fun you could have had if you had thought of patenting the 'one click' ordering process on the Internet!) Often it is easier to secure funding if you own the rights to the IPR relevant to your ideas. KPMG, in Chapter 6 on raising funds, show you what to do to get the money that you need. Not all new entrepreneurs are aware of the range of funding that is available these days, and KPMG have enormous experience in this area. Next, Andrew Millett and James Wilcox, of Mishcon de Reya (Chapter 7), cover the legal aspects of running an Internet business. Fifteen years ago few employees in small IT start-ups received equity stakes, but today it is unusual for key managers to join Internet start-ups without equity stakes. This has made the legal aspects of setting up and running an Internet business far more complex than before. So, by this stage you have your new

Internet business and it has grown, thanks to the very hard work put in by your team. Your team includes not just you and your staff but your bankers, advisers, shareholders, suppliers and customers, as well as your families and, ultimately, much of society – society at large really does cheer for the Internet entrepreneur. After all this hard work, you want an exit route, and Chapter 9 by KPMG covers this area, but it is preceded by Chapter 8 in case your market or the whole economy experiences some turbulence or even a crash landing before you get to the exit. The world is a risky place, and in Chapter 8 Sebastian Nokes reappears to provide a sort of emergency landing card for Internet businesses, the aim being to make sure that you survive and get to the exit another time. Sitting in the control tower all the while that you are preparing for the take-off of your Internet business, flying it and then exiting safely is a group of silent but powerful figures. They are the financial analyst, the fund manager, and the wealthy private investor. Edmond Jackson has been all these things, and is also an Internet entrepreneur and financial journalist. In Chapter 10 Edmond has set out a useful review of how your business is perceived and analyzed by the professional investor or the private investor. Lastly, the book closes with an Appendix containing a sample business plan, successfully used to apply for seed funding.

We hope that you find this book helpful. Please email any suggestions for improvements to me at *KY@ITVA.Net*. Finally, the editor and I would like to thank all those who contributed to this book, who have given valuable time when there were many competing demands. We also thank Stephen Temblett, Katherin Ekstrom and all the team at Financial Times Prentice Hall.

1 Understand what the Internet and the high-tech revolution are about

Sebastian Nokes

Aim

The Internet's business motto is 'Fire, ready, aim!'. There are many entrepreneurs and advisers to entrepreneurs who have made their fortunes quickly without paying any attention to what the Internet is and why it's different in some respects from the traditional business environment. However, there are even more people who have lost money because they tried to set up an Internet business or they invested in an Internet stock without trying to understand what is different about the Internet. If you are the first kind of person, skip this chapter, but if you are interested in what's different about the Internet, then read on. There is no shame in not understanding much about how and why the Internet is different. One of the world's best technology banks turned down a proposal from one of its employees, called Jeff Bezos, to found a bookstore to sell books over the Internet. Jeff started Amazon.com, made books cheaper and more accessible to millions of people, and collected a fortune. He worked with dozens of Internet experts who all missed the genius in his idea. Right now nobody understands what the Internet means for business and economics to any great extent – we're all still learning. The point is to have an idea of what some of the issues are, so that you can learn and improve your business judgement efficiently as you go along, whether you are running an Internet business or investing. The aim of this chapter is to explain the fundamental business issues concerning the Internet which are different from normal business issues.

The Internet's fundamental economic forces

The most powerful economic forces are changes in social trends or social structure. Fortunes can be made by understanding these trends (as well as having a little luck). For example, the demographic trend in the West is towards an ageing population. This trend is certain, because the 60-year-olds of 50 years hence have already been born, and so the number of 60-year-olds that there will be in 2050 can be predicted with great certainty. This means that it is a fact, or as much of a fact as there ever can be in business forecasting, that the market for products used by the elderly will get larger than it is today.

That example may seem unexciting, but the point is not excitement but to understand your market, and this example shows that in some markets it is possible to understand vital aspects of a market, such as market size, very well. In contrast, many people did not understand the true size of the Internet market. In 1995 in Europe this was perhaps excusable, but in 1998 when many business planners in large corporations, particularly banks and investment banks in Europe, did not understand the huge market size of the Internet it was inexcusable, because the evidence was already there. Why should it have been possible to have seen in 1998, or even in 1995, that the Internet would be huge in Europe? Firstly, because it already had become so in the USA. But secondly, because it was possible to use the Internet and feel its power directly. Consider the case of John Evans (not his real name), a manager at an investment bank who told the author in 1998 that rich people would never use the Internet much for banking. First of all, this was in fact not true at the time anyway, but, more interestingly, dear old John had never himself used the Internet, he had his secretary print off his email for him to read. (She would fax it to him if he was in the bank's overseas offices.) When he did get around to using email in 1999, John found it an incredibly powerful tool for communicating and managing. Once he tried it, he wanted to use email directly, himself, all the time. The point of this little story, apart from poking fun at an out-of-touch investment banker, is that there are some things that exert an extraordinary influence over how people behave. The economics, the business case, the profit/loss and the balance sheet all follow far behind the fundamentals that affect human behaviour. The English longbow was a more effective weapon in every respect than the musket that superseded it, and the longbow remained in many senses more effective a weapon than many rifles until this century. Only with the machine gun was the longbow finally made obsolete. If so, why was the longbow superseded so early on by the musket, a much inferior weapon in accuracy, rate of fire, logistic support requirement and killing power? It was superseded because the average Briton was no longer prepared to spend the enormous amount of time practising longbow technique, but wanted to play football instead.

It is human preferences and behaviour which come first, and economics second. In this chapter we will set out a few key ideas that will help you to think about what to look for with regard to human behaviour as it affects the value of business propositions on the Internet. In the context of our longbow example, the bright young manager on-the-make at stodgy old British Longbow plc might have concluded that, given the social trends of the time, he should leave and set up Manchester United FC. Nobody at the time really understood what football was, but anyone who experienced it would have realized that it was a powerful force and that there was money to be made.

A related point is our ability to notice behaviour. Changes in behaviour mean something from a business point of view only if they can be detected. If no one can tell that the people in a town a hundred miles away really want to buy your clothes rather than the clothes they would normally buy, then nothing changes. This was the situation before mail order catalogues. Mail order catalogues released a pent-up demand for new fashions and styles that had existed for a long time, but either was not detectable or was not usable. The fortunes that were made in an earlier age by the entrepreneurs who started mail order businesses were not made primarily because of improvements in postal services or catalogue printing technology or supply-chain management, although certainly all those things were necessary ingredients to success. The prime force was the untapped desire to buy a wider range of goods than was available in the provincial town. Changes in human behaviour are not the only drivers of economic change and business opportunity, but they are the most powerful.

We will look at ten areas where the Internet either changes the way that people behave or increases our ability to monitor human behaviour. We are not claiming that the list is complete, and we are certainly not claiming to understand the business impact of the Internet fully by setting out this list. The aim is to give you ideas to help you think efficiently about the Internet opportunities and the threats you face as an entrepreneur, investor or adviser. These ten areas are:

- social power;
- knowledge democratization;
- micromeasurement;
- network effects;
- disintermediation;
- global reach;
- tax arbitrage;
- market organization;
- boundaries of the firm;
- business process automation.

Social power

Summary

Social power is a term that means the power deriving from basic human wants, such as the wants for food, shelter, companionship and learning. These wants change as societies develop. Social power often precedes and causes economic change, and is the most powerful force for economic change that there is. There are aspects on the Internet that latch on to and perhaps catalyze social power, and these have been used by some enterprising individuals as great engines of business growth in a few areas of e-commerce.

We started the chapter with John Evans, the boring banker, and how his email phobia turned into a passionate embrace of the Internet. There is a basic human desire to communicate. The growth of mobile telephones exceeded the expectations of many analysts. The analysts made what seemed to them reasonable assumptions about how much people would be prepared to spend on mobile telephony, but they were wrong. Why then could their assumptions have been described as reasonable? The analysts were using data on disposable income. The problem is that the mass market is made up of ordinary folk who don't know what disposable income means and certainly are not constrained by the abstract theory studied in some large corporate strategic planning department. Ordinary people just know that they want a mobile phone, and then go and buy one. They worry about paying for it later. Other examples of social power not conforming to the tidy models of business planners include the outcry over Shell's decision to dump an oil platform in the North Sea. Economically and environmentally it was probably the right thing to do, but the decision itself and the bureaucratic handling of it by Shell triggered a strong social response in many people, and for a while damaged Shell's business. The debate in the UK over whether to abandon sterling and use the euro is not argued in terms that have much at all to do with the fundamentals of business. Successive UK governments have raped the poor average UK citizen by devaluing the pound until it is now worth less than a penny of a pound sterling from the last century. Social power has been used to manipulate a vital national debate away from the real issues. This demonstrates the magnitude of social power.

The Internet is about a shift in power – a shift so large that it is unleashing a social force that will dwarf anything seen in the debate over the euro or over a few oil rigs tossed into the wrong place. The Great War ended Europe's economic, technical and cultural superiority over the rest of the world and the United States has led in all these fields since then. The size of social forces that the Internet is unleashing has not been seen in the world since the Great War. Imagine how governments, tax, police and healthcare will have to change when every voter can give direct feedback every week or every day to their government. Think how different your life would be. Imagine also how differently wars will be fought when individual soldiers call home to their loved ones from their trenches in the middle of battle – will wars ever be the same again? The Internet could also eventually mean a return to Athenian democracy – but with women enfranchised and without slavery. This will not happen overnight, and there will be a million steps forward and half a million steps backwards along the road to this new digital Camelot (*Camelot.gov*, perhaps).

The Internet will cause massive shifts in power because, at its most fundamental, it gives people more control over their lives. In the 1960s, people who wanted numbers crunched had to rely on teams of accountants to crunch the numbers literally by hand, with manual adding machines. This was expensive and very few managers had the authority to requisition such a large pool of corporate resources. In the 1970s, data processing departments became widespread, and the managers of these temples to mainframes wielded great power because no one else had so much analytical resource available and it was not in the career interests of the data processing centre managers to tell anyone too much about what they did to manage these resources. Then in the 1980s came first the minicomputer and then the PC. At last, individual managers could take control of their own computing and didn't need to care or be interested in what the data processing department did. The data processing department cared very much that its status was sinking. It had become completely out of touch with the needs of its corporate paymasters, and of society at large.

Lotus 123 was the first commercial spreadsheet marketed on a major scale. It produced a phenomenon known in the financial world as the '1, 2, 3 Takeover!' because for a few hundred pounds a manager could analyze a potential takeover situation in massive detail in just a few days, compared with the months of work that previously would have been required to get the same level of understanding of the opportunity. But human endeavour depends on teamwork. Not the bogus teamwork of large corporate bureaucracies, where 'team player' is often used by the corporate jackal or the dissembler on-the-make to refer to his own kind, but the real teamwork where one person puts the good of the organization before his or her own interest or the political considerations of the department.

So at the end of the 1980s the manager at grass-roots level at last had real computing power at his disposal to wield as he saw fit for the good of the organization. However, he was still forced by the computer industry to work alone. Internally, the data processing department was uninterested in helping him share data and ideas with his co-workers by linking his computer to theirs. Externally, the IT industry tried to charge huge fees for membership of proprietary networks, or huge hourly rates to build point to point interfaces that would soon need updating anyway. From the point of view of a manager in the 1980s trying to do something useful for his company or the shareholders or society at large with a computer, the IT industry and the data processing departments of the time were often like a communist state, where everyone needed a passport just to travel around in their own country, and passports could be refused on the whim of some petty bureaucrat. Just as communism fell after a long period of decline, so the communist model of computing finally collapsed in the 1990s, when the Internet took off and at last the average manager was free to exchange data and set up projects with any other individual in the world who was also on the Internet. Individual managers at last had control over their own digital destiny. We believe that in thinking about the Internet it is important not to underestimate the desire of people to control their environments and lives. The desire to control one's life seems to start during the teenage years, and first manifests itself with a demand to parents for ghastly clothes and loud posters or wallpaper, but this desire is in fact in all of us, and the Internet allows people more control over how they use computing and communication power.

Table 1.1 Where to look for the social power of the Internet

Where	What	How is this an example of social power?
www.hotmail.com	Free email service	Hotmail is a completely free email service. It is unusual in that users can access it from any Internet machine. Its phenomenal growth can be attributed to social power in the form of the desire to communicate. Some Hotmail facts as at June 1998: – in India, Hotmail had several hundred thousand users, despite never having done any marketing at all in India; – Hotmail had spent only $500 000 on advertising in its whole history to that date; – Hotmail became the largest provider of free email, and its service is supported by advertising revenue, which is possible because it has so many users, and the users spend so much time looking at their Hotmail screens.
http://freenet. sourceforge.net	'Freenet is a peer to peer network designed to allow the distribution of information over [the] Internet in an efficient manner, without fear of censorship.' (*Freenet's Web site*)	Freenet can be seen as a response by some programmers to the increasing encroachment into the Internet of regulation and legislation. Freenet does not have any centralized control. As well as being likely to improve the efficiency of information distribution over the Internet, it has the potential to render censorship of the Internet impossible. The Freenet project is an example of great social power in a specifically technical context: here is a very collaborative project to which many highly skilled IT experts are devoting their time, and in some cases careers, for no monetary gain, but instead because they believe in a society of free people.
Any Internet chat room, for example *http://chat.yahoo.com*	Lonely hearts columns in real time.	People meet, date and even get married because they meet in chat rooms on the Internet. This is perhaps the clearest demonstration of the social power of the Internet. Many people find these chat rooms addictive.
www.linux.com/ whatislinux/	Linux is the next big operating system and could possibly take over from Microsoft's Windows and NT systems, just as they took over from various mainframe operating systems in the early 1990s.	Linux can be seen as the strongest case yet of two powerful trends combining. First, the social power of the Internet, and second, the Internet's potential to allow news and more effective ways to shape and manage organizations. Linux was designed by Linus Torvalds and built by a loose community of IT professionals who believe that there is a better way to develop operating systems and the world's IT infrastructure than the way that mainframe and PC operating systems have been built traditionally. Many experts said that the Linux project would fail because such a large and complex system as a major computer operating system could not be managed except within the discipline of a traditional corporation. Linux has delivered higher quality, more powerful software than traditional corporations which used project structures that worked very well up until the 1990s.

Knowledge democratization

Summary

In the traditional business environment (the 'legacy' world), the few hoarded their knowledge as a means to exert power over the many. In the Internet world, the many have access to almost as much data as the few. This is likely to mean a more meritocratic world, and a less complacent business environment. Specifically, managers will have to succeed in future much more on their competence and less on the exclusivity of the data they have access to than before. And similarly, companies will have to learn to survive while serving a much better informed customer than before.

Knowledge is power. It may seem strange to us in the twenty-first century that kings once insisted on controlling the printing and copying of books, and that states regularly proscribed books and burned them. They did this because knowledge is power. Every middle manager in a large corporation also knows this. It is a rare company that allows junior employees the same access to corporate data as senior managers. To some extent, it is necessary to restrict the access which junior staff have to information on the grounds of confidentiality and commercial sensitivity, but the restriction of access to knowledge is also practised to keep power in the hands of those who already have it. Who in their career has not met a manager who has kept an interesting report to themselves instead of circulating it, so that that manager would appear better informed or more knowledgeable? As a Machiavellian tactic, this has worked until now, but the Internet is about sharing on a scale never possible before. Long ago the church resisted sharing the Bible with its members, and kept to itself the privilege of reading and interpreting the sacred text. When printing made the mass production of bibles possible, the protestant movement took off, wreaking great change in Europe. That was probably the last time the world saw the democratization of knowledge on the scale that the Internet is bringing about.

Imagine that you have a daughter who is dying a slow death. The doctors are sympathetic but are unable to help. You have no money to take your daughter around the best teaching hospitals of the world in search of a possible cure, and even if you sold your house, which big city would you fly to first? Until the Internet, ordinary people in this situation had little choice but to watch as their daughter slowly died. The Internet has made a difference for a number of families in such tragic situations. Parents have spent hours using the Internet to research possible cures or centres of medical expertise relevant to their child's ailment, in many cases making a real difference to their children and sometimes saving their lives. Even when it has not been possible to save their children's lives, the parents have been able to put all their energy into trying to do something that might be useful, something that has worked for others, by researching on the Internet. Before the

Internet, such precious medical knowledge was not democratized: it was stored away in a university or a hospital, inaccessible to many people who wanted it. Now that the Internet is democratizing such knowledge, people will not tolerate such information being unavailable.

The old Soviet Union had secret laws, that is, some laws were not known to the population. This meant that it was possible to break a law without knowing about it. Many in the free world prided themselves on having a fairer legal system than countries like the Soviet Union partly because the law was accessible to all. However, many of those countries that once quietly prided themselves on having accessible laws are now far behind Australia: there all laws are now published on the Internet for everyone to see.

The same trend that applies on a large scale to the availability of national laws applies on a small scale to corporate data. Some businesses still try to communicate company policies and ideas through paper memos. Modern companies use the Internet to display the information so that all employees can access company information whenever it's needed at the click of a mouse. Consider Joan, an employee in a company that has changed its travel policy. Joan gets the paper memo about the new travel policy. She doesn't travel much. She files the memo, which is unusual as she normally throws such things away. The next week Joan suddenly has to cover for Martha, her boss, who at the last minute has had to go to a press conference. Joan remembers that there is a new travel policy, and remembers filing the relevant company memo. Unfortunately, Joan can't find the memo. She spends 15 minutes looking for it, gives up and books her travel the way she always used to. What has happened here is that money has been spent printing and distributing paper memos, time has been spent filing them, space for filing cabinets has been paid for, and all this time and cost has been wasted because the information could not be found when needed. Further, as a result, the information contained in the memo has been ignored, which in this case cost the company money because Joan did not use the new, cheaper company-approved airline. It could all have been different: Joan would have received an email that the corporate travel policy had changed, and that details were on the intranet. Joan would have quickly deleted the email. The following week she would have gone straight to the travel section of the intranet, looked up the procedures, and found that there was an on-line travel requisition form. She would have spent much less time on bureaucracy, and she would have followed company procedures, thereby saving money and time.

Knowledge democratization means that management must get used to staff knowing more about the company. It means trusting staff to use that knowledge responsibly. It means that staff must behave reliably enough to be trusted with such knowledge.

Table 1.2   Where to look for the knowledge democratization on the Internet

Where	What	How is this an example of knowledge democratization?
In a sense the whole Internet is about knowledge democratization.		
www.medic8.com/ MedicalDatabases.htm	A collection of medical databases.	Before the Internet, this kind of data would have been very difficult for most people to access, at least in practice. Now it is accessible either for free or for a few euros a day at the nearest Internet café.
www.austlii.edu.au/ www.hcourt.gov.au	The first site contains a comprehensive set of links to the full texts of Australian law. The second site is the site of the High Court of Australia, the highest court in the Australian judicial system.	An Australian citizen trying to find the texts of the laws of his land can log on to the Internet and read the cases himself. Citizens in other countries wanting to do the same might be forced to travel to a law library and consult hard copies instead.
www.thesmokinggun.com	A Web site that 'brings you exclusive documents that can't be found elsewhere . . . Using material obtained . . . under the [US] Freedom of Information requests and from court files'.	While much of this material has *in principle* been available to anyone who cares to go and get it, the effort required to go and get it was usually prohibitive. Consider one example of a court case where a child bit into a big-brand cake only to eat a decidedly foreign ingredient (go to the site for more details). If you buy cakes in a supermarket regularly, would you want to know which manufacturer it was? This site shows how the Internet is altering the balance of power between large corporations or the state on the one hand, and the ordinary citizen on the other. As a hypothetical example, it is conceivable that a large corporation could use its considerable PR resources to limit the spread of news about some unpleasant mistakes that it has made, but sites like *Smoking Gun* are reducing the effectiveness of such efforts to hide important news from people.

Micromeasurement

Summary

The Internet enables more relevant aspects of the commercial environment to be measured. In particular, it enables more features of human behaviour and business behaviour to be measured. This increase in measurement, or the practicality of measurement, will allow those businesses which take advantage of it in ethical ways to prosper at the expense of those that don't. What isn't measured can't be managed. By enabling more to be measured, the Internet and IT generally extend our ability to manage business and society.

Flipping a coin is an unpredictable event. The result of flipping the coin will be either heads or tails, but we cannot predict which in advance. The emission of beta particles from the decay of a radioactive isotope is also a random event, and just like flipping a coin, we can't tell in advance when a beta particle will be emitted next. There is a big difference between the reasons why these two events are *in practice* unpredictable. *In principle* the result of flipping the coin is predictable, because if we measured all the forces in your arm and hand and all the air turbulence and all the imperfections in the structure of the coin, and all the other physical factors affecting the outcome of flipping, it would be possible to predict exactly what the outcome of the flip would be. The reason that coin flipping is in practice unpredictable is simply that it is impractical, and probably impossible, to measure all the factors that affect the outcome. If these could be measured, coin flipping might not be unpredictable in practice. As far as science knows at present, the radioactive decay of isotopes is different because it is in principle unpredictable. No amount of measurement of anything at all, as far as we know at the moment, will enable us to predict when a radioactive isotope will next emit a beta particle.

Computers generally and the Internet especially greatly increase our ability to measure. In the business context this means that we can examine and act on much more than ever before. In the old, paper-based economy, it was simply not practical to record as many things as can be recorded now. Even with computers, but without the Internet, the cost of recording and sharing data could be high. Consider a retail stockbroker. In the old economy, the broker would publish research by printing it and mailing it to the customers. This was expensive, so not all customers had access to all research. The stockbroker in the new economy could email the research to customers for a fraction of the cost, but there is an even better approach: set up a Web site that allows all customers to download what they want from the research library, and record who downloads what. Analyze this in conjunction with the sales ledger data that show which customers buy which products, and the broker can begin to make informed judgement on what kind of research sells what kinds of stocks, and to which kinds of customer. With some refinement, the broker's Web site could measure which parts of the reports are of most interest, so that the analysts writing the reports could spend less effort on the low-value added parts of the report and concentrate more on what shifts stock. All of this could have been done before the Internet, in principle, but not in practice. But with the Internet and the increasing number of business tools available on the Internet to enable companies to make micromeasurements about customer behaviour, it is now not only possible but actually inexpensive to implement micromeasurement techniques.

So, when thinking about how to set up your Internet business, think about what aspects of your customers' behaviour should be measured to enable you to maximize the value of the business. The chances are that someone has already built a tool to enable you to do just that.

For an example of micromeasurement, look at the usage statistics measurement services that are part of any e-commerce package or are part of many Web site hosting services. For a simple guide, see Yahoo!'s demonstration store at *http://store.yahoo.com*.

Network effects

Summary

A network effect is where the value of a service or a good depends on how many other people have the good or use the service. Network effects can give rise to positive feedback. They may also be associated with minimum efficient scales, where network effects apply only beyond a certain minimum scale. In that case it may be advantageous for the entrepreneur to invest to get the market up to the minimum efficient scale – this is sometimes called 'pump priming'.

The classic example of a network effect is the telephone. If you were the only person in the world with a telephone, then it would be no use to you at all. The more people there are who have a telephone, the more useful it is for any one individual to also have a telephone. This may sound obvious, but note that it is not true for all goods and services, and there are some kinds of goods or services which show inverse network effects, that is, the fewer people there are who have them, the more valuable they are. (Those situations are not usually described in terms of inverse network effects, but rather in terms of luxury or exclusivity.) Part of the attraction of owning a luxury product or of travelling first class is that few other people have the same product or are using the same service. Generally speaking, the Internet and the Web-based economy display strong network effects, but when thinking through how to set up and run your business, be sure to understand which parts of it show network effects, which parts may rely on exclusivity, and which parts are neutral. For example, one exception to the general rule that Web-

Table 1.3 Where to look for the network effects

Where	What	How is this relevant to network effects?
eBay.com *QXL.com* *Priceline.com*	The world's biggest auction site is eBay, and QXL is one of Europe's largest auction sites. eBay is worth about 20 times as much as Sotheby's, and Priceline.com, which sells airline tickets, is worth more than some large airlines.	If you are looking for something to buy at an auction, there are two advantages of going to a bigger auction. First, the auction is more likely to be selling what you want to buy. Second, a large auction market is more likely to be efficient than a smaller one, which reduces the risk of you overpaying. Conversely, it also reduces the 'risk' of you underpaying – but this is an advantage if you are a seller. Another advantage from the seller's point of view is that there is more likely to be a buyer in a larger auction than in a smaller auction.
Mysimon.com *Evenbetter.com*	Price comparison services which can tell you where to buy the cheapest toothpaste or toaster.	The more outlets a comparison service covers, the more accurate and the more valuable it is. Of course, this may be valuable to you the consumer, but it may not be valuable at all to the retailer or the manufacturer because it may force them to reduce prices. Network effects can be one-sided.
www.cpb.nl/nl/pub/pubs/ werkdoc_122	A page giving a formal description of network effects and related topics. See Section 4.2.	Relates network effects to externalities (three kinds) and excess inertia. May be useful for entrepreneurs who are about to pitch to trained economists.
www.aol.com	AOL (America Online) was one of the largest proprietary bulletin boards in the days before the Internet took off. It has managed to become one of the world's leading Internet service providers (ISP).	AOL's old business model was to use the network effect to build its own proprietary network. The Internet arrived and made this impossible. AOL realized this, and unusually for a large corporation, was able to abandon its previous business model relatively quickly and embrace the different network effects of the Internet, and today it is one of the largest Internet companies in the world. The moral of this story is to watch out for rapidly changing network effects in your market.

based businesses show strong network effects is bandwidth. The more people there are who share the same bandwidth, the less valuable the bandwidth service. A practical instance of this is in cable modems. Access to the Internet by means of cable modems is often sold as providing very high bandwidth. However, the way that the cable networks have been built tends to mean that if you are the only person in your street using a cable modem, then it is true that you will have huge bandwidth, but the more people in your street who join you in having a cable modem for Internet access, the worse the service becomes.

One corollary of network effects can be positive feedback, which means that the more people there are on a network, such as a telephone network, the more likely it is that another person will join. When there is only one other person in the whole world with a telephone, there is much less attraction to having a telephone than when there are hundreds. This example also introduces the idea of a minimum economic scale. The minimum economic scale of a network is the scale below which it is uneconomic for the network to operate. Continuing with the example of the telephone, suppose that in the world when there was only one telephone, a widget factory had calculated that there would need to be 100 other businesses with a telephone to justify the cost of the widget factory installing a system of its own, perhaps because the factory believed that if there were 100 other businesses then it could make enough cold selling calls to generate sufficient widget sales to justify the cost of having a telephone system. In this case, from the point of view of the widget factory, the minimum efficient scale of the telephone system is 101 telephones. This in turn means that it would not be viable for any business to buy a telephone in our example until 100 other businesses had a telephone. The positive feedback aspect here is that as more other businesses have a telephone, it is more valuable for the widget factory to have one. From the point of view of the telephone manufacturer, it may be worth giving away the first 100 telephones or at least subsidizing them if it helps to get the telephone network started. This is known as 'pump priming'.

For the entrepreneur, identify network effects in your business space. How does your idea take advantage of them? Where might pump priming be required?

Disintermediation

Summary

Any transaction can be either direct, between two contracting parties (e.g. buyer and seller), or it can be indirect, in which case there is at least one intermediary. Intermediaries are not free, they come attached to a cost. In the legacy economy it was often the case that intermediaries could be justified because the cost of having an intermediary was lower than the cost of not having one. The Internet is changing this for many intermediaries, either by providing a lower cost automatic intermediary, or by eliminating the need for any intermediary.

In the 1990s many middle managers in large and small organizations argued that the Internet would never amount to much, and especially not in their particular industry. Why? A charitable explanation is that these professional business managers had simply not understood the Internet. A less charitable explanation would be that many of these people were painfully aware of their own shortcomings as managers and knew that the Internet would do them out of a job, perhaps for life. Middle managers add value by interpreting the decisions of senior managers and controlling their execution by lower-level managers or workers. If things change so that the decisions of senior managers can be executed directly by the workers or lower-level managers, then there is no point keeping middle managers on the payroll. This might sound somewhat brutal, but the word 'disintermediation' means getting rid of the middle man, whether the middle manager within an organization or the broker or retailer that stands between one organization or individual and another. Amazon has disintermediated the high street book shop. E*Trade has disintermediated the traditional retail stockbroker. Lastminute.com is trying to disintermediate some aspects of what the high street travel agent does. First-e and many other banks are disintermediating the high street bank.

In 1994, senior management in British Telecom's Martlesham Heath research laboratories noticed that by using email, a manager could manage nearly 100 subordinates effectively, whereas previously a manager's 'span' had been a maximum of about 30 subordinates. There was apparently scope to disintermediate two managers for every 100 direct reports, though we do not know if this did in fact happen. However, if British Telecom as a company had not acted on similar opportunities to reduce cost by eliminating jobs made redundant, then some other telecoms company would have done, which would have given the other telecoms company a cost advantage over British Telecom.

Disintermediation is always painful. At best, it means that individuals must adapt quickly to performing a brand new job in a restructured or different department. At worst, it means that individuals lose their jobs. Whether disintermediation effects put at risk people in the same organization or people in the suppliers and customers of an organization, there are very few people who do not find it unpleasant to have to work out and implement the consequences of disintermediation. This is where the Internet entrepreneur has an advantage. It is always easier for a new organization to take advantage of the opportunities for disintermediation than it is for an existing player. The existing player must find people who will plan and implement the redundancy of colleagues and business partners. The new Internet start-up merely has to set up an organization that takes advantage of the latest opportunities for efficiency.

The point for you the Internet entrepreneur is to look at what opportunities the Internet creates for disintermediation. What are the opportunities it creates within the internal structure of your competition, your suppliers, and your customers, and how can your new business exploit those? Secondly, what are the opportunities that the Internet creates for disintermediation in the structure of the market in which your business will operate? Look particularly at the supply chain, and the marketing channels and the

Legacy process

| Customer telephones broker | —1 min→ | Customer places order | —1 min→ | Broker gets quote from system | —2 mins→ | Broker calls market maker and deals | —1 min→ | Broker writes ticket | —3 days→ | Certificates posted to customer | —2 days→ | Postal service delivers certificates |

Internet process

| Customer logs on to the Internet and his on-line brokerage | —2 mins→ | Customer places order | —30 seconds→ | System emails customer to confirm trade | —1 hour→ | Shares transferred to customer's nominee a/c |

Not only is the Internet-based process much faster, there is less risk of miscommunication, and it can be at a much lower cost.

Fig. 1.1 Disintermediation: retail customer buying a publicly quoted share

distribution channels. Two-thirds of successful Internet businesses are successful because they have disintermediated someone else.

Global reach

Summary

Much of the way that business is done now assumes that geography matters. Before the Internet geography mattered for finding customers, fulfilling their orders and for the regulation of the two foregoing activities. On the Internet, geography rarely matters for finding customers, but it sometimes matters just as much as it always did for fulfilling orders from customers. Many regulators would like to pretend that geography will always matter for regulation, but it is not clear that this is or should be the case.

The Internet is global. Or is it? If it is global, why is there an Amazon.co.uk as well as an Amazon.com? Why do the European subsidiaries of the big US on-line retail stockbrokers behave as if they are not part of their parent companies, for instance, by charging more to sell a US stock to a European investor than selling a US stock to a US investor? There are three relevant factors: *communication*, *fulfilment* and *regulation*.

For communication, the Internet is global. Communication costs over the Internet are not affected by distance, and access to all sites is in principle the same from all countries.

Fulfilment means delivering the good or service that was ordered. Fulfilment will not always be global. The foreign exchange market is global and a Swiss franc is worth almost the same whether it is given to you in Singapore, Basle or Rio de Janeiro. Swiss francs can in effect be transmitted anywhere in the world by the SWIFT electronic payments system, so that you can move Swiss francs in and out of your accounts in Singapore, Basle and Rio de Janeiro easily and almost immediately. Books and CDs are easy to ship, but not as easy as Swiss francs can be 'shipped' over SWIFT, whereas haircuts don't ship at all. Amazon.com can fulfil orders for books from anywhere in the world, at a price, by using the postal services of the countries of the world or a courier service, but haircuts cannot be sold over the Internet in anything like the same way because a haircut is a service that doesn't travel, which means that even if orders for haircuts were taken, they could not be fulfilled.

Having discussed selling goods and services and then fulfilling those sales orders, let us turn to legislation. In some industries, such as retail financial services, it is the case that in most countries there are severe legal restrictions on the provision and fulfilment of goods and services: no matter what it is practical to fulfil, it is only legal to provide and fulfil rather less. There is no reason why US stockbrokers should not sell US stocks to people in the UK directly from their US sites. The British government does not like this idea, but as the US brokers are breaking no US laws in doing so, they can. However, most US on-line brokers won't sell stocks to customers in the UK, though some do. Those that won't tend to be the ones that have set up or are interested in setting up a retail financial service operation in the UK. The point is that even when something is legal, not all the established players will take the advantage offered to create and fulfil orders. This may mean that there is a gap for you the entrepreneur.

Case study

Global reach

In the legacy world, if you moved away from home to get a better job but wanted to stay in touch with your roots by listening to your local radio, tough! Worse, if you lived somewhere with poor local radio – the DJs had all the charisma of a parking ticket – there was nothing you could do. All that has changed with the Internet. Whether you live in Sevres or Scunthorpe, Schaffhausen or Bad Toltz, you can listen to local radio from London, San Francisco and Tokyo easily and cheaply on the Internet. People in Peebles and Peenemunde can now listen to the sounds of downtown Nashville, Tennessee (which may make them think twice about emigrating).

http://wmbr.mit.edu/stations/list.html – a comprehensive list of Internet radio stations from around the world

http://realguide.real.com/stations – more radio stations

Tax arbitrage

Summary

Tax has always been a major consideration in business and politics. The Internet poses new challenges to those setting taxes and offers new opportunities to businesses and individuals to manage their tax affairs. It will take some time for the fiscal community to adjust to the Internet's impact.

Assume that you are not a millionaire. Assume that you have £117.50 to spend. Further assume that you have very little time, you are treasurer of a charity for sick children, and you like taking your aged parents to tea at the local hotel. You are checking the performance of your stock portfolio on the Internet one day when you see an advertisement for a piece of software that looks like just what the children's charity really needs to manage its next publicity campaign. The software is provided by a firm in the USA and costs the equivalent of £100. It downloads over the Internet. You spend a few minutes investigating the software's Web site, and it is precisely what the children's charity needs. The only problem is that right now the children's charity has no money. But you are a generous sort, and decide that you are prepared to spend some of your own money to buy the charity for sick children what it needs in this case. Now you have a decision. Do you (a) buy the software, go through the bother of telephoning Her Majesty's Customs and Excise to report the transaction for Value Added Tax purposes, thereby costing yourself £17.50, a lot of time and half a tree's worth of form filling? Or do you (b) download the software, forget about trying to pay VAT, and spend the £17.50 thus saved on taking your beloved parents to tea that afternoon, which also uses up the time that would otherwise have been spent filling in the VAT paperwork and trying to explain what the Internet is to some remote tax bureaucrat? There is little doubt that most readers of this book would have no hesitation in choosing option (a), but there is some evidence that a small number of people would choose option (b). This horrible little story keeps many bureaucrats awake at night.

The problem that the Internet poses to tax authorities is severe. Their immediate reaction is to legislate to impose taxes on the Internet. In this the tax authorities have the support of many politicians and some lawyers. The question is whether legislation and the will of national governments are sufficiently powerful to achieve the hopes of the tax authorities. There are many precedents where governments have tried and failed to legislate or coerce the world to behave in a particular way. The Eurobond market owes its very existence to the US government's doomed attempt to tax its domestic bond market in the 1960s. Governments can be slow to learn, and the UK government is close to destroying the livelihoods of tens of thousands of people in London who work in the Eurobond market by repeating exactly the same mistake that the US government made. The English poll tax, the German withholding tax, the UK's support for the EMU – there are many examples of where governments have found they lacked the power to enforce a tax or quasi-tax.

What does this mean for the entrepreneur? We advise against using the Internet to evade tax. Apart from being illegal, it is a high-risk strategy. But it is also not where the greatest opportunity lies for the entrepreneur who thinks through the tax implications of the Internet for his or her business. The debates about tax and the changes in tax regimes are played out slowly and on a large scale, and the big corporations make much of the running. The opportunity for the entrepreneur is to see which way taxes on the Internet are likely to go, and then to use this understanding to structure the business efficiently. For example, in the 1960s the money made in the bond market was not made by evading the new US tax on bonds, it was made by people who were the first to shift their bond operations from the US to London, and also by entrepreneurs in London who got ready to receive the influx of US bond business. If your business needs 20 programmers to update and manage a Web site, don't assume that they need to be in the same country as your marketing people or your fulfilment people. Programmers can sometimes work remotely, and it may make sense to hire them in a country with lower taxes on employment than the country where you intend to have your head office. Similarly, look at where you hold your intellectual property rights (in some jurisdictions they incur stamp duty), where your billing systems are based (this may affect Value Added Tax in some jurisdictions) and where your servers sit (in some jurisdictions, capital allowances against corporate tax). The 10% to 20% difference in all these taxes and allowances can soon add up to a reduction in several years for the time it will take you to make your first millions.

Market organization

Summary

Markets are central to any economy, ancient or modern. The Internet lowers the cost and other barriers to running a market. This means that existing markets can be made more efficient, and new markets can be created to serve parts of the economy where it was not feasible (uneconomic) to have a market previously. Markets have a number of functions: they set prices, bring together buyers and sellers, provide information and encourage standards. All of these functions can be made more efficient by the Internet.

The concept of the market is central to modern business. The private sector worries about how its products compete in 'the market', its managers worry about how its shares are performing in the stockmarket, or, if not quoted on the stockmarket, the management is probably worrying about how and when to make an initial public offering (IPO) on the stockmarket. A few specialist managers in multinationals are paid to worry about nothing but the foreign exchange market. The public sector is forced to confront the market, either by being sold into the private sector, like Deutsche Telekom, France Telecom, Telecom Italia and most other telephone monopolies that existed in Europe, or by being 'market tested', that is, having their output measured against a benchmark from the private sector. Today we take the existence and operation of many markets for granted. But what is a market? And why should the Internet entrepreneur be particularly interested in markets?

Markets can be regarded as having four core functions:

- to introduce buyers to sellers;
- to provide liquidity;
- to propagate customs or rules; and
- to exchange information.

Particular markets may have other functions in addition to these, and not all markets have all of these functions, but most markets have most of these functions. The primary function of a market is to introduce a buyer to a seller, but sometimes intermediaries are involved or even take the part of buyer or seller or both.

Providing liquidity means making a market, that is ensuring that for every buyer there is a seller, and vice versa. In formal markets, such as a stock exchange, there may be a law that requires certain parties to ensure liquidity, but in less formal markets less formal mechanisms guarantee sufficient liquidity most of the time. For instance, in the residential property market estate agents ensure liquidity by marketing their services to potential sellers and raising their estimates of a property's value when there is a shortage of property and by writing to potential buyers and freezing or lowering their estimate of property valuations when there is a glut of property on the market.

The rules or customs of a market help buyers and sellers by making the process of buying and selling more efficient and reducing the risk involved. A housebuyer is interested in the house being bought and the price to be paid, and the seller is usually only interested in the price to be paid. Neither is especially interested in the details of the process, except to the extent that the cost of the process increases the price paid by the buyer and reduces the price received by the seller. Standard forms for conveyancing property, standard training for surveyors, and even a standard set of euphemisms among estate agents (everyone who has bought a house knows that 'open sunny aspects' can mean 'a hole in the roof') all help to reduce the cost for buyer and seller.

Finally, the fourth function of a market is to convey information about the goods or services being exchanged. We don't use the property market just to buy and sell houses, we use it to value our houses when we have no intention of selling them but wish to remortgage or to assess the value for tax purposes. Similarly, the antiques market sets guide prices for insurance purposes for antiques that do not pass through the market. When researching and planning your new Internet start-up, examine the structure of the existing market for your product and determine what opportunities exist for that structure to be changed by Internet-based mechanisms.

Table 1.4 Examples of new markets made possible by the Internet

Chemdex/Ventro *www.chemdex.com*	Chemdex is a 'vertical market', providing a source for many supplies and inputs required by businesses operating in the life sciences industry by linking suppliers, researchers and enterprises through a customized Web site. It had great success in one vertical market, and recently decided that it should expand and use the expertise gained in its home chemicals and life sciences market to move into other markets. The group had been called Chemdex, and has renamed itself Ventro to reflect this evolution of its strategy.

Table 1.4 *cont.*

VerticalNet *www.verticalnet.com*	VerticalNet targets niche business communities and builds vertical market Web sites tailored to the needs of those industries – in a way replicating Chemdex for other industries. So far, VerticalNet operates in 11 niches: advanced technologies; communications; environmental; food packaging; foodservice and hospitality; healthcare and science; manufacturing and metals; process; public sector; service; and textile and apparels.
ecFood.com *www.ecfood.com*	An on-line exchange/vertical market for the food industry. If you need four gross of chickens really quickly and cheaply, this is the place to look. When we last looked, there was a special on 38 919 lbs of powdered eggs, Kosher certification optional.

Boundaries of the firm

Summary

Every business depends on many processes, but to be organized for maximum efficiency and effectiveness, only some of those processes will be within the firm, and others will be bought in from other firms or performed by related but legally separate entities. The boundary of the firm distinguishes which processes are within the firm and which without. However, progress, and especially technological change, means that the optimal boundaries of the firm change all the time. To survive, an organization must constantly review where its boundaries are and make adjustments. The Internet is causing the biggest change that has been seen in the boundaries of the firm in most industries since the 1950s.

The idea embodied in the concept of the boundaries of the firm is that there are some things a firm should do and some things that it is better to buy in from another firm. Of course, these boundaries are not precisely defined, they change with time, and they are subject to local factors and special circumstances. There was a time in the past when conglomerates were fashionable, but then starting in the 1980s in Europe, and slightly earlier in the USA, it became fashionable to break conglomerates up into different businesses. A possible explanation for this is that in the period after the Second World War until the late 1970s firstly, management talent and secondly, analytical resources were in short supply and that thirdly, the capital markets were less efficient than they became after the late 1970s. The evidence for these three claims is that the proportion of managers with MBAs, the availability of cheap digital business computing and the availability of financial instruments such as commercial paper were relatively much lower in the first period than the second period. When the supply of these resources and financial instruments changed, it meant that the sorts of things that had been wise for many businesses to do in a large and centralized headquarters were better done in small decentralized business-specific headquarters. That explanation of the reasons behind the trend away from conglomerates is only a theory, albeit a widely held theory, but there are many other examples of how the boundaries of the firm change. The outsourcing industry is precisely about changing the boundaries of the firm, and a vast range of activities that were once done in house are now outsourced by many organizations: office cleaning, IT support, pensions management, payroll, employee benefits management, PR, expatriate HR services, distribution, catering, telecoms management, travel agency services and many more.

The Internet allows the firm to change its boundaries in many ways. Part-time workers can be utilized and controlled in new ways thanks to Internet tools, which means that organizations can expand their boundaries to include part-time workforces where before this was impractical; that teams of programmers can be hired on contract to work in low-cost countries such as India, but thanks to the Internet their work can be monitored and used as well as if the programmers were sitting in the firm's own headquarters; and that whole supply chains can be automated and managed by a fraction of the staff previously needed. Is your Internet business helping your customers to optimize the boundaries of their firms? Where should the boundaries of your own start-up firm be to maximize the efficiencies which the Internet offers? What can be outsourced on the Internet?

Business process automation

Summary

A firm takes inputs, processes them and produces outputs. One way to automate processes is to add a computer to them to speed up the manual process. Often a better way to automate a process is to redesign the whole process to take advantage of what the latest technology, especially computer technology, can do, and then implement this improvement. For instance, voice-recognition software is in many cases a better automation of the typing-pool function than adding a word processor to the typist's tools. Business process automation is about obliterating manual processes and replacing them with newly designed, different automated processes. The Internet allows the automation of business processes on a scale never seen before.

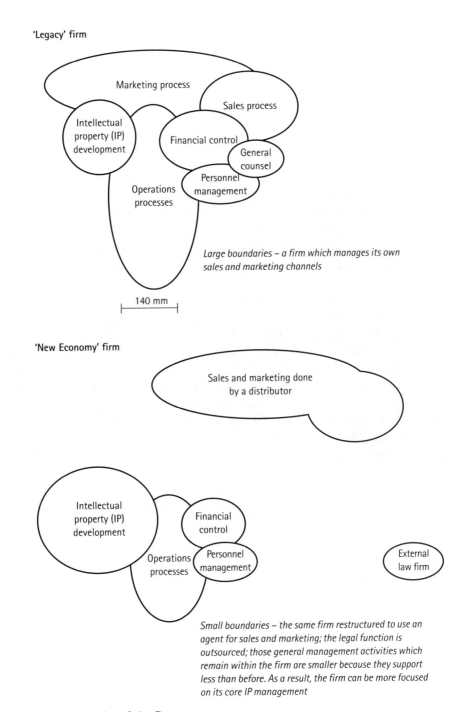

Fig. 1.2   Boundaries of the firm

Business process reengineering always promised much, but it really began to deliver business benefits on a massive scale with the Internet. The first of our ten key aspects of the Internet was its social force, because, we argued, social force underlies all economic and business profit or loss. Our last key aspect of the Internet is business process automation, because more than any other aspect that we have looked at, this one encapsulates exactly how it is that the Internet is such a powerful channel for changing social forces to act on and change business profits and the value of a firm. More than anything, the Internet is about automating business processes. As an extreme case of business process automation, consider the process of buying 100 shares in IBM. Before the Internet, a European would telephone his or her broker, that broker would then telephone a broker in the USA, the broker in the USA would telephone a floor broker on the New York Stock Exchange, who would go to a specialist, who would write the order in his book . . . you get the picture – many manual processes. Now, all you need to do is to log into your Datek account and buy the shares. Datek's back-office systems are fully automated, and often the shares are bought and registered to your nominee account without the order ever touching human hands. The result is massive cost saving, massive time saving, and a greatly reduced risk of improper execution of the order ('Oh sorry Jack, I only bought 5000 shares at five pence not £5000 worth of shares – I didn't hear you properly. Yes, I know they've gone up 300%, well done for buying them Jack.')

So many processes can be automated by using the Internet. As a start-up entrepreneur, you will probably have thought out which of your customers' processes you are trying to automate with the Internet and which of your own. Make a list of these processes, and another list of key business processes that you are not going to automate, whether because they are already automated, because it is not feasible to automate them, or because it is not part of the scope of your new business to automate them. Then rank those processes from most valuable to least valuable. Are you trying to automate the most valuable processes, that is, the processes that will earn you most revenue if they are successfully automated? If not, why not? Should you consider refocusing your new business to capture some of the higher-value processes? For instance, the retail banks could have used the Internet to communicate with their customers ages ago, but it made more sense for them to introduce Internet-based banking for only some of their processes first – in fact, the processes involved in dealing with their richer customers because that is where the banks could make the most money. Once they had fully exploited that opportunity, it was worth their while to look at using the Internet to automate banking processes for ordinary customers like you and me. For the processes you are planning to automate, are you sure that you understand the process fully? What are the dependencies of the process? What is the output of the process? How is the process measured?

Conclusion

This chapter suggests that there are ten features of a business that can make it an exceptional opportunity for exploitation as an Internet-based business. These are:

- social power;
- knowledge democratization;
- micromeasurement;
- network effects;
- disintermediation;
- global reach;
- tax arbitrage;
- market organization;
- boundaries of the firm;
- business process automation.

When assessing your idea, try to understand which of these features apply, or how some of these features could be exploited by your idea. Your idea needs to exploit only one of these ten features, as demonstrated by Hotmail, which very quickly became a multi-million dollar business because the idea of Hotmail exploited social power – specifically, the human desire to communicate. To evaluate and refine the quality of your idea and to prepare it for presentation to potential employees, management, backers and customers, take the feature from the list that your idea exploits the most, and for that feature make a list of where your idea is better than the competition or the traditional way of doing things. Having made the list, try to estimate the cash value of the difference – how many people would your idea affect, how much is it worth to them?

extract from *The Economist*

The following article on the impact of IT and the Internet on the future is reprinted from *The Economist*, 1–7 April 2000.

INTERNET ECONOMICS, A THINKER'S GUIDE

It is supposed to reduce distances and bring people closer. Yet the Internet seems to have the opposite effect on economists. The profession is divided on the effects of the Internet. Some predict that it will hugely boost global growth and kill inflation – hence the boom in technology shares. Others retort that inflation is determined solely by the money supply, and that Internet share prices are overvalued. On this basis, when the bubble bursts, it will leave behind little more economic benefit than did the 17th century's tulip bubble.

Recent gyrations in the stockmarket might seem to support this second view. Many dot.com shares, particularly those of Internet retailers, have fallen off a cliff; some once-bright prospects are finding it hard to raise enough cash to stay in business. Yet the really big impact of the Internet is likely to be felt not among dotcom firms but in the wider economy. And in this area, the truth probably lies between the economists' two extremes. The Internet will boost efficiency and growth, but not enough to justify current stockmarket valuations. Faster economic growth will not automatically mean faster profit growth, because margins may well be squeezed. As with most technological revolutions, the biggest benefits of the Internet will flow to consumers and not, in the end, to producers.

In practice, the Internet cannot easily be separated from information technology (computers, software and telecoms) in general. In America, the European Union and Japan, business spending on IT is growing at an average annual rate of 12%, much faster than overall investment. This promises additional productivity gains. This article will, however, focus on what is special about the Internet itself, and how it may deliver benefits above those from IT generally.

The economic impact of the Internet has often been described as an oil shock in reverse. The jump in the oil price in the 1970s increased inflation and pushed the world into recession. The Internet reduces the cost of another input, information, and so has positive economic effects.

[. . .]

The nude economy

Economists at Warburg Dillon Read, an investment bank, suggest that the new economy should be called the 'nude economy' because the Internet makes it more transparent and exposed. The Internet makes it easier for buyers and sellers to compare prices. It cuts out the middlemen between firms and customers. It reduces transaction costs. And it reduces barriers to entry.

This last point may surprise dotcom firms that reckon the huge marketing and technical costs of setting up a business, and the supposed advantage that comes with being a first mover, constitute big barriers to entry. In practice, it remains to be seen how big such barriers are: some established dotcom firms have lost market share. But the real point is that the Internet is reducing barriers to entry in other parts of the economy.

To understand this, go back to Ronald Coase, an economist, who argued in 1937 that the main reason why firms exist (as opposed to individuals acting as buyers and sellers at every stage of production) is to minimize transaction costs. Since the Internet reduces such costs, it also reduces the optimal size of firms. Small firms can buy in services from outside more cheaply. Thus, in overall terms, barriers to entry will fall.

In all these ways, then, the Internet cuts costs, increases competition and improves the functioning of the price mechanism. It thus moves the economy closer to the textbook model of perfect competition, which assumes abundant information, zero transaction costs and no barriers to entry. The Internet makes this assumption less far-fetched. By improving the flow of information between buyers and sellers, it makes markets more efficient, and so ensures that resources are allocated to their most productive use. The most important effect of the 'new' economy, indeed, may be to make the 'old' economy more efficient.

Economies will still be some way from the frictionless world of perfect competition. In some industries, low marginal costs (e.g. the extra cost of selling software over the Internet is close to zero) and network effects (e.g. the more widely an operating system is used, the more people will want to use it) will result in increasing returns to scale, and thus the emergence of monopolies. But because the Internet will in general reduce barriers to entry, making markets more contestable, competition and efficiency are still likely to increase across the economy as a whole.

It is hard to test this conclusion, but some studies seem to support it. Prices of goods bought on-line, such as books and CDs, are, on average, about 10% cheaper (after including taxes and delivery) than in conventional shops, though the non-existent profits of many electronic retailers make this evidence inconclusive. Competition from the Internet is also forcing traditional retailers to reduce prices. The Internet offers even clearer savings in services such as banking. According to Lehman Brothers, a transfer between bank accounts costs $1.27 if done by a bank teller, 27 cents via a cash machine, and only 1 cent over the Internet.

Internet retailers and other business-to-consumer firms, such as Amazon or eBay, tend to hog the headlines, but the biggest economic impact of the Internet is likely to come from business-to-business (B2B) e-commerce. GartnerGroup forecasts that global B2B turnover could reach $4 trillion in America in 2003, compared with less than $400 billion of on-line sales to consumers.

B2B e-commerce cuts companies' costs in three ways. First, it reduces procurement costs, making it easier to find the cheapest supplier and cutting the cost of processing transactions. Second, it allows better supply-chain management. And third, it makes possible tighter inventory control, so that firms can reduce their stocks or even eliminate them. Through these three channels B2B e-commerce reduces firms' production costs, by increasing efficiency or by squeezing suppliers' profit margins. In the economic jargon, the economy's aggregate supply curve shifts to the right.

2B or not 2B

The biggest savings are likely to come in procurement. A recent report by Martin Brookes and Zaki Wahhaj, at Goldman Sachs, estimates that firms' possible savings from purchasing over the Internet vary from 2% in the coal industry to up to 40% in electronic components. British Telecom claims that procuring goods and services on-line will reduce the average cost of processing a transaction by 90% and reduce the direct costs of goods and services it purchases by 11%. B2B exchanges also offer big savings: Ford, GM and DaimlerChrysler are setting up a joint exchange to buy components from suppliers over the Internet, and this week the biggest aerospace firms said they would follow suit.

Messrs Brookes and Wahhaj reckon that doing business with suppliers on-line could reduce the cost of making a car, for instance, by as much as 14%. Their report looks at industries that account for about one-quarter of America's GDP, and uses input–output accounts to include second-round effects of cost savings – i.e. that lower costs in one industry will reduce the price of inputs for other industries. They conclude that, in the five big rich economies, B2B e-commerce could reduce average prices across the economy by almost 4%. And this probably understates likely cost savings because it is based on lower procurement costs alone.

What does all this mean for inflation and growth? As lower costs encourage firms to produce more at any given price [. . .], the long-term equilibrium level of output will rise and the price level will fall. But note that it is the level of prices and not the level of inflation that falls. To the extent that this happens gradually over a period, inflation may be reduced, but only until prices reach their new, lower equilibrium level.

The Internet cannot permanently reduce inflation, because this is a monetary phenomenon. If central banks continue to aim for the same inflation target as before, then, beyond the short term, inflation will stay unchanged. If inflation drops below target because the Internet pushes prices down, the central bank will reduce interest rates, allowing faster growth while leaving inflation unchanged. Prices of goods exposed to the Internet may fall, but prices of other goods and services will rise faster than before.

By boosting productivity, the Internet can lift the economy's safe speed limit before inflation starts to rise. But how much? The Goldman Sachs study, the most comprehensive to date, estimates that B2B e-commerce will cause a permanent increase in the level of output by an average of 5% in the rich economies, with over half of this increase coming through within ten years. That implies an increase in GDP growth of 0.25% a year. If the benefits of Internet use spread to other industries not included in the study, the eventual gains would be larger.

In historical terms, an extra 0.25–0.5% of annual growth would be hugely significant. Estimates suggest that the carriage of freight by rail over a couple of decades in the late 19th century added perhaps 10% overall to American output. But if the Internet by itself seems unlikely to boost economic efficiency by as much as this, the productivity gains from information technology and the Internet together could easily come close. Computers, software and telecoms now account for about 12% of America's total capital stock, not far short of the share accounted for by railways at the peak of America's railway age in the late 19th century.

Moreover, information technology has some advantages over previous technological revolutions. First, unlike the railways, which affected only the movement of goods, it can be applied across a broader section of the economy, including services. The Internet, for example, offers a new information system, a new marketplace, a new form of communication and a new means of distribution. The power of digital distribution may even lead to wholly new products and services that nobody has hitherto imagined, offering the hope of further increases in economic growth.

A second positive factor is that the prices of computers and telecommunications have fallen more rapidly than for any previous technology. This is encouraging firms to adopt the Internet more quickly. There is always a lag before new technology lifts productivity growth, because it takes time for firms to reorganize their business to take advantage of new ways of doing things. The recent spurt in American productivity may be the productivity pay-off from the computer revolution, which started 50 years ago with the invention of the transistor. But because the Internet is now spreading extremely rapidly, productivity gains linked to it could arrive pretty quickly.

Inflation and profits

So far this article has argued that the Internet may push down inflation in the short run, and that in the longer run it will boost growth. However, this assumes that the Internet affects only aggregate supply. In reality, it could also boost demand. If equity investors expect faster growth in output and profits and so push up share prices, this will boost households' wealth and encourage them to spend more, even before the increase in supply has materialized. Higher share prices, and hence a cheaper cost of capital, may also boost investment. [. . .]

This may describe the situation in America today. Alan Greenspan, the Federal Reserve chairman, recently argued that an increase in productivity growth could indeed boost demand via share prices. The risk is that, if this increase in demand outstrips the productivity-led boost to supply, the equilibrium price level, and so inflationary pressure, could rise in the short term, not fall.

Some economists even argue that, following a technological shock, the previous inflation target is no longer appropriate. An essay in the 1999 annual report of the Federal Reserve Bank of Cleveland suggests that if rapid productivity gains pull down the costs of production, prices should also be allowed to fall, so workers can enjoy the benefits of higher productivity through increases in real wages. If central banks stop prices falling, and nominal wages, being stickier than prices, lag behind productivity gains, this will inflate profits and share prices will soar on the (false) expectation that profits will go on rising, spurring excessive investment. This suggests that central banks should aim for lower inflation targets than before.

Investors certainly seem to have inflated expectations about future profits. But faster growth and lower costs do not automatically justify a leap in share prices. Yes, there will be big cost savings, but to the extent that the Internet lowers barriers to entry and increases competition, this is likely to squeeze profit margins, so passing the benefits on to consumers. History shows that, although the share of profits often rises during the early years of technology-led expansions, as it did in the 1990s, it then usually declines as a result of competition from new entrants attracted by high returns.

Consider again the example of railways in the 19th century. Most schemes made little money and many went bust, largely because overinvestment had created excess capacity and fierce competition. Britain's railway mania of the 1840s certainly had much in common with Internet fever. Share prices soared, then spectacularly tumbled as many lines failed to deliver expected profits.

There is a big risk with the Internet, similarly, that boom will be followed by bust. But the good news is that, long after share prices crashed, railways continued to function, to the benefit of the economy, if not of the original investors. In all technological revolutions, from the railways to the Internet, the only sure long-term winners are consumers who gain from lower prices and hence higher real wages. There is no reason to expect the Internet to be any different.

Indeed, by reducing search costs and increasing the flow of information, the Internet explicitly shifts power from producers to consumers and so looks even more likely to squeeze profits. As with railways, stockmarkets currently seem to think that Internet firms will be the ones that reap the biggest rewards. But consumers and old-economy firms, from cars to chemicals, that use B2B e-commerce to reorganize themselves are likely to gain most. The overall rate of profits may be little changed, but profits will be redistributed.

Catchup.com

It is often argued that America's lead in the Internet age will give it an economic edge for many years to come. After all, corporate spending on IT is considerably higher as a share of GDP in America than in Japan or the EU, and the proportion of households with Internet access is three times as high. Some economists also reckon that the success of America in exploiting IT partly reflects its flexible, competitive markets. The Internet may yield smaller benefits in more tightly regulated economies with rigid labour and product markets and inefficient capital markets, which prevent labour and capital shifting in response to new opportunities.

To turn this argument round, however, the potential for cost savings and productivity gains from the Internet should be much bigger in the EU and Japan than in America. The impact of the Internet on growth could thus also be more powerful in Japan and Europe than in America. This is because the Internet, by increasing price transparency and competition, will directly attack the inefficiencies in their economies.

Countries with high distribution margins are likely to see the biggest price reductions and the biggest gains in efficiency. By exposing firms to more intense global competition, the Internet should force governments and businesses to rethink their old, inefficient habits and seek new ways to get around or eliminate market rigidities.

In Japan the Internet strikes right at the heart of many archaic business practices that hold prices high and hinder productivity. Take Japan's famously inefficient and expensive distribution system. Suppliers and retailers tend to be tied to manufacturers, through cross-shareholdings. This allows manufacturers to control prices by restricting distribution to their own retailers. However, by increasing price transparency, the Internet will give more power to consumers. Japan often seems to be a nation of middlemen. The longer the supply chain, the bigger the potential gains from B2B e-commerce, since it allows firms to eliminate the many layers of middlemen that hamper economic efficiency. Structural failings in Japan may hinder productivity gains from the Internet at first – but they cannot block them.

The Internet allows producers and consumers to seek the cheapest price in the global market. This will make it harder to maintain higher prices and higher taxes. In Europe especially, by making cross-border purchases easier, the Internet will increase tax competition and so put pressure on governments to reduce taxes.

The Internet could also give a boost to growth in emerging economies. Echoing Coase's theory, Andy Xie, an economist with Morgan Stanley in Hong Kong, argues that because the Internet cuts transaction costs and reduces economies of scale from vertical integration, it reduces the economically optimal size of firms. For example, lower transaction costs will make it possible for small firms in Asia to work together to develop a global reach. In this way, the Web could open up more opportunities for emerging economies to catch up with richer ones.

Smaller firms in emerging economies can now sell into a global market. It is now easier, for instance, for a tailor in Shanghai to make a suit by hand for a lawyer in Boston, or a software designer in India to write a program for a firm in California. One big advantage rich economies have, their closeness to wealthy consumers, will be eroded as transaction costs fall. Mr Xie argues that this will help emerging Asia to catch up.

The Internet could also accelerate the process of economic catch-up by speeding up the diffusion of information, which will help new technologies to reach emerging economies. The Internet is spreading rapidly throughout Asia, Latin America and Eastern Europe. In contrast, it took decades before many developing countries benefited from railways, telephones or electricity. If America can look forward to significant gains from IT and the Internet, then the rewards to other economies could be even bigger.

2 Planning your Internet business

KPMG

Editor's introduction

KPMG is one of the world's largest professional advisory firms, whose purpose is to turn knowledge into value for the benefit of its clients, its people and its communities. The firm has more than 100 000 partners and professionals who provide a wide range of assurance, tax, financial and consulting services. KPMG has worked with many clients of all sizes to create, plan and implement both Internet start-up businesses and e-commerce initiatives for existing businesses. One of the many examples of KPMG's Internet expertise is the NetAid Web site, which was deployed faster and had greater capability than any other site when launched – it is capable of handling 60m hits per hour and was developed in just 90 days.

KPMG can be contacted through its Web site at www.kpmg.com.

Aim

Investors, incubators and potential trade partners are key to an early-stage Internet business, but to maximize both the probability of receiving funds, and to achieve minimum dilution to the founders' shareholdings, it is critical that these groups understand the business proposition clearly. Time spent preparing a plan is, therefore, invaluable to the entrepreneur in several ways:

1. funders are, in the absence of any track record, looking to evaluate the quality of the management team. The latter's ability to convey their idea and the associated business proposition is therefore one of the key credibility statements that investors are looking for and judging;

2. using a framework for a business plan in effect creates a 'checklist' of items which the entrepreneur needs to have thought through in order to obtain funding; and

3. it is not possible to create a business plan for a concept – hence, the preparation of a plan inevitably moves the idea from vision to business proposition. Conversely, the lack of a detailed plan can suggest to investors that the team has not necessarily properly developed the implementation and commercial implications.

This chapter illustrates how, by using a staged process, entrepreneurs can quickly develop an idea into a viable proposition that can be presented to potential partners or investors. The planning process serves a number of purposes: to develop the idea, to identify risks, issues and solutions, to identify the funding requirement, and to formulate how this will be approached. A good plan will also identify a detailed implementation timetable with actions and responsibilities, together with some indication of key risk factors, means of mitigating these and some sensitivity analysis to understand the consequences.

For most commercial operations, and particularly those which develop as quickly as most Internet proposals, a single operator is unlikely to succeed. It is, therefore, essential that at an early stage, the skills base required is identified, prioritized and candidates identified. Funders will expect to see a team – incomplete potentially, but with a structure proposed and at least a couple of key personnel in place. In terms of the business plan, to have both a division of labour and an internal sounding board is helpful in providing a balanced perspective.

Planning properly also allows the team to be fully prepared before talking to third parties about the development of the business. There are very few second chances. The plan should state quite clearly how the business will make a return, what is required to achieve this and what are the key hurdles to be overcome.

During the planning process the team will also need to think about issues to be considered at different stages and potentially to revisit areas once they have progressed a stage. The team should have flexibility in the process and to a great extent it is an iterative process. However, a staged process encourages discipline, and the fundamental proposition should not be altered unless identification of a key risk or issue results in the original concept becoming obsolete.

Tools and methods to assist in the planning process

Using an adviser

Having the support of a professional adviser at the funding stage can be invaluable in adding to the credibility of the proposal, providing a sounding board on alternative funding options and assisting in introducing and negotiating terms offered. At an earlier stage, advisers can also add significantly to the planning by:

- guiding the process;
- facilitating thinking;
- providing industry-specific knowledge;
- helping to create financial models;
- acting as a sounding board.

They therefore help to reinforce the process and can add significant value when polishing and presenting the plan. However, it is vital that funders appreciate that the plan is owned by the team – they do not want to feel that they are evaluating the calibre of the advisers. It is therefore critical that the management team create the business plan themselves, if necessary with advisory support.

Business planning workshops

A popular approach to planning, which enables the analysis to be broken down into a manageable set of activities, is to hold a series of planning workshops. In formal terms, these workshops are team meetings where a mechanism is established to:

- brain-storm issues;
- bond the team;
- share thoughts and tasks;
- delegate responsibilities;
- update the team;
- install quality control by setting objectives and time deadlines;
- agree commercial solutions to major issues.

They are often advantageous in the early stages when not all of the team members can devote 100% of their time to the project. Trusted specialists can be introduced at workshops to provide knowledge of specific elements. Whilst a structured approach can be effective, these workshops often work best if they are not in the style of formal board meetings but group exercises to achieve a common goal.

The aim of such workshops should be to divide the work into manageable portions, rather than to generate meetings for meetings' sake. Individual tasks to be performed outside the workshops will therefore include:

- recruiting people to the project;
- carrying out research;
- obtaining costs;
- talking to customers, suppliers and potential employees.

Whether or not workshops are used, one person should be delegated the responsibility of collecting the thoughts to compile the written document. Ideally, this should be the key entrepreneur who can shape the document to reflect his or her personal style and to maintain control of the planning process.

1. Workshops

Workshop 1   *Setting objectives and brainstorming ideas.*
Workshop 2   *Analyzing customers, revenue and competition.*
Workshop 3   *Analyzing supply, risks and success factors.*
Workshop 4   *Thinking through the numbers.*
Workshop 5   *Writing the executive summary and review.*

The written business plan

The entrepreneurial team members should remember throughout the process that they need to prepare a written document which encapsulates their plan. This document should be driven by the conclusions from workshops and individual research. Example 5 (p. 48) illustrates some standard headings which are most frequently used.

It is tempting for the entrepreneur to take the headings and try to complete each section in turn. This is a dangerous strategy because it does not focus on what is of prime importance when planning an Internet business. It is important to formulate the idea and build the commercial and financial case before finalizing the plan, to avoid redrafting whole sections as different issues and risks are evaluated. Writing the business plan will then be a case of inserting these thoughts and conclusions and completing other sections required.

Writing the plan should generally be the last part of the process. The steps below cover many of the areas which need to have been completed before the written plan can be finalized.

Formulating the idea

At the earliest stage of the process the team should formulate the following elements of the idea:

■ What is the idea – how can it be described in five sentences?

■ Who is the customer and user?

■ What will they be buying?

■ How will products or services be supplied and distributed?

■ How adaptable is the proposition to Internet technology?

■ What is unique about the proposition?

An understanding of these items will guide and provide focus for the commercial review. Thinking through these basic principles of the business will provide a starting point for the proposition. The team should adapt and modify the idea as more is learnt about the customer, products and supply issues.

The idea pitch

The team should agree a few sentences which summarize exactly what the business will be doing. This is often referred to as the 'elevator pitch'. It should be possible to reduce the proposition to a few simple lines – existing businesses, for example, may sell drinks, sell electronic goods, provide Internet access or publish books. This elevator pitch should be revisited throughout the process and adapted as the idea is thought through and more is understood about the market.

Customers and revenues

All key potential products or services will need to be thought through, prioritized and key potential customers identified. The revenue streams may revolve around:

- the selling of goods;
- the sale of information;
- the sale of advertising space;
- facilitating transactions;
- brokerage commission.

Internet businesses are generally either focused towards the consumer or businesses. As the Internet is developing, there are businesses focusing on a combination of the two. In such cases it will be necessary to be clear as to what products will be sold to each class of customer. It is important to identify the specific profile of the customer. In the case of consumer-focused businesses, this will include analyses of customers':

- age;
- sex;
- location;
- buying habits (what, where and how).

In the case of business-focused propositions, the analysis should include:

- size of business (small, medium or large);
- industry;
- location;
- customers' buying habits (what, where and how).

It is also important to be clear as to whether customers (who pay) are the same group as users – who may view but not pay. In many e-businesses the two are different constituencies and a failing of some business plans is to focus substantially on users, with far less analysis of customers, or the links between the two.

Supply and distribution

Once the products or services have been identified, the team will need to establish how they will be sourced from suppliers and how they will be delivered. In the case of consumer goods, this would involve understanding who the manufacturers are. Other products and services may be sourced from the following:

- building a database of information;
- generating a user base for advertising space;
- providing a solution for executing transactions;
- forming alliances for services supply.

Distribution and payment for Internet-based businesses are areas that customers are still uncomfortable with. Solutions to tackle these problems will need to be identified for the business since logistics and distribution problems can often be a major stumbling block for Internet businesses. In addition to order or service delivery, there are problems with cancellations and returns. This type of day-to-day operation must not be forgotten.

It is also essential to consider some financial risks in association with supply and distribution:

- How does the cashflow work?
- Is the business carrying the working capital risk (i.e. needing to pay suppliers before receiving payment from customers)?
- Who is accepting the credit risk (i.e. is the liability of the customer to the supplier and the business acting as an intermediary taking commission, or is the liability on the business to pay the supplier and hence accepting the credit risk)?

'Internetability'

It is important to understand, and to be able to explain, how the Internet will facilitate the business proposition. This should include:

- a review of how the method of distributing the product or supply will be received by customers;
- what technology is required to make the business work.

Unique selling points

A common area overlooked in Internet business plans is consideration of the uniqueness of the proposition. The entrepreneurial team should focus on understanding what it is that makes the idea special. One of the most common arguments is that they are the first mover. As time goes by this is becoming increasingly difficult to argue as the range of existing propositions broadens and business models become established. Other reasons that can make an idea unique include:

- introducing solutions to market inefficiency;
- cost reductions;
- new value to customers;
- patented technology.

This should become clearer and be reinforced once the commercial case has been evaluated.

Developing the commercial logic

Developing the commercial logic involves evaluation of the market environment, management, resources and building strategies to achieve critical success factors and overcome the key market risks. The areas of focus are shown below.

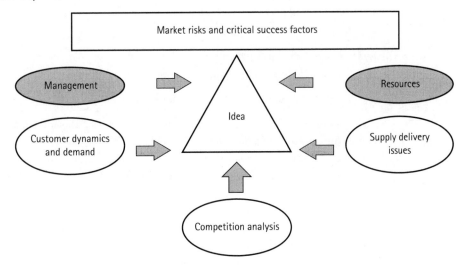

Fig. 2.1   Developing the commercial logic

The market environment

The business proposition must illustrate a clear understanding of:

- the dynamics of the customer;
- demand for the product or service;
- forecast growth for market demand;

- supply and distribution issues;
- resource requirements (including management and technology);
- current and potential competition.

Where possible, supporting evidence either from publicly available research or more targeted and focused evaluation should be incorporated in the plans. If independent research is used, it is helpful in providing funders with independent corroboration of forecasts and trends.

Customer dynamics and demand

It is essential to understand details about the customers and what the scale of their demand will be. The team will need to understand:

- how many customers are likely to want the product or service;
- how strong their demand will be;
- how they will be won;
- where they will be located;
- how they feel about pricing;
- how their demand will change over time;
- how they will select and purchase in the on-line environment.

In a number of business plans, the relationship between this information and the forecast volume/pricing parameters is not clearly defined. Pricing models, in particular, need to be explained. If the decision is simply to replicate, or even to reduce the traditional pricing model, then this should be presented as a conscious decision – too often it appears to be assumed.

If a member of the team is aware of the industry, it will be easier to identify the key issues customers will have in the market, what they are paying and how sensitive they will be to new ways of doing business or new prices. It may be that such issues are the factors driving the business idea. If this information is not available, it is a good idea to speak to potential customers and find out more about them – and it may still be difficult to persuade funders that a genuine market understanding exists within the team without management experience.

Supply and distribution issues

The majority of Internet business plans do not focus on how the business will source supply for the products or service or how they will be distributed. It is important for the team to understand how the products are distributed through channels and identify who will supply them and whether there will be any difficulty in obtaining supply. This is a key issue not only for products companies but also for service businesses.

Competition

An understanding of competitors is extremely important. It is very difficult to know all the competition, especially given that some of them may be developing their plans in garages or overseas. An analysis of current competition and potential competition involves analyzing their operations, market share and strengths and weaknesses. This understanding will help guide what market share can be expected for the business and how this share can be protected.

Potential competition is more difficult to evaluate. A key exercise which can provide useful insights is to evaluate who in the industry could benefit from adopting this way of doing business or who else has been researching and developing similar technology advances. The team also needs to monitor ongoing developments by speaking to people in the industry, reading trade and general press and monitoring investments made by investors. It is vital to detail the differences between the competitor's and the team's idea. There is usually space in any marketplace for more than one business.

Management

A good team is needed not only to provide valuable input during the planning process but to execute the plan and build the business. Good management will bring credibility to an idea and is one of the key areas that partners and investors consider when evaluating propositions.

A good management team brings a balance of skills and experience to cover management and finance, sales and marketing and technology. The best people to have in the business are those most likely to make it work – this means people who have a good track record in their field, who have relevant industry experience, valuable networks and commitment, and these people must work as a team to make the business work. With all start-up operations, it is difficult to persuade people to join until they believe in the proposition. For this reason, it may not be possible to secure all the key positions from day one. A substitute is to seek advice from contacts during the planning process to ensure that thorough research is carried out. The plan may then also be used to seek the buy-in of key personnel.

Corporate names and non-executives

There is an increasing trend to concentrate on deciding who should be the Chairman, CEO, Managing Director or Vice-President of Sales, rather than to focus on the skills and expertise required. Ideally, the team should focus on getting the right mix of skills to build the business. However, such titles are often valuable in attracting people to join the team and demonstrating to the outside world that the management plan to operate like an established business. A wide group of non-executives, or advisory board, has been used successfully in several instances to provide cover for areas of expertise missing in the core management team, or as an interim measure or to provide a degree of 'gravitas' in a young management team. Such groups can be invaluable – but the key to any management structure is to demonstrate that each member of the team is bringing different but complementary skills, and that, as a group, there are no omissions.

The importance of a good management team should not be underestimated. The entrepreneur should try to lock in the commitment of key members. This is usually done by a form of incentive scheme, either through an initial share in the business or a right to a future share of success, either through structured bonuses or participation in the ownership of the business. Professional assistance should always be sought for implementing such schemes. It is not essential at the business-plan stage to have the scheme thought through in detail – but it is important to demonstrate that it has been considered.

It is also useful to analyze other staffing requirements for the business and how easily staff can be recruited.

Other resources

An analysis of the strengths and weaknesses of available resources should be included. This can include an evaluation of specific technology to be developed, patents or trade marks to be obtained or applied for, trade alliances in place or agreed or an evaluation of an existing business supporting this proposition. The specific requirements for resources should also be identified and detailed.

A common omission from Internet business plans is an evaluation of the technical requirements of the business. It is important for the team to identify the technical requirements to both build the on-line environment and manage the business when trade commences. This should include an evaluation of:

- technology security;
- payment facilities;
- data protection and management;
- product or service distribution.

Market risks and critical success factors

A good understanding of the market environment should identify key issues the business faces. The industry understanding should highlight specific risks to the business. Industry-specific risks may revolve around certain laws and regulations (including tax) or particular strengths of suppliers or customers.

As well as industry-specific risks, there are general factors such as how easy it is to replicate this business and whether there are any alternative products or services. All risks should be identified and strategies to overcome them evaluated. A well thought through business will have plans and monitoring procedures set up to achieve those items critical to the success of the business.

2. How market risk identifies the critical success factors

Market risk	Critical success factor
Low barriers to entry	*Capitalize on first-mover advantage*
Supplier power	*Form key alliances*
Specific regulations	*Obtain regulatory approval*
Large number of competitors	*Differentiate the proposition*

Strategy

Through a combination of highlighting the risks and the requirements of the business, the team should start developing a strategy. It is important that the team separates out the long-term strategy for the business and short-term objectives. It is important to demonstrate how the business will get off the ground in the first 100 days and to picture the longer-term direction. The team should be able to explain where the larger revenue streams are and who the biggest customer will be in 3–5 years and beyond.

It is useful to prepare a milestone analysis, spelling out the key objectives over time for the following:

■ technology development strategy;

■ recruitment strategy;

■ product development strategy;

■ supply and distribution strategy;

■ market entry strategy.

Of specific importance is the market entry strategy. This should be based around how the business will enter and win in the market. This can include detail on branding, advertising, PR or trade-alliance strategies. The related funding and financial strategy can then be developed through building the financial case.

Building the financial case

Building the financial case involves understanding and detailing the potential revenue, costs and cash requirements of the business. The financial assumptions should be driven from the basic idea and conclusions from the commercial logic analysis.

The financial analysis can present difficulties to a core management team which does not have any financial training. However, it is absolutely key to persuading funders that the idea has some genuine commercial potential. One reason that some entrepreneurs struggle with numbers is that the commercial logic has not been properly addressed and therefore there is a lack of comprehension as to the value drivers in the financial model.

One of the best ways to analyze the financial numbers for a start-up Internet business is to prepare a one-page cashflow analysis for three years, rather than focusing instantly on profitability. This can be supported by a monthly cashflow analysis for the first year, either presented in the main section of the plan or in the appendices. This type of analysis will clearly demonstrate funding requirements, and indicate the revenue and profitability potential. If the entrepreneur or a member of the team is financially literate, he or she may wish to prepare a financial model which incorporates fuller profit and loss analysis with balance sheets. This type of detail will be needed at some point in the future but a cashflow will be sufficient for the start-up business. Example 4 (p. 46) illustrates a typical annual cashflow.

The assumptions within the financial analysis provide a number of functions for funders. There are two key aspects which can be overlooked – firstly that the assumptions provide the funders with an opportunity for them to assess whether they have understood the commercial logic presented in the text; secondly, it is frequently the easiest way for funders to test the coherence and credibility of the business plan. In Example 3 below, for instance, are some of the logical relationships which funders would consider.

Example	**3. Logical relationships in the business plan**

Commercial logic	Financial analysis
Customers × price × volume × growth	Revenue stream
Market entry strategy	Include marketing costs
Seasonal sales activity	Include seasonal revenue
Need for regulatory approval	Include professional fees
Need for distribution warehouse	Include property costs
Increased revenue through the year	Include increased costs

The burn rate

The burn rate is the amount of money that will be spent in the business. This can be an annual amount or a monthly figure. Given that most Internet businesses do not generate revenue during the development stage, it is important to separate out the initial monthly burn rate before any revenue is achieved. After this stage it is appropriate to discuss the net burn rate, which is the difference between revenue receipts and expenditure.

In order to get the burn rate correct, the team should spend time considering and analyzing the costs required to build the business. All potential costs should be captured and their likely timing placed appropriately in the cashflow.

Example 4 (p. 46) identifies some of the common cost captions that businesses incur.

Revenue assumptions

Different revenue streams should be separately identified. Whilst it is tempting to simply extrapolate the revenue as predicted market share x size of market, it is important to analyze what this means in terms of volume x price, i.e. a bottom-up approach which complements the top-down review. Volume can be easier to relate to timing than market share – and a combination of volume and price can also be more susceptible to sensitivity analysis. It is also vital to understand from the revenue model when the cash will actually be received, and what discount or commission will be payable on receipt.

Margin analysis

A cashflow does not include specific margin detail. The margin is the profit that can be achieved. The gross margin is the amount of profit after the costs relating directly to revenue have been deducted. It is useful to understand the assumed gross margin forecast to be achieved in the business and how this compares with current margins in the industry (both traditional and electronic) and the direction in which the margin is forecast to go.

Sensitivities

Every effort should be made to make the financial analysis as accurate as possible given the commercial evaluation of the proposition. However, it is appreciated that it is difficult to predict these numbers with 100% accuracy. It is, therefore, important to detail the main sensitivities and the impact of change on them. For example, the team should consider the impact of different prices or market share on the numbers. Several scenarios of numbers should not be provided in the plan. The exercise should be carried out by the team and a list of key sensitivities and a summary of their impact should be understood and detailed. For example:

- if the business manages to capture an additional 5% of the market share, revenue will increase to £x million with an increase in profit of £x thousand; or:
- if the technology is not developed within the projected timescale, the revenue will be deferred and the business will need to support the monthly burn rate of £x thousand.

Example

4. Cashflow projections

Financial projections of XYZ.Com

	2000 £'000	2001 £'000	2002 £'000
Revenue			
Advertising revenue	50	150	300
Product sales	20	200	1200
Commissions	10	50	300
Technology licences	5	50	100
	85	450	1900
Expenditure			
People costs	150	200	350
Property costs	55	60	65
Fixed assets	50	50	40
Technology	30	25	20
Product costs	10	100	600
Marketing costs	100	75	75
General costs – including professional fees	30	15	15
	425	525	1165
Net cashflow	(340)	(75)	735
Cash introduced	500	0	0
Cash brought forward	0	160	85
Net cash position	160	85	820

Valuation

Internet businesses often use the business plan to obtain funds in exchange for a share of the business. For this reason, entrepreneurs are keen to know what the business is worth. It is best practice to avoid including a valuation in the business plan. This is not a straight-forward exercise and there is a high probability that the business will be either overvalued or undervalued by the entrepreneur.

Polishing and presenting the plan itself

Once the commercial logic has been developed and financial projections and requirements understood, the team should write the business plan. It needs to be professional, factual and to include an understanding of all the factors influencing the business. The document should be readable within 30 minutes, and ideally the plan should be a concise 20 to 30 pages written with simple, clear sentences. Table 2.1 sets out useful tips to remember when writing the plan.

Example 5 sets out a typical format for a business plan. These headings should not be followed religiously but used as a skeleton structure. They should be adapted to the business and personal style of the team.

Table 2.1 – Presentation tips

Do	Do NOT
Prepare a smart document.	Prepare a hand-written document.
Include a title and contents page.	Use coloured or unusual fonts.
Include your contact details.	Spend too long on graphics.
Number all pages.	Prepare pages of financial analysis.
Underline headings.	
Provide sources for supporting research.	
Bind or tie the plan together.	
Check all spelling.	
Date and prenumber the document.	

Confidentiality and purpose statement

The team should include a statement at the front of the plan which sets out the purpose of the plan and details the confidential nature of the information contained within it.

Example

5. Business plan headings

Title page

Confidentiality statement

Contents

1 Executive summary

2 Current status

3 Idea
  3.1 The pitch
  3.2 Operating model
  3.3 Products and revenue streams
  3.4 Customer profile

4 Management
  4.1 Current team
  4.2 Requirements

5 Market environment
  5.1 Customer dynamics
  5.2 Forecast demand
  5.3 Supply-chain analysis
  5.4 Competition
  5.5 Market risks and critical success factors

6 Other resources
  6.1 Technology
  6.2 Alliances
  6.3 Requirements

7 Financial analysis
  7.1 Cashflow projections
  7.2 Burn rate and costs assumptions
  7.3 Revenue assumptions
  7.4 Sensitivities

8 Appendices
  8.1 Press reviews
  8.2 Milestones
  8.3 Web site graphics
  8.4 Intent letters
  8.5 Organization structure
  8.6 Further market research
  8.7 Exit plan

The executive summary

The executive summary should be written just before the business plan is completed. It should communicate in simple language a balanced summary of the idea, management, market environment, financial highlights and the current status and requirements. The summary can be made easier to read by using headings and capturing the persuasive arguments constructed in the individual sections of the plan.

Invitation to the party

The executive summary, in many cases, will be the first and sometimes only section of the plan read in significant detail. The executive summary needs to persuade people to invest – and needs to be written in the expectation that funders will have considerable pressures on their time, and potentially competition from not dissimilar proposals. It, therefore, needs to be accurate, honest, pithy and persuasive.

Owing to time restraints, investors, incubators and trade partners often ask only for an executive summary at first. However, best practice suggests writing the whole plan having been through the business planning process first, then finalizing the executive summary. In this way, not only is the team prepared to address more detailed questions arising from funders, but they are also confident that the more considered response will be consistent with the executive summary.

Exit planning

The members of the management team will have their own views on the future. Financial investors are concerned with making a return – for which they need to be able to identify a point of exit when they can (if they choose) realize this. It is important to provide them with comfort on two aspects – firstly, that the opportunity will arise, and secondly, that the ambitions and objectives of the management team are aligned or at least not incompatible with that opportunity. To date, most exit opportunities have arisen on IPO and this has not been an issue.

Current status and background

The current status section should be used and updated once the plan is in circulation. This saves incorporating new activities within individual sections. It also allows clear communication to the reader as to what is happening in the business today. This section can include activities like the appointment of an advertising agency, the injection of some seed funding, the formation of the company, securing the intent of a customer or supplier and latest information on competition.

Alongside new activities, it is also recommended that the stage of development is indicated. For example, is this a concept proposition? Has the technology been developed? Is there an existing business supporting this venture? Is there a Web site or prototype that can be reviewed? This is important background information to include. If the proposition involves new concepts for future markets, it might be appropriate to cover a brief overview of the new marketplace.

Idea and market

The core content of the business plan will be the presentation of the commercial case. The conclusions and supporting evidence from the workshops should be included under the appropriate sections of the plan.

Management – what to document

The business plan should provide details of the management team. The key items to include are the industry experience, Internet experience, entrepreneurial track record, reputation and any personnel risk undertaken to pursue the proposition. If there is a gap in either a key position, like finance or personal limitations with respect to sales and marketing, it should be highlighted in the business plan as a requirement. Whilst this is not the ideal scenario, it is understood that human resources are limited in the Internet world and that most business plans currently carry management requirements in their plans.

Generally, high first-year salary costs for the team and management are not looked upon favourably. The reasons for premium salaries should be documented. It is also recommended that comment be made in the plan of the intended contribution of any non-executives and specialist management in the business.

Financial analysis

A detailed cashflow should be included alongside a summary of the assumptions supporting each of the revenues and costs. It is important to demonstrate to the reader that the financial analysis is driven by the commercial analysis presented in the idea and market sections. To achieve this, the description titles for revenue and costs should be the same as those used in the commercial analysis sections.

Appendices

The appendices provide a useful way of removing bulky information from the main body of the plan, allowing the reader to focus on the important elements. Items that can be included in the appendices are:

- milestone analysis for the next 100, 200 and 300 days;
- copies of letters of intent from trade partners;

■ detailed financial analysis;

■ scanned copies of Web site;

■ copies of media write-ups about the business or management;

■ full curriculum vitae of the management team;

■ detailed organization chart;

■ detailed market research;

■ legal documentation (e.g. patent application or ownership structure);

■ detailed information on technology capabilities.

Checklists and review

Once the plan has been finalized, each member of the team should critically review it. The plan should also be reviewed by a trusted outsider whose role is to ensure that the plan spells out clearly what the idea is, who is behind the business, what the market is for the business and what the business needs are.

Business plan review

Funders will be examining the plan for answers to some very specific and basic questions. If the answers are not clearly visible, then barriers to further progress are erected in their minds. The type of questions being considered are:

■ Has a demand for this product or service been identified?

■ How big is that demand likely to be?

■ What is the potential revenue for the business?

■ Is it a business that can grow rapidly?

■ What are the revenue streams?

■ Who is the customer? How much will they pay for the product or service and why would they buy from this business?

■ Who else provides this product or service? Does this business provide a superior ability to generate profit or rapid growth?

■ Is it clear what stage the business is at?

■ Is it clear what the business needs to do in the next 100 days?

■ How credible is the management team – what is their experience?

Common mistakes

Plans frequently suffer from some common mistakes, which can readily be avoided:

- Imbalance:
  - too much focus on one area of the business plan;
  - making the executive summary as long as the rest of the plan;
  - irrelevant information;
  - focus on presentation not content.
- Omissions:
  - not including developments in the business or its competitors;
  - lack of a clear long-term strategy;
  - lack of industry understanding;
  - lack of competitor understanding;
  - requirements not spelt out clearly;
  - lack of market risk understanding.
- Financial issues:
  - unrealistic growth forecasts;
  - numbers not relating to commercial logic;
  - ignoring key costs.

What to do next

Presenting the business plan

Once a document has been prepared, the team should be ready to also present their proposition. It is becoming increasingly popular to invite businesses to pitch their ideas to allow investors or incubators to assess the management and their understanding of the proposition. It is important that the presentation is both internally coherent (i.e. each team member presents a complementary view of the proposition) and consistent with the business plan.

A talk book or slide show is most frequently used in presentations. Many funders prefer that the actual presentation is comprehensive and clear but brief, allowing them more time to pursue questions on particular aspects.

The contents of any presentation should focus on explaining strengths and weaknesses of the idea, team and resources available, alongside building the commercial and financial case with a summary of requirements. The slides should contain the key messages from each section of the plan. The team should talk around the presentation to demonstrate their understanding of the proposition.

The future

Once the members of the team are comfortable that they have reached the end of the planning process, they should start to implement the 100-day plan contained within it. The business plan should then be used as a benchmark document to look back at and evaluate whether the business is following the plan. As the business develops, there will be a need to revisit the direction of the business. An ongoing planning process which evaluates the strategy, commercial environment and financial position and performance of the business is encouraged, as it can facilitate growth of the business in the same way that it can help to launch it.

A extract from *Tornado–Insider.com*: the new economy

The magazine *Tornado-Insider.com* is Europe's leading Internet and high-technology venture capital magazine. A similar magazine with a US bias is *RedHerring*. The article

reproduced below (from *Tornado-Insider.com*, June 2000) presents a new way of doing business, where personal relations, flexibility and innovation have taken the lead

over standard qualifications and experience. Ironically, this is from Michael Jackson, an accountant and lawyer by trade, who plays down his background in favour of a more positive, open-minded working experience.

MICHAEL JACKSON – TAKING SWEET EQUITY

by John Dunn

The world is changing its mindset. A decade ago, it would of been considered eccentric for a venture-capital outfit managing tens of millions of euros to declare on its corporate profile that it started life in a down-at-heel part of London working from a single room above a Korean takeout restaurant. Today such beginnings are almost a badge of honour, proof that you worked your way up from the financial equivalent of the 'Street'.

This is how London-based Elderstreet started out in 1990, founded by one Michael Jackson after what he describes as a 'bust up' with his former employers, a nameless 'small investment bank'. The investment company he describes as 'entrepreneurial venture-capitalists' is now based in an elegant Georgian terraced property in an intimidatingly high-rent part of central London. Not a takeout in sight.

Apart from starting Elderstreet, Jackson was also one of the founding investors in the Sage Group, currently capitalized at billions of pounds on the London Stock Exchange and considered, along with ARM and Psion, one of the UK's 'blue-chip' technology stars. He is currently chairman of Sage, and after a 17 year involvement is as close as it gets to being a father figure for the business.

He plays down his background in accountancy and law. 'I realized that the one thing I really hated was accountancy and the one thing I was good at was marketing.' But what's wrong with accountancy? 'I think if people knew I was accountant they would be put off,' he maintains.

Later in the conversation he returns the same theme in a different guise, discussing some well-regarded business leaders from the UK's old economy past. 'I just never got it because to me they were just cost cutters. They never looked at the top line. That's the way accountants think. What's more interesting to me is growing a company. That is a fundamental difference between the old economy and the new economy.'

It remains an unspoken sentiment, but you get the feeling some traditional old school VCs might figure in his reckoning as accountants of sorts. 'What happens is the VCs of the past had to park themselves and haven't any more.'

The straight-talking but humorous response is typical of Jackson. He admits rather sheepishly to being a US Civil War 'buff' and having a passion for tennis. In a profession known for its formality and a 'money talks' attitude, he is laid-back, spontaneous and clearly enjoys talking to and about people. This gives a clue to what may be his main investment skill. 'Someone walks in here and there is every reason in the whole bloody earth why you shouldn't invest in that company. But there is something [about them] that makes me want to do it.'

It would be hard to pin the mainstream VC badge to Michael Jackson; at times his outlook is more like that of the enthusiastic investment angel one suspects still lurks behind his VC mantle. He relies on his own judgement about people, eschewing systems, financial analysis and rounds of research. 'I'm not a great proponent of reading business plans. If you're not careful you can lose some of the personal touch.' Then comes the punch line: 'If someone's boring and tedious we tip them out early. I like people I can have laugh with.'

He suggests that new economy mores have had a positive effect on the way business gets done. People are not necessarily more relaxed but they are perhaps more open minded. 'Five years ago my business card would have had qualifications on it. Now I don't have qualifications on it,' he observes.

He wonders aloud whether failure is too far from the minds of a new generation of entrepreneurial VCs. 'The very first deal I did when I started Elderstreet was a complete disaster. I called up all of my mates as it went under. I thought you couldn't go much lower than starting your own business and having your first deal be a disaster. It was probably quite good for me.'

Tornado-Insider.com – Magazine, June 2000

3 Hiring for Internet start-ups

Iqbal S. Bassi, Charles E. Bruin and Mannie Gill

Renaissance Search & Selection

Editor's introduction

The Internet boom has created a critical shortage of talent in two areas for all firms, whether involved in the Internet or not: experienced managers who know how to run a business and what sorts of controls need to be implemented to reduce the most serious risks of a new venture, and experienced technologists who can build and maintain the technology required. At the time of writing this introduction, managers of both sorts are receiving several calls a week from headhunters, sometimes when they have been in a new post for only a few days. And, at the time of proofreading, Boo.com went spectacularly bust.com – as if to prove both points. In most business plans, one of the major risks is being unable to find suitably experienced management. Finance is not a limiting factor (at the time of writing); junior employees are not a limiting factor; and even well connected finance directors, general counsels and non-execs are not a limiting factor for most new Internet ventures, but finding talented operational and general management is. In consequence, the HR and hiring functions have assumed an even greater importance to the Internet start-up process than they normally do for new businesses in general. A fortiori, it is worth noting that the first thing a venture capitalist or banker looks at is the quality of the management. A rule of thumb is that a second-rate idea with a first-rate management team will always be backed before a first-rate idea with a second-rate management team behind it. People matter. It is vital that you, the entrepreneur, hire the right people.

Renaissance Search & Selection Ltd is an unusual headhunting firm (I trust that they will forgive me for using the term that everyone but the executive-search industry itself uses) in http://www.renaissance-search.co.uk/ *two ways. First, all the principals have succeeded in another field before entering the headhunting business. Second, they have always specialized in the Internet and high technology.*

Renaissance is a boutique executive search firm, serving clients in European private equity and early-stage technology companies. The executives at the firm have previously gained experience within professional services, including strategic and technology consulting, investment banking and executive search.

Iqbal S. Bassi is founder and director of both Renaissance Search & Selection and

Renaissance Ventures. Prior to this, he worked as a strategic consultant with Monitor Company advising Fortune 500 companies on technology ventures, and as a mergers and acquisitions executive with Broadview International, on cross-border high-tech transactions. He is 30 years old, holds two first-class honours degrees and was an Economic and Social Research Council scholar at Cambridge University. He serves as a non-executive director at European Technology Ventures.

Charles E. Bruin *is founder and managing director of Renaissance Search & Selection Ltd and founder of Renaissance Ventures. Prior to this, he was a strategy consultant with The Boston Consulting Group (London), dealing with Fortune 500 companies across several industries. Previously he worked as a strategic change consultant for Reckitt & Colman on projects worldwide, and he is a graduate of the Harvard Business School (MBA).*

Mannie Gill *is founder and executive director of Renaissance Search & Selection Ltd. Prior to this, he worked for PSD Group plc, where he focused on international search assignments for leading private equity and M&A firms across many sectors, including technology. While at PSD, he established strong relationships with a number of key clients. Previously he was a management consultant with Framework Consulting in its London office. He is 28 years old holds a bachelor's degree in Business Management, focusing on strategic marketing.*

Aim

Knowledge itself is Power
Francis Bacon (1597)

The Internet revolution is causing an unprecedented shift in employment attitudes across all professional levels in Europe. Partner-level executives in investment banks and leading consulting firms, as well as entry-level graduates, are leaving the corporate and professional service sectors to join the Internet revolution. As with most revolutions, there are tremendous risks and high levels of disruption from puncturing an existing order.

What distinguishes good historians from mediocre ones is their ability to study the dynamics of a revolution, not just by their recording of events. Equally, it is critical for Internet entrepreneurs to arm themselves with an understanding of the Internet landscape so as to craft a winning strategy. This is as equally important for acquiring human capital as it is for the crafting of competitive strategy.

Examining the critical process of recruitment to build great teams in isolation to other aspects of the firm will prove a major disadvantage in the longer term. This is particularly true for Internet companies, where human capital is a key determinant in a company's success. This chapter outlines the methods for hiring an outstanding team, and the often overlooked and critically important aspect of retaining outstanding professionals. These are examined in the context of understanding two important issues: (i) people and knowledge as a source of competitive edge, and (ii) managing knowledge workers.

The Internet revolution

The Internet and related technologies are rapidly changing the methods of business organization and with it, attitudes of risk-taking. The whirlwind effect of the Internet revolution that gripped North America several years ago is now taking root in Europe. Simultaneously, it is bringing extraordinary rewards to some, but not to all, risk-takers. http://www.qxl.com/ Innovative entrepreneurs like Tim Jackson of QXL and Brent Hoberman and Martha Lane-Fox of Lastminute.com have become multimillionaires in a very short space http://www.lastminute.com/ of time. The 'dotcom mania' is encouraging other risk-takers to cash in on their experience and join the start-up revolution, often as equity holders or with the promise of becoming one over time. The frenzy has even reached the upper echelons of the corporate world with high-profile executives leaving their careers to join dotcoms. http://www.priceline.com/ One such executive is Heidi Miller, who left Citigroup as CFO to join Priceline.com, and another is George Shaheen, the former head of Andersen Consulting, http://www.webvan.com/ who joined Webvan in 1999. It's fair to say that the Internet has acquired near celebrity status across Europe; even governments are seeking to become 'e-governments' http://www.davidbowie.com/ and rock stars are establishing their own banks!

Even ambitious executives with opportunities to study at leading business schools, such as the Harvard Business School, are either deferring or abandoning education due to the 'high opportunity cost'. Traditional employers, the so-called 'bricks and mortar' companies, consulting firms and investment banks are all experiencing the downside of the Internet revolution. Executives have abandoned their firms in droves to seek greater personal challenges and financial rewards. Pricewaterhouse/Coopers' e-business unit has witnessed a 50%[1] churn rate in the last year alone. In a bid to keep talent, many firms are deploying new and far-reaching retention strategies such as creating venture capital funds, http://www.labmorgan.com/ accelerator units or incubator funds, and by promising to finance employees' strong ideas. Examples include JP Morgan's creation of LabMorgan, e-finance for great http://www.bainlab.com/ ideas, and BainLab, an incubator fund created by leading consulting firm Bain and Co. Others are simply paying more money in order to retain staff.

There is a shortage of qualified staff in Europe,[2] which matches the risk profile often perceived as necessary in Internet start-ups. This reflects a lack of development in the e-commerce and e-services markets in general, and slow European adoption in particular. As a result, companies most at risk of employee defection are the e-consulting units at professional service firms and technology and telecommunications companies such as Cisco and British Telecom. However, an increasing number of executives are making the transition from 'bricks-2-clicks', as some of the risks associated with the net diminish through: (i) better understanding and validation of business models, (ii) the greater availability of funding, and crucially (iii) the ease of returning to the bricks and mortar world.

Finding great hires is probably the most important task for the founders of any company, particularly for Internet companies, as these human assets are *the* central assets in a firm's early days. Also, the human-asset element in a firm's survival equation is becoming increasingly important, and will have a tremendous impact on ownership and innovation patterns in these firms over time.

The age of knowledge

Internet start-ups need to appreciate some of the fundamental shifts in technology and business strategy to fully capitalize on the Internet age. We are constantly reminded that we live in a 'post-industrial' economy or 'information society', a change reflected in the dramatic rise in the service sector. Essentially, this translates into knowledge and people becoming more central to new methods of organization and wealth creation. Up to recent years, there has been a strong relationship between wealth and the ownership of 'physical' assets. However, through advances and dispersion of cheaper and faster technology, future wealth creation will be generated in large part through 'intangible' resources, principally knowledge assets. Knowledge has become an important new wealth generator.

Knowledge assets in companies, in the form of intellectual capacity and innovation, reside within people (human capital), and these are accessed through the presence of processes, procedures and routines of knowledge deployment. Great companies are being

http://www.microsoft.com/ built through the understanding of how to utilize knowledge and the chief knowledge bearers – people. These include leading companies such as Microsoft, Silicon

http://www.sgi.com/ Graphics and SAP. A brief examination of capital markets highlights the value attached to knowledge companies versus that attached to bricks and mortar companies. For

http://www.sap.com/ instance, Microsoft enjoys a market capitalization of $581 billion, against General Motors' value of $53 billion, yet the software giant has only one-tenth of GM's workforce and one-ninth of its revenue. Often the defection of a key knowledge worker can have a profound impact on a company's valuation, much like the impact of a celebrity cook who defects from a leading restaurant. Interestingly, technology and knowledge have parallels – both can become redundant rapidly, both need constant updating and re-inventing, and both need to be applied in novel ways to achieve superior economic returns.

Knowledge and strategy

A greater understanding of the role of knowledge has had a major impact in explaining the performance of companies. In the past, it was a widely held belief that the key to achieving competitive advantage centred in the product/market arena. However, this did little to explain a key question: why are there differing levels of performance across companies in the same sector? A key to answering this question is found by looking outside the product/market arena and inside companies themselves.

Examining the 'internal dynamics' of companies quickly led to new frontiers in thinking about what a firm should do and, more importantly, what it should not do. New concepts like core competencies and strategic outsourcing became the guiding mantras for determining the optimal boundary of a firm, and establishing with whom and under what conditions to create strategic alliances.

As knowledge capital became a central component to a firm's success, greater attention was paid to teams, skills, decision-making processes and the organization of the firm. In short, knowledge-based firms sought to align competitive strategy, organizational design and human strategy in order to gain an edge and stay ahead in dynamic markets. Today, intelligent firms recognize that capabilities and competencies are not inherent in the firm, but grow internally, through the unique combination of assets with flexible structures – this, firms now realize, combined with a powerful product/market strategy, will lead to success.

To use a biological metaphor, knowledge and competencies can be regarded as 'genes', confronting the same environmental challenges as other firms. Successful genes evolve and adapt to their environment, seeking to mutate in order to survive. Likewise, if knowledge companies are to avoid mediocre performance (or extinction), they need to pay *careful* and *constant* attention to the dynamics between competitive strategy, organizational design and human strategy, and ultimately to the ownership pattern of the firm.

Human assets and Internet start-ups

In light of the above, the strategic issue centres on what asset combination and market strategies lead to success. Three principal assets are required:

> Ideas – Capital assets – Human assets

Most Internet firms begin with an idea. Innovative and commercially sound ideas in today's buoyant market will find some form of funding, but unfortunately many great ideas wither away. Market forces will determine the cost of funding, a trend which currently favours entrepreneurs, due to the heavy supply of risk capital. Access to suitable human assets is probably the most difficult problem facing Internet start-ups in the current climate. Unlike acquiring capital assets, which is a fairly transparent process and is, moreover, easily utilized, humans are more complex and, consequently, hiring decisions are based more on intangibles such as judgement and intuition. Yet, the tolerance for making a mistake is very low and can imperil an early-stage company.

Start-ups should be aware of the following considerations when dealing with human assets:

■ People with knowledge and competencies are highly *transferable*, *mobile* and much sought after. Knowledge workers find themselves courted by numerous firms both in the Internet and in the bricks and mortar world, thus strengthening their ability to switch jobs.

■ Carefully selected knowledge workers can be critical 'architects of value' for the firm. In order to extract and cultivate this value a firm must align the interests of the knowledge worker with the firm and its team. Providing the knowledge worker with the opportunity to own part of the firm creates a powerful impetus to work harder, innovate, and lower the likelihood of job switching. For example, there are over 2000 millionaires at Microsoft Corporation.

■ Finally, firms should ensure that knowledge workers understand the risks associated with early-stage companies, especially in the Internet sector. Most people have a risk threshold, beyond which they feel uncomfortable. Most Internet firms are unique in their risk profile *vis-à-vis* traditional companies and can be characterized by:

– rapid and real-time decision making;

– shorter product/service life-cycles;

– disruption through disintermediation;

– market uncertainty and high competitive intensity.

The above trends have an important bearing on the process of hiring great people. The following section focuses on some of the practical steps and considerations all start-ups will go through in hiring people. Often, the recruitment process is rather 'mechanical' and it is easy to fall into a formulaic mode. However, start-ups should pay particular attention to the above considerations, remembering that the quality of the people is paramount and not just 'quickly ramping up the company'.

Teamwork means having a team

It is well documented that the success or failure of any organization, be it an Internet start-up or a more traditional enterprise, is a function of how well the individuals within that organization can work together. This is particularly true of Internet start-ups where the environment is unstructured and unpredictable, and where roles and responsibilities are by necessity fluid. Hence, it is imperative that entrepreneurs focus their attention on building flexible and cohesive teams.

Everyone at some point in his or her working career has been part of an exceptional team. It is an experience most people look back on with relish, where they really felt that the whole truly did exceed the sum of the parts. The curious aspect of many high-performing teams is that they tend to be exceptions as opposed to the rule and many people fail to re-discover the 'secret sauce' that seemed to make that incremental difference.

Entrepreneurs who have been successful in convincing capital providers of the validity of their business proposition often lack experience in recruiting and managing an

http://www.hbs.edu/ effective team. According to Professor Linda Hill at Harvard Business School[3], those who are new to managing and leading a business tend to neglect their team-building responsibilities, incorrectly believing that managing one-on-one relationships is sufficient in building a cohesive team.

This section offers practical advice on hiring individuals and on building outstanding teams within Internet start-up organizations. It argues that organizational analysis should be less concerned with personalities or filling generic positions in the 'organagram', and more with finding those people possessing the necessary skills and knowledge for the organization, and who, when brought together, form a balanced team.

Recruiting and retaining those people who drive organizations forward is one of the greatest challenges a business faces. This task is made more problematic by today's tight labour market, increasing premiums on the best people and the difficulties in locating them.

Figure 3.1 provides an overview of the various stages involved in the recruitment process.

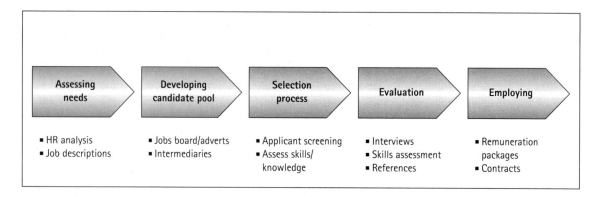

Fig. 3.1   Overview of the recruitment process

Stage 1: Assessing needs in the context of a start-up's development

The skill-set required in a start-up organization varies according to the stage of development. Figure 3.2 lays out the different stages of the start-up's development as defined by its advancement in the funding process.

An entrepreneur should not think to himself, 'I need a business development person', but rather, 'I need to acquire a skill-set that enables the business to develop a number of external beneficial commercial relationships . . .'

Given this approach, the entrepreneur is looking to identify skill-sets that might reside across a variety of organizations, as opposed to focusing on narrowly defined positions (see Fig. 3.3).

Development phase	START-UP	SEED CAPITAL	FIRST ROUND	SECOND ROUND
Existing team	Founding team of entrepreneurs, consultants, advisers	Founding team of entrepreneurs	Founding team of entrepreneurs and initial hires	Founding team of entrepreneurs and senior professional managers
New hires		*Business development* *Technical hires* *Back-office support*	*Professional managers:* *CEO* *COO* *VP marketing* *VP technology*	*Professional staff:* *country managers* *VP sales*
Skill-sets	▪ Business conceptualization ▪ Market sizing ▪ Product prototyping ▪ Investor selling	▪ Product development ▪ Identifying vendors and commercial partners ▪ Pitching customers ▪ Building office infrastructure	▪ Product launch and delivery ▪ Managing business complexity ▪ Scaling business ▪ Resetting organization direction and culture	▪ Business roll-out ▪ Implementing robust processes and systems ▪ Managing next level of complexity

Fig. 3.2   The key developmental stages of an Internet start-up

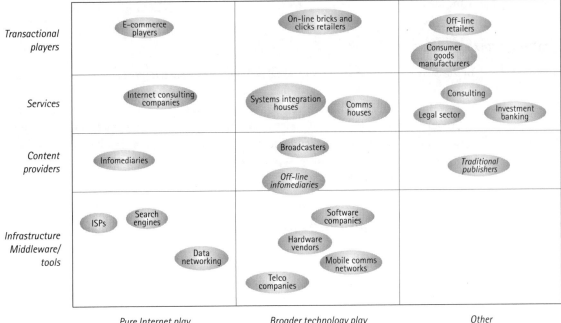

Fig. 3.3   Sources of intellectual capital in the information age

Equipped with the context of the organization's development and the skills necessary to propel the organization forward to the next stage, the entrepreneur can start identifying where the skill-sets reside and how to access them.

Identifying where key skill-sets reside in the technology and non-technology universe is a crucial next step in the process. Figure 3.3 maps out a taxonomy of the different types of firms that exist in that universe.

Recruiting for an Internet start-up does not necessarily mean raiding so-called 'technology companies'. In addition, extracting executives from leading technology companies, such as Amazon, Yahoo! or Psion, can prove prohibitively expensive.

Would-be recruiters are encouraged to search further afield where the same transferable skills can be acquired more cost effectively. Many large corporate enterprises or professional service firms are filled with smart individuals with Internet experience or knowledge. Moreover, they have the ability and skills to fill such a role.

Additionally, the allure of an Internet start-up opportunity for these individuals may be more appealing than to incumbent technology executives, and the ability to extract them is increased. Mapping out the sources of intellectual capital also demonstrates that process and content knowledge for particular industries can also reside across a highly diverse set of executives.

Having a broader understanding of where skills reside is particularly important, as many entrepreneurs start out with unrealistic expectations, believing they can recruit the CTO at a leading search engine, only to discover that 100 other funded start-ups had the same idea.

Creating a mix of talent

In the early stages of an organization's development it is also important to be aware of the overall skills mix. A skills audit should provide a strong indication as to the make-up of the total hiring needs. This requires an understanding of the subtle blend of strategic, operational, and organizational design requirements, with a sound grasp of the roles and responsibilities of each and their potential overlaps. Entrepreneurs should never lose sight of the fact that the cohesiveness and strength of any team derives from collective and individual strengths of its members.

Stage 2: Developing a candidate pool

Having identified where the desired skills reside, the next task is to gain access to the right people. Herein lies one of the largest problems for would-be recruiters: opaque informational flows, highly protective employers and tight labour conditions make it very difficult for entrepreneurs to identify with any real clarity which specific candidates to approach. Listed below are a number of strategies which an entrepreneur can pursue.

Personal network search

Most entrepreneurs actively use their personal network, which generally involves staying in touch with former colleagues, professional institutions and attending networking events, such as First Tuesday.

http://www.firsttuesday.com/

It is more cost effective to use personal network search methods. However, these tend to have a limited reach and more often than not entrepreneurs have a core network which is either technically or commercially biased. The inability for founders from either camp to transcend other disciplines (technical or commercial) can make a personal network search limiting.

In addition, many companies create internal reward programmes for recommending successful candidates. This is an easy option and benefits from combining multiple personal networks.

Use of on-line and off-line infomediaries

Traditional off-line sources such as newspapers and industry journals are useful tools for identifying potential executives in a particular sector. However, these fail to capture the entire candidate pool and companies are increasingly reluctant about what they publish. On-line infomediaries, particularly on-line job boards, do go some way to overcoming the informational asymmetries that exist between potential employer and recruit. However, job boards do not necessarily have access to the highest calibre of candidates and there is a large amount of information to filter.

The most successful of the on-line job boards include: *http://www.monster.co.uk/*, *http://www.stepstone.com/* and *http://www.topjobs.net/*. The key limitation of this approach is the time and resources required to research various job boards and the rudimentary filtering services offered, though these are continually improving.

Retaining an executive search firm

The executive search industry exists because of the highly inefficient information flows between buyers and sellers in the labour market. This inefficiency allows search firms to charge up to 35% of a candidate's first-year compensation. In the current conditions, it is not unusual for this figure to be higher and to include a claim on equity compensation.

Accordingly, should a company decide to retain the services of an executive search firm, the company should be highly disciplined in how it chooses, briefs and manages that search firm.

Choose and manage an executive search firm

Executive search is a highly fragmented industry in which practitioners require no professional qualification. Not surprisingly, there is a huge variance in the quality and repute of firms that practise in this area.

Segment your market

Identify which executive search firms deal with senior-level hires and those that deal with mid-tier hires. Also, identify those firms that profess to have sector expertise useful to your organization. Remember, there isn't one firm that will meet all your needs.

For key senior hires, such as a CEO (*chief executive officer*) or CTO (*chief technology officer*), it is advisable to retain a high-end executive search firm. An entrepreneur should also look to personal referrals when drawing up a shortlist of firms, to determine the ability of firms to successfully fill positions.

Draw up a shortlist and test content knowledge

A high-end specialized executive search firm should either employ industry-experienced executives or have a high level of content knowledge. Potential recruiters should assess a search firm's ability to source suitable candidates and determine what skill attributes these candidates should possess.

Write a clear yet flexible brief

Writing a brief is a subtle mix of ensuring that the client firm sees only candidates with the appropriate skills but does not become so specific that the potential candidate universe is prohibitively small. A good executive search consultant should provide guidance on the usefulness of a brief.

Manage the search process

Search firms typically charge a non-refundable retainer, hence it is important to ensure that resources committed by a client firm are suitably employed. The process must be project managed with regular reviews of progress and agreed timeframes for producing a candidate shortlist.

Stage 3: Selection process

The most crucial hiring decisions for an entrepreneur are those concerning the senior management team: CEO, COO, CTO, CFO and head of marketing/business development. These positions tend to be filled after a significant round of funding has been completed. They often represent the entry of professional management into the organization.

These decisions result in the initial founders having to cede control to outsiders, thus making the process more difficult. The following provides a list of key traits and skills that start-ups should look for in senior hires. Understanding what each should bring into the organization is also necessary for an effective interview process.

Chief executive officer (CEO)

Responsibility centres on setting the strategic direction and leadership of the company.
Key skills/abilities:

- successfully led an organization in a start-up or corporate environment with visible results;

- excellent understanding of either the industry sector or ability to grow a young organization to maturity;

- ability to communicate internally (articulate a vision) and externally (credible with investors and the City of London);

- well networked – can potentially open doors to major customers and strategic partners;

- correct risk orientation – required adequate base salary but keener on long-term upside;

- can motivate and inspire employees and co-workers who will need to feel that their needs are understood and appreciated in a start-up/pressure-cooker environment;

- must be a role model for the organization with the ability not to be deflected by the many roadblocks that will be presented.

Chief operating officer (COO)

The COO is responsible for running the day-to-day operations and execution of the business plan.
Key skills/abilities:

- ability to manage operational complexity as the organization grows;
- experience of implementing new processes, procedures and systems;
- excellent content knowledge of the product and the industry;
- ability to staff and organize the company through its development;
- excellent problem-solving skills – highly pragmatic and operational in orientation;
- experience in handling operational roadblocks and using a network to seek outside advice.

Chief technology officer (CTO)

The CTO is responsible for managing the technical 'build' and 'run' – chiefly concerned with product delivery and bridging the technical and commercial objectives of the business.
Key skills/abilities:

- key qualifications in a technical discipline from a leading institution;
- strong knowledge of the underlying technology;
- led and managed product development teams;
- track record of product delivery and disciplined project management;
- ability to think strategically and contribute significantly at board level.

Head of marketing and business development

Responsible for growing the top line of the business and should be externally focused on customers and commercial partners.

Key skills/abilities:

- outstanding track record in growing the top line of a business;
- ability to articulate customer needs internally and execute campaigns or align with key strategic partners;
- excellent negotiating skills;
- very good networking skills, deal sourcing and knowledge of the sector;
- ability to hire and manage a motivated sales team.

Stage 4: Evaluation

Interviewing candidates

Having been presented with an interesting shortlist, which prima facie appears to offer the right skills, the entrepreneur must intelligently and systematically manage the interview process.

The interview process typically involves a number of key stages:

- *skills and content knowledge:* being satisfied that the candidate brings the right skill levels and content knowledge for the role under consideration;
- *cultural fit:* assessing the candidate's 'fit' with the organization, which includes his/her appetite for risk, and personality fit with the rest of the team;
- *investor approval:* certain key management hires require investor approval.

The importance of hiring decisions, especially for senior positions, is amplified in Internet companies as the cost of making a poor decision may seriously hinder the progress of the company.

Entrepreneurs can increase the chances of making a high-quality decision through being rigorous in how they conduct the interview process. Many entrepreneurs underestimate the time and effort required to meet, assess, discuss internally and provide feedback to the candidate over a period of little more than eight weeks.

Many outstanding potential candidates are actually lost due to the inability of companies to turn around a decision or at worst the inability to manage the logistics of meeting several times with a candidate in order to make an intelligent and informed decision.

The entire process should be rigorously project managed. The following provides a checklist for preparing for an initial interview:

- set the objectives of the interview and the specific areas to probe. In an initial interview this should focus on content knowledge and track record;

- prior to meeting, collate all submitted candidate materials and review these against the initial skills audit;

- scrutinize to an extent the qualifications and experience that have been listed by the candidate. Identify the key institutions and use personal networks to gather more information about their credibility and achievements;

- identify the interview technique that will be employed – case study, one-on-one, panel interview, etc.;

- ensure that the administrative arrangements for the venue are confirmed – it may seem trivial but re-arranging meetings is one of the most time-consuming activities. Many entrepreneurs fall into the trap of being so busy that they neglect basic courtesies of postponing interviews with acceptable notice periods, or at worst not turning up at all. There is a fine line between a hectic and rapidly changing environment and being unprofessional with outside parties;

- calibrate the expectations of the interviewee as to the process of the interview.

Different approaches to interviewing

The interview format should be adjusted to reflect the seniority of the candidate, the stage of the interview process and whether the interview focuses on cultural fit or skills and abilities.

The following provides a brief list of different techniques that can be deployed in an interview situation.

Content/industry knowledge

When testing content knowledge the interviewer should push for specifics and detail within a particular area. Test the candidate's understanding of a particular product, etc. If the interview is likely to become technical in nature an entrepreneur should use an adviser or consultant.

Problem solving/process skills

The use of case studies is a favourite for professional service companies, as case studies aim to test how candidates address problems and apply analytical skills, often in industries where they have little content knowledge. Case studies tend to be far more interesting and useful if they are based on real scenarios experienced by entrepreneurs. The key is to seek out the approach and methods of problem solving, using logical and reasonable assumptions and conclusions.

http://www.mckinsey.com/

http://www.bcg.com/

http://www.monitor.com/

Analytical/numeric skills

For mid-level hires a written or verbal test is a good filter to examine analytical skills. Increasingly, these tests can even be conducted on-line.

Interpersonal/influencing skills/personal fit

These interviews are conducted once a candidate has satisfied the initial criteria (content, experience and analytical skills). The interview is intended to assess a cultural fit with the company. Approaches to organizational issues, understanding of company culture and personal empathy are aspects to be probed at this stage. Leading companies offering such services include: *http://www.shlgroup.com/, http://www.test.com/*, and *http://www.psl.com/*.

Stage 5: Employing

Pulling it all together – creating a high-performing team

Having successfully managed the recruiting process and having identified a number of suitable candidates, the next task centres on formulating compensation structures and thinking about how the hires will fit into the team.

http://www.pfdf.org/

Peter Drucker a leading management thinker, draws a useful analogy of teams using sporting metaphors. A baseball team can be a team of all-stars, each with his own individual strengths, without the need to worry about assuming the skill-set of other participants, i.e. a third baseman will never have to pitch a game, etc. Likewise, skill shortfalls in an organization can be filled with outstanding individuals with no regard to team dynamics.

The second comparison he draws is to a football team, where greater interdependence is required, but where roles are still tightly defined. Finally, Drucker talks about a pair of tennis doubles where the players' skills are almost identical, and their roles are interchanged and improvised at will.

The team environment in an Internet start-up probably lies somewhere between the second and third analogy. The environment is such that everyone in the early stages must be prepared to get their 'hands dirty', whilst retaining a key role in the organization. The organization finds itself constantly under-resourced, but stretches its people to manage the shortfall.

Creating a common perception of the working environment before participants join crucially calibrates the expectation of the hires, and begins to build a sense of common purpose.

Compensation and reward within Internet start-up firms is a highly written about topic. As an entrepreneur, getting this right is crucial to motivating and retaining employees. Interestingly, many studies have revealed that when people talk of their most rewarding and enjoyable professional experiences, they quote the most important factors as the people they have worked with, the highly charged and motivating atmosphere, the belief in themselves and team members, etc. – i.e. there is no mention of financial motives.

Frederick Herzberg, a leading organizational theorist, contested in his *motivation-hygiene theory* that factors giving rise to worker satisfaction and motivation such as those above (*intrinsic factors*) were very different to those that reduced dissatisfaction such as salary, working conditions and company procedure (*extrinsic factors*).

However, we are reminded from the initial discussion in this chapter that mass migration of talent into the Internet world has been brought about by the promise, or chance at least, of significant financial return as by intrinsic personal fulfilment. An entrepreneur would be foolish to imagine that creating an intrinsically pleasing environment would be sufficient to attract and retain top talent.

http://www.cisco.com/   Further research has also revealed the dramatic difference ownership has on the behaviour of individuals engaged in an enterprise. Aligning an individual's interests around http://www.sun.com/   the long-term financial health of the organization through a minority ownership stake has now become one of the most popular means of attracting talent into an Internet http://www.antfactory.com/   organization. The use of stock options – giving employees a stake in the companies that they are helping to build – has proven to be a highly influential 'carrot' in the http://www.tweisel.com/   war for talent. Many knowledge-based companies are taking this approach seriously, including the leading technology and technology investment firms, such as Cisco, Sun, http://www.internetcapital.com/   Antfactory and Internet Capital.

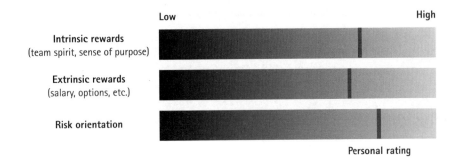

Fig. 3.4   Factors affecting motivation in Internet start-ups

Figure 3.4 outlines the three key factors affecting employee motivational levels. The key goal for entrepreneurs is to actively track and manage all three influences. Problems tend to arise when any one factor slides too low and creates a tension significant enough for the employee to consider job switching. Throughout the recruitment process, entrepreneurs need to assess where individual candidate ratings lie and whether this is consistent with the firm. This needs to be an objective process, as inconsistent expectations quickly lead to employee dissatisfaction and waste precious time.

In consequence, the entrepreneur faces the subtle task of casting an environment that plays to the intrinsic and extrinsic needs of the identified talent pool. Interestingly, it may still be the former that convinces people to stay in an organization as long as the opportunity cost/intrinsic reward tension does not become too great. This explains in part why so many of the professional service firms are investing huge resources in adjunct incubator funds to their main business and company gymnasiums in order to retain their employees. Netscape, for one, has its own dentist, and Sun Microsystems has an in-house laundry service.[4]

`http://www.netscape.com/`

`http://www.sun.com/`

It is important that employers also fulfil the administrative tasks of issuing share options, contracts and other promised benefits in a reasonable timeframe. Start-ups should NOT underestimate the time required to achieve this, NOR be ignorant of the fact that not completing this task does have a detrimental effect on the motivation of new hires.

Levels of compensation (at the time of going to press) are being pushed ever skywards as the competition for particular skills intensifies. Smart entrepreneurs should be more circumspect in their quest to acquire human capital, recognizing that financial reward is only one element of the recruitment and retention mix.

Here is a checklist for determining team dynamics and compensation structures:

- establish the nature of the desired team environment;
- map the skills profile and 'fit' of individuals on to the organization before extending offers;
- scrutinize the risk orientation of candidates carefully;
- calibrate the expectations of all candidates before they join;
- ensure compensation structures for key hires address intrinsic and extrinsic reward and take account of the difference minority ownership makes to an individual's incentives;
- ensure that all issues of compensation and employment are checked thoroughly by experts, such as HR consultants and legal advisers.

Conclusion

Hiring and retaining outstanding teams is a complex task, especially in dynamic environments such as technology markets, where management time is limited. There is no single template for successful recruitment and it is essentially a confluence of intuition, judgement and vision. Furthermore, the knowledge base inside technology companies requires constant updating and renewing and, like all assets, it needs 'depreciating' or re-allocating. Finally, it is worth drawing upon the observations of another organizational theorist, Robert Michels, who in 1915 asserted that all organizations ultimately are reduced to oligarchies through self-interest and opportunism. However, entrepreneurs MUST realize that in an 'age of knowledge' such tendencies in knowledge-based companies will lead to failure.

Listed below are five key themes which should permeate the recruitment process and to which entrepreneurs should pay close attention when building an outstanding team:

- knowledge is assuming a central role in the success of companies;
- recruitment should complement competitive strategy and organizational design;
- recruitment is a continual and evolving process;
- recruitment should be rigorously project managed – success depends on it;
- successful retention requires a mix of financial and non-financial incentives.

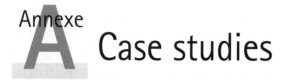

Case studies

Case study | ## 1. Internet start-up

How PremierFind.com built its team (Eleanor Chadwick, CEO)

PremierFind.com is creating the definitive source for fine art, antiques and contemporary http://www.premierfind.com/ design on the Web. The company's vision is to create a truly international on-line source, which attracts the highest quality dealers and designers as our partners, and the most discerning individuals, collectors, and interior designers as our clients. The site brings together several previously fragmented markets, mixing the old with the new, and breaking down traditional barriers in the fine and decorative arts.

PremierFind.com was founded in September 1999 and, in addition to our full-time team, includes an advisory board of international industry experts.

Building a team for any Internet start-up is a delicate business, and even more so when dealing with the heady sums and strong personalities that define the art and design worlds. Members of the team were chosen both for their expertise in a certain facet of the business, be it art, marketing or technology, and a willingness to tackle what is often unbroken ground with our dealer partners, the press, and the business and technology communities.

In a small team, individual initiative is the key factor. Decisions are made at what might seem like lightning speed in a more traditional business environment. The willingness to put forward ideas and carry them through, and to adapt to new situations with grace and good sense are as important as any amount of previous experience. Rising to the occasion is often the order of the day, and it is vital that each employee is hired not just for the here and now, but for his/her growth potential within the company. People who respond well to challenge and flourish under increased responsibility are the most positive additions to a young team.

If we have learned anything in the past few months, it is the importance of personal recommendation and use of personal networks.

On the issue of compensation, Internet start-ups are famous for tipping the cash versus options scales. As a rule, anyone who is in it solely for the money, the stability or the '9 to 5' should stay at home. Options are a very effective way of making everyone feel a part of the project, both with its risks and rewards. When people feel they have a real stake in the company, it makes the mission stronger – and the good ideas flow faster.

Summary points

- Recruiting criteria are a mix of technical skills and ability to work in a dynamic un-chartered environment.

- Personal network searches can be a highly effective means for acquiring the right mix of talent.

- Rewarding employees is not just about financial incentives, although sharing ownership in the company creates a strong common sense of purpose.

Case study

2. A view from the investor community

Apax Partners & Co (David Latter – London Office)

Apax Partners & Co is one of the leading private equity firms in the world with 130 venture capital professionals operating across Europe, the USA, Israel and Japan. Apax Partners invests in high technology and growth companies at all stages of development, from start-up to buy-out. Founded in 1972, Apax has currently over $7 billion under management or advice. Recent Internet investments include NetDoktor (UK, Denmark), Beenz.com (USA and Europe), Talk City (USA), moneyextra.com (UK), Independer.com (Europe), PaperX.com (Europe), Clicksure (Europe) and QXL (Europe).

http://www.apax.co.uk/

The importance of excellent management for a venture house looking to invest in an Internet business cannot be overrestimated. At Apax Partners, the quality of the management team is generally the single most important factor in the investment decision.

Typically, a core management team would comprise initially a chief executive officer, chief operating officer, chief technical officer and head of sales and marketing. A finance director would likely be the next major hire. The team should collectively encompass the breadth and depth of skills and experience needed to make the business a success. These will include strategic flair, strong sales and marketing abilities, technical expertise and financial know-how, backed up by deep industry experience. Obviously, different members of the team will bring different strengths to the party, but it is crucial that all share the vision and culture of the company, are results oriented and have previously demonstrated their abilities. Apax's view of the management will be built up further through management presentations during the fund-raising process, backed up by referencing. Vital to clinching the investment deal is the team's ability to communicate its vision and excitement for the business during these presentations.

An example of a recent first-round Apax-led investment is PaperX.com, an independent business-to-business exchange in the €50 billion European paper and packaging market. The two founder entrepreneurs are MBAs with experience in a start-up and consulting respectively (including consulting to the paper industry). The team was bolstered initially by the addition of non-executive directors from the paper industry and a top-rated paper-sector analyst, and later by the hiring of the ex-CEO of a major European paper company, as CEO of PaperX. The advisory board has proved to be very useful in identifying and attracting other key personnel for the business. This combination of new entrepreneur vision and energy together with deep off-line industry experience made the team an attractive investment proposition.

Apax does not expect every component of the management structure to be in place at the time of the investment; indeed, many key hires are often made concurrently with the first major funding round. However, it is important that management recognize the need to build a complete team, and that they are open to the concept that the balance of the team may need to be altered during the course of its evolution to a mature company. This provides the basis for a trusted relationship with the company's investors, so that ongoing changes can be implemented to the satisfaction of both sides.

Apax's philosophy towards retention reflects our belief in the importance of hiring the best people and rewarding them well. It is essential that the team are committed to the success of the business on a long-term basis. In common with most venture houses, Apax sees share options as the most important element of the remuneration package. This helps to foster a results-driven organization and enables key team members to reap rewards from the company's success. We also like to see share options distributed widely, ideally to all employees in the organization.

Finally, we seek to assist our portfolio companies in their recruitment activities throughout the time we are with them. As an established private equity house with a long history of technology investing, we are able to draw on our extensive resources, networks and industry contacts on a global basis. We also have established relationships with numerous search firms and can help companies identify those that are most suited to fulfilling their needs.

Endnotes

1 *The Economist*, 25 March 2000, 'The Real Meaning of Empowerment', p. 101.

2 New estimates by International Data Corporation and Microsoft predict a European shortage of IT workers of 1.7 million by 2003. European governments are seeking new measures to address this shortage through granting additional visas to non-EU nationals, fiscal measures and education. (See *http://news2.thls.bbc.co.uk/hi/english/business/newsid%5F688000/688138.stm*, *http://news2.thls.bbc.co.uk/hi/english/uk%5Fpolitics/newsid%5F699000/699504.stm*, *http://news2.thls.bbc.co.uk/hi/english/world/europe/newsid_689000/689410.stm*.)

3 Hill, Linda A., 1992, *Becoming a Manager: Mastery of a New Identity*, Harvard Business School Press.

4 *The Economist*, 25 March 2000, 'The Real Meaning of Empowerment', p. 102.

4 You and your new dotcom business

Alastair Shaw

Editor's Introduction

Alastair Shaw is an experienced entrepreneur, having set up or co-founded a number of companies in various different corporate sectors. He has been closely involved with a cable TV investment company, an interactive video production business, a quoted investment trust that backed privately owned commercial radio stations (where he was Chairman), a joint venture between the legal profession and the BBC, a City-based public relations organization and an asset management company in France. He has been advising a fledgling Internet-related company for the past year and is currently helping to establish a venture debt partnership which will advance loan packages to fast-growing, IT-based entities in Europe. Prior to working with start-ups and newly formed businesses, Alastair worked in international banking, both in the UK and the US. In addition to his banking and entrepreneurial experience, he has also conducted research into executive stress and into the skills-sets of successful CEOs. The ability to manage stress is critical to anyone who tries to found a new business. In this chapter Alastair writes about what it takes for you, the entrepreneur, to make it in the Internet world. He has seen both sides of the entrepreneurial endeavour many times, both as an entrepreneur himself and as an adviser and investor in start-ups. He has worked with budding chief executives at all stages, from day one to exit and has seen what works, what doesn't work and everything in between. He is thus well qualified to write about you and your new dotcom business. Alastair may be contacted at Shaw@Start-upWWW.com.

Aim

So, you want to start and run a dotcom business! An Internet company with a sparkling future. You are not alone. Many people, not just whiz-kids wishing to make a fortune in cyberspace, constantly dream of starting up on their own, of creating something worthwhile from an original idea, of being their own boss, of giving the orders for a change, of entertaining in the executive dining room, of taking the company public and of making a fortune in the process. They may even be older than 30 when they get these wild and fanciful notions! But do they have what it really takes? Do *you* have what it really takes? Probably you have not had time to consider the matter. There is too much to do to get things up and running. But pause before you take the plunge. Think very carefully about the journey that you are about to embark on. There are many rewards along the way, but there are also many pitfalls for the unwary and those unsuited to the challenge. It would be worth your while to focus carefully on the material in this chapter, as it may eventually save you time, effort and money, and may ensure as well that the confidence that you have in your own abilities and in your unfolding career is not dented or even destroyed. If your self-esteem is to be preserved and built up, and if your enthusiasm and drive are to be properly channelled, it is essential that you make the right decision. Are you made of the right stuff to become a true entrepreneur, a leader of others intent on building a growth-oriented company, or should you team up with others and pool your talents, or should you work as an employee for someone who does have the necessary mix of CEO-type skills? Assuming that you are a complete novice in these matters, let's help you to answer these questions and begin the analysis that should lead to your making the correct choice. In short, let's see if you are up to the task in hand.

Creative genius or effective executive?

It is often said that what the corporate world constantly craves is new ideas, based perhaps on a mixture of original thinking, lateral thought processes, inspiration and luck. The Internet world, in particular, thrives on new ideas or, more precisely, on the application of Internet technology to old ideas. We all used to book holidays and plan our leisure time way in advance, using travel agents and booking agencies, where the service was not all that speedy and discounts were not always available. Now we can book flights, hotels, restaurants and shows at the click of a mouse, at the very last minute, invariably at a significant saving (*www.lastminute.com*). The new idea was that computer-delivered convenience in the home, ease of access to a wide range of products, an instant booking capability and attractive discounts all added up to a service that would attract significant consumer interest. The new venture, at least to date, is undoubtedly a great success story for Brent Hoberman and Martha Lane Fox, the entrepreneurs who came up with the new application, and is a good example of creative genius in the dotcom context. (It has yet to prove a success story for the investors.)

Some people come up with fresh ideas all the time, many of them unworkable, a few of them sensible, sometimes the occasional gem that everyone knows is great the moment they hear about it. Other people rarely devote any time at all to coming up with something novel. They are either sure that they have no talent in this direction or they simply can't be bothered. Many of you reading this book will already have an idea in mind, or be heading a team that has collectively come up with one. You probably have had other ideas in your time, but this is the one that is exciting you right now and is the one you want to run with. The question to be addressed here is not whether that idea is a good one and potentially commercially viable (that is a separate analysis), but whether the person who dreamt up the idea, that is you, is the right person to take it forward. The point at issue is whether the individual who shouts 'eureka' in the bath is the person to turn that idea into commercial reality. The creative genius may indeed become the effective executive but how can we tell in advance whether that is how it will turn out?

Deciding which you are

In the UK, Sir Clive Sinclair, the inventor and entrepreneur, has been responsible for some remarkable inventions in the consumer-electronics field in recent decades but he did not go on to head up a highly successful organization that exploited his creative talent. In Germany, too, a country known for its innovation, particularly in technical areas, there have been countless examples of original thinkers who came up with brilliant ideas but who were unable to take those ideas much beyond the drawing board. That task had to be carried out by others. And much the same story is true across the whole of Europe, France and Italy, in particular, being home to innovative design and style on the part of individuals who did not go on to found successful corporations. It seems quite often to be the case that the source of the *inspiration* is not also the source of the *perspiration*, the sweat that makes the original idea or new application work in the commercial cauldron. The two activities are really quite different.

On the other hand, worldwide there are powerful examples that prove the opposite, Mike Bloomberg in America being one. Bloomberg set up Innovative Market Systems (now Bloomberg Inc., *www.bloomberg.com*) in 1981, his idea being to bring a range of financial information and services to the international financial community via specially designed terminals. He still heads up that highly successful corporation which today serves clients in over 90 countries. David Potter of the British company Psion plc (*www.psion.co.uk*) is another example. He established his ground-breaking portable and hand-held computer hardware and software company years ago but runs it to this day. In France, Marcel Dassault founded his famous aircraft company after the Second World War and went on to develop it into a world leader in the aeronautics field (*www.dassault-aviation.com*). Around the same time, in Italy, Enzo Ferrari, a motor-racing champion who worked first for Alfa Romeo, soon went solo and began to design and build racing cars that became famous throughout the world. He built the company (*www.ferrari.com*) into a formidable one before selling a significant stake to Fiat in 1969. The inspiration and the perspiration, in these four cases, went hand in hand. And there are many other examples across Europe of 'ideas people' going on to run their own businesses very successfully, just as there are examples of 'ideas people' who for one reason or another were not suited to the executive role and management challenge.

As regards today's start-ups, therefore, it is vital to determine whether the person or persons involved, the ones who hit on the new idea, approach, concept or application, are capable of running the company that will subsequently evolve. Such a determination can

Table 4.1 Innovator or CEO?

The successful 'ideas' person	Character trait	The successful CEO
Quite likely	Curious	Not necessarily
Quite likely	Experimental	Not necessarily
Quite likely	An original thinker	Not necessarily
Quite likely	A lateral thinker	Not necessarily
Quite likely	A constant learner	Quite likely
Quite likely	A driven character	Quite likely
Not necessarily	Passionate about the business*	Quite likely
Not necessarily	Commercially minded*	Quite likely
Not necessarily	Vision-led	Quite likely
Not necessarily	Ambitious	Quite likely
Not necessarily	High achiever	Quite likely
Not necessarily	Confident	Quite likely
Not necessarily	Enthusiastic/committed	Quite likely
Not necessarily	Organized	Quite likely
Not necessarily	Determined/dedicated	Quite likely
Not necessarily	Resourceful	Quite likely
Not necessarily	Self-reliant	Quite likely
Quite likely	Open-minded	Quite likely
Not necessarily	Hard-working/productive/efficient	Quite likely
Quite likely	Persistent	Quite likely
Quite likely	Tenacious	Quite likely
Not necessarily	Resilient	Quite likely
Not necessarily	Decisive	Quite likely
Not necessarily	Adaptable	Quite likely
Not necessarily	Fast-acting	Quite likely
Not necessarily	Tough-minded	Quite likely
Not necessarily	Single-minded	Quite likely
Not necessarily	Willing to work all hours	Quite likely

* Possibly the most important.

only be made by highlighting the character traits and the personality of what could be described as the typical CEO of a successful business, and contrasting them with the character traits and the personality of what we can describe as an 'ideas person'.

The list in Table 4.1 is not exhaustive, but it makes the point. Those who come up with the idea do not necessarily have the right qualities to turn that idea into a successful business. Decide which camp you fall into and if you are more of an ideas person than an executive type, team up with a budding CEO. If you are less an ideas person and more of a CEO, you'll need an original thinker on board before you can make a sensible corporate move. If you are both an ideas person and are made of the right stuff to run the company, then well and good, although two heads with complementary skills are usually better than one when it comes to implementing that new application and making a commercial fist of it.

Superman or Bionic Woman?

Whether or not you were the one who thought up the original idea or application on which the new venture is based, let's suppose that the new company is now set up and the

Table 4.2 The successful CEO's skill-set

The ability to:

> Develop a concise business plan.
> Deviate from that plan when necessary.
> Think clearly, both strategically and tactically.*
> Think creatively.
> Select and manage a team/teams of people.
> Build and nurture networks of contacts, advisers and backers.*
> Make a long-term commitment to the business.
> Enjoy responsibility.
> Communicate effectively.
> Delegate.
> Listen.
> Welcome feedback.
> Learn from experience.
> Pay attention to detail.
> Thrive in a competitive environment.
> Form partnerships with other businesses.
> Experiment, innovate and reinvent.
> Challenge the status quo in all matters.
> Test rules and regulations to the limits.
> Create a relaxed yet vibrant and challenging office atmosphere.
> Make the company a fun place to work and develop a career.
> Handle change.
> Fire people who do not pass muster.
> Take criticism constructively.
> Recover after being knocked down.
> Not take things that go wrong personally.
> Not take himself or herself too seriously.
> Keep his or her ego in check.

*Possibly the most important skills.

day dawns when you turn up for work and you are the new CEO or the Managing Director. Actually, these titles smack of the 'old economy' and, more probably, recognizing that a modern company is not that concerned with titles, you will opt for a 'new economy' title, such as Web Chief, Net Head, Chief Energizing Officer, Head Coach, Chief Tecchie or Head Geek! Whatever title you decide on, you are Chief Honcho. To fulfil that role, what sort of a person ought you to be to succeed?

We saw above in Table 4.1 that the successful CEO, whatever else he or she is, needs to be quite a character, a high achiever, commercially aware, a decision maker, able to absorb new information and continually learn new skills, an ambitious person, driven in many senses, wanting above all to succeed, to fulfil the vision, enthusiastic, resourceful, highly organized, determined, resilient in the face of adversity and willing to work flat out to achieve defined goals. The reader might well be forgiven for concluding that the successful CEO needs to be the corporate equivalent of Superman or Bionic Woman. The list of attributes and strengths required is daunting and clearly very few people will be all of these things. Without doubt, few dotcom CEOs, or any other commercial sector's CEOs for that matter, that you have come across in your career will exhibit the majority of Table 4.1's long list of traits, but it is true to say that success in the world of commerce, whether Internet-based commerce or any other type of commerce, demands from those who run companies as many of the traits listed in that table as possible. Worse still, the list of requirements doesn't end there! Budding CEOs of dotcom companies, in particular, are going to need yet more in their armoury if progress is to be made in the cyberspace corporate battle.

Again though, as stated earlier, whatever talents and skills you must possess to be a successful CEO, clearly you cannot possibly be all of these things all of the time and you need a lot of support. You need a team or most likely several teams. The teams you assemble around you will be of the greatest importance and help in establishing the company on a sound footing and in driving your and their ambitions forward. In selecting candidates you will, in part, be gathering round you key people who will complement your own capabilities, character traits, mind-set and personality but people who are also ambitious and forward thinking in their own right and who are likely to deliver against goals. So assembling those who will work with you is of the greatest importance.

Chapter 3 ('Hiring for Internet start-ups') gives advice on recruitment that, in the 'new economy' world, very definitely demands that you seek specialist support. An example of an international executive search company which can help in this connection is *www.heidrick.com*. Assemble the wrong team and you may be in deep trouble. Assemble the right team, and the company will quickly prosper. It may take time to get the right team, or teams, together, but it will be time very well spent. After that, building and keeping the management team is all a matter of leadership.

Leadership in the super-fast dotcom world

Many of yesterday's leaders thought they had, or pretended to have, all the talents that were needed for the job, as well as all the answers to questions posed to them by shareholders, analysts, suppliers, customers and so on. Top-down management was normal and a rigid hierarchy and a deferential relationship pervaded every level of business. Today, it is different. The 'old economy' model of leadership is very definitely obsolete. A new *modus operandi* is taking its place. In the middle to late 1990s, it became apparent that no leader, no matter how talented, could possibly have all the answers and was wise to admit as much at the very start of operations, particularly if they were dotcom operations. The reason for the change in attitude, of course, was the arrival of revolutionary changes in the commercial world, and what may have worked pre-Internet and pre-World Wide Web simply does not apply in this brave and demanding wired-up universe. In addition to the characteristics that a successful CEO needs to exhibit, therefore (see Table 4.2), modern leaders must develop a new approach and a new attitude and a new way of leading. This process is already under way and the latest generation of business leader is totally rewriting the rules of commerce and enthusiastically redefining leadership as well. Dotcom leaders are at the forefront of this revolution as running an Internet-based company takes special talents over and above those normally and formally associated with being a CEO.

However, today, leadership is being thrust on young entrepreneurs who have had little or no formal business training. They haven't had the time. The sheer speed with which the technologies, the competition, the revolutionary selling techniques, the demands of customers and much else are being altered and changed means that ideas and novel applications have to be pounced on and exploited at break-neck pace. The challenge for the Internet-inspired newcomer is, therefore, tremendous. But it is at the same time incredibly exciting, as the company of the future will look very different from the company of the past. So, faced with this prospect, and with the opportunity to head up a newly established dotcom company, how will tomorrow's leaders cope and how will *you* cope?

Trying to define leadership in the modern context

Recognize first that the subject of leadership is a huge one, to which countless erudite and useful books have been devoted. You will need to resort to this source of material. Recognize second that leadership, while ultimately rewarding and self-fulfilling, is difficult, demanding, at times gruelling and painful and itself perhaps the greatest challenge that you will ever take on. The transition from the cyber café where the great idea was hatched, or from team player in a previous corporate existence, to overall team leader in a new dotcom business is going to be tough and you are going to need help. That help may come either from people within the new organization that you now head up or from reputable outside sources, but much of what you need to know as

Table 4.3   Elements of effective dotcom leadership

You as leader

    Knowing your own self, where you are in life, where you want to go and what your values are.

    Keeping your integrity intact, doing what you believe to be morally and ethically correct.

    Being able to read your emotions, as well as those of others around you.

    Spotting when you are acting in character (the essence of who you are) and when your persona (the coping part of your personality) is influencing your actions.

    Understanding that you can't get around life's inherent contradictions.

    Learning to reconcile the often brutal realities of business with basic human values.

    Being honest with yourself about what real leadership demands of you.

    Placing a high value on the reputation of your company and its integrity.

Courage

    Having the courage to make things happen and to stand by unpopular decisions.

    Having the courage to face reality and helping the people around you to face reality.

    Being unafraid to make waves and accepting that confrontations will occur within the company.

    Having the stomach for conflict and uncertainty outside the company.

    Developing a steely nerve.

    Sometimes having the courage to initiate action based on minimal information.

Character and charisma

    Being passionate about what you are doing.

    Being able to communicate your passion for the business to those around you.

    Having the charisma to affect those around you in a positive and energizing way.

    Having a vision, delivering on it and getting others to share it.

    Thinking big, thinking new and thinking ahead.

    Creating a culture of urgency in response to the hectic pace of the dotcom world.

    Being able to create momentum in the company, to bring energy to the workplace, to create energy in yourself and in other people.

    Being able to inspire loyalty, trust and confidence.

    Creating an optimistic, 'can do' atmosphere.

    Getting those around you to focus on the company's core values and to avoid getting side-tracked.

    Motivating people around you to tackle tough challenges, bringing out the best in them.

    Learning how to abandon your own ego to the talents of others.

Table 4.3 *cont.*

Being intellectually stimulating to get others to use reasoning and evidence to problem solve.

Showing initiative.

Mobilizing those around you to handle continual change.

Communication

Communicating effectively, in a transparent way, and constantly improving your interpersonal skills.

Being able to communicate purpose.

Sharing information with those around you whenever possible.

Providing direction, posing well-structured questions and not definitive answers.

Fostering an atmosphere in which people ask for help when they need it.

Dealing effectively with shareholders and venture capitalists.

Choosing suitable non-executive directors and then working constructively with them.

Overall management

Not being a control freak.

Learning to prioritize.

Being able to simplify matters for those around you and to offer guidance.

Being able to set targets, milestones and yardsticks for those around you, explaining how they have been set and how they will be measured.

Being concerned about quality.

Being willing to try something to see if it works and canning it if it doesn't.

Never forgetting (as many British businesses do) that the greatest products and services do not sell themselves.

Letting those around you have an impact on the business.

Praising where praise is due and admonishing where it is deserved.

Making sure that the work environment is conducive to work and enjoyment but that it is also demanding and full of expectation.

Creating a loose discipline that focuses on responsibilities and performance rather than orders.

Being considerate to those in the company, coaching, advising and supporting.

Being able to handle the anxiety caused by the constant need to choose between various options, tough choices being a daily requirement of leadership.

Having an experimental mind-set, knowing that some decisions will work out while others won't.

Being dependable, following through on commitments.

Having respect for those around you.

Table 4.3   *cont.*

Creating opportunities for continual education within the company.

Focusing on tomorrow's problems as well as today's and acting ahead of the curve.

Constantly reinventing yourself in terms of learning from experience and acquiring new skills.

Team management

Recognizing that people are the company's most important asset and that keeping them is one of the biggest challenges you face.

Allowing people to have their say as then they're more likely to accept and support a decision.

Recognizing the critical role that technologists play in your company.

Ensuring that the tecchies and other employees are not at odds with each other.

Recognizing that tecchies and non-tecchies alike may not make good managers and may not want to be managers.

Being accessible and encouraging everyone in the company to email you with ideas, suggestions and complaints.

Creating an environment that allows people to think for themselves.

Letting natural leaders come to the fore and creating grass-roots leaders all over the organization.

Getting the compensation packages right but remembering that money does not buy total loyalty.

Finance

Having a working knowledge of forecasting, budgeting, cashflow analysis and financial accounting, which may change as the employees and intangibles become more and more important elements in a company's asset structure.

If your own numeracy and financial skills are not up to scratch, hiring suitably qualified people to undertake these tasks.

Choosing the right venture capital backing and dealing effectively with venture capitalists on the board (an entire chapter could be devoted to this).

leader may have to be learnt the hard way, that is on the job. So in a sense you will be teaching yourself and the better you come to understand yourself in your new role, the better leader you will make.

No two leaders are that alike, no two companies are that alike and no long list of helpful hints and 'dos and don'ts' will be just right for a particular leader in a particular company, but drawing up a list is the only way to tackle this large subject in a short chapter which deals with other matters. Table 4.3 should prove a useful guide to help you on your corporate way.

Remember that being a good leader is a very difficult thing to be but, hopefully, you can rise to the challenge if you keep the above in mind and if you can find time to read up on the subject and if you can find time as well to take some appropriate courses. Success in this respect does not of course presuppose that you are brilliant or that you have the whole panoply of attributes that are listed in the tables in this chapter. But it does presuppose that you know how to make the best use of whatever talents you do have, that you know how to plug the gaps in your capabilities by bringing in people who have the necessary skills, and that you know too how to bring out the best in all the teams that you have brought together, by leading them, empowering them, challenging them and providing them with the resources that they need to do the job. Above all, so far as you yourself are concerned, if you are prepared to accept yet more advice, have courage and learn to believe in your own capabilities.

Table 4.4   A few other pointers – platitudes and aphorisms that work

Don't expect anyone to give you a helping hand, ever.

Network constantly with your peers in the industry.

Be risk aware, not risk averse.

If you're not a natural, learn to work with other people.

If you're not a natural, learn to negotiate hard.

Establish a work pattern for yourself that you feel comfortable with.

Be alert to people's body language, especially during meetings.

Be firm but courteous in the office.

Admit that you're wrong when you are wrong.

Learn to arrange your time efficiently.

Try to make no more than one mistake a day.

If you don't understand something, keep asking until you do.

Be prepared to change direction.

Keep a sense of proportion.

Dump your pride and be pragmatic and sensible instead.

Anticipate the future.

Take time out when you need to (see below).

Play sport or indulge in a mind-absorbing hobby once a week at a minimum.

Keep fit – e-commerce is a demanding occupation.

Develop both mental and physical stamina.

Strive to be happy in your work.

Don't burn the candle at both ends.

Laugh a little every day.

Time off and holidays

However else you try to prepare yourself for life as a dotcom leader, talk to as many up-and-running CEOs as you can get in to see. There is no substitute for hearing the good and the bad first hand. They can tell tales of the highs and the lows of running your own dotcom business. A part of their hands-on experience would encompass their views on taking time off from the fray. A common thread would very definitely run through their advice. However much you love the company that you have set up, no matter how brilliantly things are progressing, however good the teams that you have moulded and fashioned, how devoted you are to making the business work even better, if you are true to type, you will fail to take enough time off. All the experts argue that in so doing you will be storing up lots of trouble for the future.

In today's fast-moving world there is, of course, never enough time. In the dotcom industry, as they like to say, time flies past four times more quickly than it appears to do in any other sphere of commercial activity, three months in the dotcom world equating to one year elsewhere. So, it's rush, rush, rush, time manage, time manage, time manage. But as a dotcom CEO, you should be aware of one time-related factor, in particular, if you are to be successful, no matter that you are young, energetic, have boundless ambition, endless enthusiasm and can party until dawn and still be in the office next day at eight o'clock bright as a button. That factor is burn-out. Burn-out is a killer, or more precisely a job loser, and there is a trick you can learn to help you avoid it. As they say in America, 'play more golf'. In other words, make sure that there is a firm dividing line between work and the rest of your life, take time off, go on holidays. Do not become a workaholic to the exclusion of all else.

Table 4.5   Reasons not to take a holiday vs. the truth

There are a million reasons why I can't leave the office now.	True but untrue.
I know I need a holiday, but . . .	You need a holiday, no buts.
I'm too busy.	Simply not true.
There isn't enough time.	Simply not true.
The business would fall apart if I went away for a week.	Smacks of poor management.
This industry moves too fast for me to be away from my desk.	It doesn't.
I get stressed-out on holiday.	Learn to relax.
My partner can't get away at the same time.	Start planning together.
I've got to be at that meeting next week.	Reschedule it for the week after.
I just don't need to take a holiday right now.	You may well need one.
I like working all the time.	Your brain/body doesn't.
The competition won't be taking a holiday.	Possibly true but foolish, and short-sighted on your part and theirs.
I'm indispensable to the business.	Nobody's indispensable over a long weekend, or even over a week.

There's little excuse these days for not taking enough time out to relax. Even if you cannot bring yourself to go away for a fortnight or even a week, there are literally hundreds of short-break holidays on offer over the Internet and in the press. But, you are not convinced. Your every instinct tells you that you must work seven days a week, at least until the business is on a very firm footing. Besides, it's so exciting being at work, even if you are beginning to feel overly tired and perhaps a touch overwhelmed. It's worth it, you say, not going away, as when success has been achieved, there'll be plenty of time to snow board in 'Les Trois Vallées' and soak up the Malaga sun. Yet, you must take stock, even at this early stage in your career. Why? Because otherwise your job will take over your life and undermine your health. Table 4.5 goes through the list of reasons why you say you can't or shouldn't take a complete break and tests their validity, noting how the experts on executive stress respond to your reluctance to unwind properly.

If you don't take this advice, you may not notice the effects of stress building up in your mind and body, though others around you most certainly will. Check out Web sites such as the Health & Safety Executive's (*www.hse.gov.uk*) to see what effects prolonged periods of executive stress can have on your well being. You may be surprised at how serious the medical consequences can be. Whatever else you do, try not to take papers home every evening. If you have to work at home, don't work until late and then immediately go to bed. Your mind will be racing and you will have difficulty getting to sleep and sleeping soundly. Turn off your mobile, say, at eight in the evening and don't talk shop with your partner after that. Certainly, unwind when you first get home and tell your partner what happened during the day, good and bad, but then switch off from the office. Try as well to keep the weekends free to do something completely different and for you and your partner to party. Book up a mini holiday, a three to four-day break, perhaps as often as once a quarter. You will return to your desk refreshed, relishing the task ahead and be better able to make the right decisions and progress the business.

Time for others to take over the reins

Whether or not it is due to the effects of stress suffered over a longish period, or that your own particular skills and talents are no longer, frankly, up to the job, the dotcom CEO, as any other sector CEO, should recognize that there may come a time when he or she should step down or step aside. While such a move might not be in his or her own best interests, although conversely it could be, the chief executive's departure might be best for the company and for the shareholders. It might simply be recognition of the fact that someone else has come into focus who could better serve all interested parties.

A recent, well publicised example makes the case. It is Bill Gates' stepping aside at Microsoft in early 2000 (*www.microsoft.com*). Steve Ballmer took over as CEO from co-founder Bill Gates in a move that surprised almost everyone, not least because it was announced immediately before some terrific quarterly net earnings, up 22% from the previous year. In an email to all employees at the time, Ballmer was reported to have stated that Microsoft's success had been built on its commitment to graphical user interfaces, or GUIs, in its Windows operating system and the Office applications that work with it. He added that it was now time to bet on using software to improve the way that people use the Internet. What he was saying was that Microsoft had to develop a new kind of operating system, one in which Windows will pervade the Internet, in much the same way as until now it has pervaded the hard drive of virtually every PC in the world. On the management front, Gates had decided that he was not the right man to lead the company in this new challenge. His colleague, Steve Ballmer, was the man for the job and Gates himself would free up his own time to laterally think about the future of this famous, ground-making corporation.

Giving over the reins is never an easy thing to do but, if there are tell-tale signs that an executive change needs to be made, for reasons other than those illustrated above in the Microsoft example, and you are the one who should go, then accept that circumstances have altered and depart. What are some of these tell-tale signs?

Table 4.6   Sunset signs

You –

> No longer enjoy going to work.
> No longer care much about the company.
> No longer keep abreast of industry developments.
> Show some of the classic signs of executive stress.
> Become irritable, argumentative and dogmatic in the office.
> Get annoyed with clients, joint-venture partners and suppliers.
> Can't think and plan strategically.
> Start making wrong decisions.
> Stop listening to colleagues and the market.
> Lose the fighting spirit.
> Upset the relationship with partner and family.
> Rely on drugs, booze, cigarettes and coffee to get through the day.

Once you accept that it's time to go, the most constructive thing you can do is to help the board and the major shareholders to identify and appoint a suitable successor. And don't despair, your own career isn't over. Don't spiral down into deep depression. Take stock of where you are, learn the lessons of your recent past and move on. You'll undoubtedly live to fight another day and succeed in a new company.

One final point on giving up the reins: normally, you would expect a decision to step down to take place years after you have founded your dotcom company. However, it may take place far, far earlier, even quite soon after the business has been established. You may indeed have been the right person to found the business and to get it up and running, but you may well not be the right person to take the company to the next stage. Your character and skills-set are just not what are required at this juncture and you should recognize this and give way. You could still remain an executive rather than be Chief Honcho, or you could leave and go on to establish another successful dotcom business!

Conclusion

Dreaming up, setting up and running your own dotcom company is at once wildly exciting and incredibly challenging. Possibly, you are both the creative genius behind the business idea and the soon-to-be effective executive who will power the newly formed company to great heights. Either that, or you are teaming up with one or two others whose skill-sets complement yours. Hopefully, too, a team of more junior people, tecchies and non-tecchies, is being assembled to ensure that the business plan can be implemented aggressively. As Net time flashes past, you will either slot into the role of leader with the greatest of ease or, more likely, you will have to learn as you go along, seeking outside advice when you can and learning from your mistakes. Being at the helm, or near it, will be fun though and the rewards should be there in time as well. If you overdo it, play more golf, and if you find the going tough, consider honestly whether you are the right person to continue doing the job you are doing. In the interim, which may last months or years, think of it as a journey and try to enjoy the trip. Rise to the challenge. All it takes is courage and integrity and lots more besides. And when the time comes to depart, leave, enjoy the proceeds and seek a new frontier.

A extract from *Tornado-Insider.com*: how a winner wins

Many of the points that Alastair Shaw makes in this chapter are echoed in the articles,
reproduced below, which appeared in the April and June 2000 editions of
Tornado-Insider.com. Both articles review the new business process from the point of
view of the entrepreneur. The magazine, *Tornado-Insider.com*, is Europe's leading
Internet and high-technology venture capital magazine. A similar magazine with a US bias
is *RedHerring*.

www.tornado-insider.com

www.redherring.com

OF GRASSROOTS AND REVOLUTIONS – KAWASAKI AND OMIDYAR ADVISE STARTUPS

by Guy Middleton

Tornado-Insider.com's 'UpStart Europe' conference opened Tuesday with keynotes from
two people with a claim to having played a revolutionary role in the technology business.

www.ebay.com

First off was Pierre Omidyar, the French-born entrepreneur who founded eBay in the
US. In a speech that concentrated on the success of his own company he spoke of the
brutal forces of evolution that 'selected out' weak business models on the Internet.

Omidyar contrasted the approach of his own company with Amazon and Yahoo!,
which also offer trading platforms. Omidyar said that while Amazon spent vast sums on
marketing and Yahoo! could offer its own auction and its massive brand awareness,
eBay had built itself through its interest in grassroots customers. eBay looked to build on
this community approach through a network of local sites.

Though US-based, the company is enjoying success in Europe, notably Germany. eBay,
which is targeting the five largest Internet markets outside of the US, rather than opting
for blanket coverage, currently has a greater sales volume through its German operation
than all the other online trading companies have globally, Omidyar said.

www.garage.com

Guy Kawasaki, ex-Apple evangelist and founder of Garage.com, used his 45 minutes
to rattle out advice and anecdotes to an audience of around 1,000 entrepreneurs and
investors. Opening with the admission that during his tenure Macintosh was 'the biggest
collection of ego-maniacs in history' he went on to describe how revolutionaries must, in
the interest of speed – be prepared to release a less-than-perfect product – under the

motto, 'don't worry, be crappy' – but then must quickly improve the product with later releases. Kawasaki cited the first Macintosh released in 1984 as a personal example.

Networking and a voracious appetite for information were also necessary if a company is to succeed. Business development advice followed, with Kawasaki exhorting the audience to avoid over-cautious legal advice in favour of the maxim, 'this is what we want to do – now keep me out of jail'.

Startups pitching to VCs should ditch non-disclosure agreements, according to Kawasaki, as few will sign them. 'They won't sign NDAs – at any one time there might be five companies doing the same thing, and they might be seeing three of them.' In an environment with few unique ideas implementation was what counted, he added.

Kawasaki's take on the vexed question of valuation was straightforward, 'Look for value not valuation'. Kawasaki encouraged people to take funding from well-connected sources and accept dilution rather than go for enormous valuations from advisers ill-equipped to take a venture to market, but was slightly wrong footed when he presented Omidyar as an example. Omidyar responded from the wings with the assertion that he still personally owned 'over 30 per cent' of the trading giant. Another tip was brevity. A first approach to a VC should be a one page e-mail, business plans should be no longer than 20 pages and Powerpoint presentation should be restricted to an absolute maximum of 12 slides.

While he said startups should take money when offered, rather than hold out for a higher valuation and risk being the victim of a change in investment fashion, he advised startups not to aim too high when drumming up money, for fear of an embarrassing shortfall.

'Ask for less than you need . . . create the illusion of scarcity,' said Kawasaki, and the investors that missed out the first time will come to you.

Tornado-Insider.com – Magazine. April 2000

GUY KAWASAKI – A MASTER OF HIGH TECH THEATRE

by John Dunn

Guy Kawasaki is amiable, relaxed, and self-deprecating, in touch with what feels like a laid-back trend in contemporary company zeitgeist. Hailing from the US (of course), and in a more professional sense from California, Kawasaki is not far off being the sort of avuncular, unthreatening head most Europeans would like to have running their company.

Officially, Kawasaki is the CEO and chairman of garage.com, a US-based VC capital linker. Unofficially, as evinced by his recent *Rules for Revolutionaries* presentation at Tornado-Insider.com's UpStart Europe event at Disneyland Paris, he is the master entertainer bearing a serious message.

Visiting US high-tech CEOs of the 'You've got it all wrong' school, have an unfortunate reputation for speaking down to their European counterparts. Everybody gets mightily sick of this unsavvy species of sales pitch but carries on smiling nonetheless. Kawasaki and his ilk are more at ease crossing the tank traps that are cultural barriers. What's his secret?

Aim high but punch low

'Lots of people can do one key note so I thought I would try to outdo most people. I want to set a standard for Europe about key note sessions at high-tech conferences' he announced to the assembled hall of delegates from every corner of Europe and beyond. Of course, Kawasaki has an ace in his pack which gets him an audience wherever he goes; he once had the good fortune to work for Apple, the most interesting 'failure' in Silicon Valley's recent past. This punches all sorts of important buttons for any audience over 25 years old. He worked for Steve Jobs; enough said. He also worked at the beginning of Silicon Valley's PC era when the sixties generation's high-tech dream was being lived at full tilt. Kawasaki can speak with the authority of having 'been there' when the democratic computing age began and of having played his part in its ultimate success.

Hit home, when people least expect it

'Revolutionaries do not care about making things better, cheaper, faster. They care about changing the world.' This sentiment neatly encapsulates what kept the Apple vanguard going through the dark days of Microsoft's ascendancy. They wanted to get rich but somehow that wasn't going to be enough. This remark formed the centrepiece of the presentation, and contained perhaps his most important message to European entrepreneurs if you truly want to be big you have to think on a cosmic scale. Those of a pragmatic disposition need not apply.

State the obvious, no matter how embarrassing

'The Macintosh division was the largest collection of ego maniacs in Silicon valley. That record was recently broken by Netscape which was even more arrogant than we were.' This was followed by: 'The truth is that we [Apple] were trying to send IBM back to the typewriter business holding its electric balls.' Distil this down a little: you have to have an enemy, so welcome competition.

Trash yourself – it's good for your image

'If you look for the first product shipped at Apple it had no software thanks to my efforts.' This sort of deprecating assessment is a good antidote to business complacency. He followed it with his most astute gem, inspired, he said by a Bobby McFerrin song. 'Don't worry, be crappy.' Revolutionaries don't worry about whether the products or service they are selling is perfect, they worry about getting it on to the street. They fret about whether it is perfect when the time comes for version 2.

Kawasaki's UpStart presentation struck a chord with its audience that many similar presentations don't. This has everything to do with a style and delivery – his comic, even satirical timing is finely honed over long calendar of main US events. As one delegate commented at the end of the Kawasaki experience, 'If he'd been selling Macs at the door I'd have bought one and I hate Apple'. The high-tech scene in Europe needs to find some showmen in the Guy Kawasaki mold if it is ever to truly flourish.

Tornado-Insider.com – Magazine. June 2000

5 Create and protect intellectual property rights

Michael Cover, Mishcon de Reya

Editor's introduction

Mishcon de Reya is a commercial law firm based in central London. The firm has recognized that new economy-based companies, in technology, e-commerce and communications, are capable of very fast growth and are heavily dependent on their people and their intellectual property rights (IPR). They require advisers who share their vision and understand their technology and the market in which they operate and who are able to take them from start-up to IPO.

The firm is working with clients who have established businesses to develop their on-line strategies and e-commerce capabilities. Its corporate and commercial practice is primarily focused on the technology, e-commerce and communications sectors. The firm works closely with entrepreneurs, investors and intermediaries clustered around these sectors, including incubators, investment bankers, venture capitalists and corporate financiers, as well as the sector-specific regulators and other government organizations. Many of the partners have direct experience as managers and advisers in industry, or as investors or directors in entrepreneurial ventures. The firm's Internet and technology experience extends into Europe and the United States.

Mishcon de Reya can be contacted via its Web site at www.mishcon.co.uk.

Aim

It is symptomatic of knowledge-based companies that, at least in the early days, they are likely to have not only relatively little turnover and a modest if non-existent profit but also virtually no assets of a tangible kind. However, they will almost certainly have substantial intangible and 'human assets'.

Assets may be divided into two categories – those that you can touch (all tangible assets) and those that you cannot (intangible assets). Tangible assets would generally consist of real property and tangible items, such as plant and machinery. Intangible assets will generally comprise so-called intellectual property assets (which sometimes used to be called industrial property). Such intellectual property assets will have been created by the intellectual effort of the company's employees (or consultants or other third parties retained by it) and generally arise once an idea has been expressed in a particular form. As such, knowledge-based companies, including e-commerce businesses of all types, will generally only have these intellectual property assets (or intellectual capital) and the expertise and skills of their people (so-called human capital).

Table 5.1 Five characteristics of valuable IPR

1. Originality and novelty.
2. Owned by the company (or at least available to the company by licensing).
3. Registered, in the case of IPR which has to be registered (or at least well down the track to registration).
4. International coverage – achievement of the right level of investment for the right level of reward.
5. 'Clear blue water' between the company's IPR and that of competitors.

As items of property recognized by law, both tangible and intangible assets are capable of being assigned and also charged (or mortgaged). There is another parallel in that it is possible to grant licences and other rights falling short of 100% ownership in these rights.

Obtaining IPR

Certain intellectual property rights come into existence automatically; others have to be registered. There are also some what might be called hybrid rights, for example, those which give rise to actions for passing off in common law countries, such as the United Kingdom, and unfair competition actions in most of the rest of Europe or the United States.

Table 5.2 Five significant differences: USA/UK/Europe

1. Better protection for methods of doing business/computer software in the USA but Europe is catching up.
2. Unregistered marks protected in USA, first-to-register now in UK and Europe.
3. Patents not published until grant in the USA, i.e. at least one year later than the UK and Europe.
4. Choice of jurisdiction for litigation – more flexible funding arrangements in USA and more comprehensive discovery process looking for the 'smoking guns' amongst the other side's documents.
5. Originality in copyright – requirements and standards in Europe are generally higher.

The species of intellectual property

Table 5.3 The main characteristics of IPR

Category	Term	Ownership	Registration
Copyright: artistic and literary includes computer programs; infringed by copying; Database rights	Author's life + 70 years	The author/originator; employee's copyright belongs to employer	No
Patents: novel process or product capable of industrial application; Can include software with a technical effect	20 years	First owner is inventor; employee's invention belongs to employer	Yes
Registered Trade Marks mark (word or sign) capable of distinguishing a person's goods	10 years, renewable	First applicant	Yes
Registered Designs: features which appeal to the eye	15 years	First applicant	Yes
Design Right: functional features	15 years maximum		No

Table 5.4 Quasi IPR

Category	Term	Owner/enforcer
Passing off: common law action in UK to protect goodwill in a name or sign. Elsewhere in Europe, statutory basis to sue for unfair competition taking the form of imitation of getup, business process and the like	Indefinite	Proprietor of goodwill to protect
Confidential information: in UK, contractual and common law remedy where information of a confidential nature is disclosed in circumstances of confidentiality	Term of contract	Disclosing party
Domain name: protects identical name only – evidence only of some proprietorial right	Indefinite if renewed	First registrant

Copyright comes into existence automatically on the creation of the copyright work. The term of copyright is typically the life of the author plus 70 years and *artistic copyright* covers visual works and *literary copyright* covers written works. Curiously, computer software is generally protected under literary copyright. What distinguishes copyright from other intellectual property rights is that, for infringement to be shown, there must be copying or, at the very least, there must have been access to the right that is infringed. Database rights are a sub-division of copyright and they protect, as their name suggests, databases.

Patents protect novel industrial processes and products and generally have a life of 20 years. Unlike copyright, which has a very long period of protection and which requires no action to renew, patents generally have to be renewed once per year, on an increasingly expensive scale. The first owner will generally be the inventor or inventors but inventions made by employees will generally belong to the employer. Inventions of non-employee directors may also belong to their company, for example, by it being established that such inventions are held by them on trust for the company. The Patent Office, where the application is filed, will conduct a search of the prior art and provide a report to the applicants. There may be considerable negotiation about the correct ambit of protection before the patent is granted.

Registered trade marks, as their name suggests, require an application to register. In many countries, the national trade mark office will conduct a search and will refuse to register trade marks which are confusingly similar to marks which are already on the register. A registered trade mark is the one piece of intellectual property that is of indefinite duration, provided that it is used properly and renewed. Periods between renewal are generally ten years. For registration purposes, goods and services are divided into 42 classes. Relevant classes for e-commerce are *class 9* (software), *class 35* (retail services on the Internet), *class 38* (telecommunications gateways to the Internet), *class 41* (training and education, entertainment, publishing on-line) and *class 42* (writing Web pages on the Internet). Curiously, it is not yet possible to register trade marks for purely retail services, though this may be about to change.

In many countries, designs are given distinct protection. In the United Kingdom, this is by means of an application for a registered design, which is to protect features which appeal to the eye, or the unregistered design right, which will protect more functional features. In both cases, the maximum life of these intellectual property rights is 15 years. For further information, visit the UK Patent Office site at: *www.patents.gov.uk.*

Passing off has already been mentioned. This is a common law action in the United Kingdom which protects the goodwill and reputation in a particular name or sign. In each action for passing off, that goodwill and reputation have to be established afresh. This contrasts with a registered trade mark, where the reputation will have to be established at the point where the mark is registered but thereafter a monopoly is granted. Actions for unfair competition are available in European countries and, in the United States, actions will generally be available for not only infringement of registered trade marks but also infringement of unregistered trade marks (an action which has some similarity with passing off) and unfair competition as well.

Ownership and assignment

Table 5.5 Trade marks matrix

Territory	Who is the owner?	Unregistered trade marks protected?
UK	First to register/use	Effectively yes – action for passing off
EU	First to register	As such no – but actions for unfair competition
USA	First to use/register	Yes

The position on ownership of intellectual property will vary according to the intellectual property rights involved. The basic approach is that intellectual property devised by employees in the course of their employment will belong to the company, whereas intellectual property originated by third parties, such as independent consultants (whether individuals or companies), will belong to them. Accordingly, it is vital to consider the question of ownership of intellectual property and put in place the necessary assignments right at the beginning. There are many tales in the old economy of advertising agencies being sacked, with the client thereafter finding that the copyright in all the advertising material, including television commercials, was vested in the agency and those materials were unavailable for use by the client without further negotiation and payment.

On assignment generally, all intellectual property is assignable. It is important to register such assignments, as it may be possible for a subsequent purchaser to come along and to claim that it has a better right than the assignee whose assignment has not been recorded. There are also various means to take security over intellectual property. These will range from the entering of a formal security interest, which is possible with a registered trade mark, to the chargee taking an assignment of the intellectual property right in question, with an assignment back on the fulfilment of the conditions of the charge or mortgage. In circumstances where e-commerce start-ups may only have valuable human capital and intellectual property, such start-ups may well be requested to give a charge over their intellectual property by lending institutions. This probably happens less often than it did, in that much financing is currently provided by equity rather than debt.

The international dimension and 'priority'

There are many treaties and conventions which regulate the treatment of intellectual property rights. Generally, these are designed to put nationals of various different countries on the same footing in each other's countries and third countries. They are also designed to ensure that vital priority dates are protected across the geographical spectrum.

There are also several treaties which deal with patents. These either set up transnational registration systems in their own right or require the contracting parties to observe a particular set of standards in their own national laws. A further category provides not a replacement for national registration of intellectual property rights but a system whereby applications can be made centrally, leading at a later stage to a 'basket' of national rights. The (European) Community trade mark system, with its trade mark office situated in Spain, is an example of a transnational system. One application lodged in the Community Trade Mark Office in Alicante should lead to a trade mark registration which is valid in all the member states of the European Union. The second category is evidenced by the European Community Trade Mark Directive, which was a harmonizing provision, designed to ensure that all member states' trade mark laws were generally the same. The third category is illustrated by European patents. An application to the European Patent Office in Munich, Germany, will lead to the 'basket' of rights, in this case patents, across the contracting states for the European patent (*www.european-patent-office.org*).

Whilst the basic concept of intellectual property rights transcends national borders and the World Intellectual Property Organization (WIPO), based in Switzerland, promotes this, there are some striking differences in different countries. (See, for example: *www.wipo.org* – the home page of WIPO; *http://ecommerce.wipo.int* – devoted to electronic commerce and intellectual property; and *http://ipdl.wipo.int* – which provides access to various intellectual property data collections.) Perhaps the most important of these is the contrast between a so-called 'first-to-use' trade mark system and a so-called 'first-to-register' system. In common law countries or countries observing a common law tradition, such as the United States, it is generally the first user of a trade mark who gets the first rights. By contrast, it is the first registrant who will generally obtain the best right in continental European countries and this approach has now made some in-roads into the United Kingdom. This means that registration of trade marks should be considered at the earliest possible opportunity, as the loss of a day's priority could be fatal.

Priority is an important concept in the international sphere. The way priority works is that, if an applicant makes an application in its home country, it subsequently has a period of grace within which to file applications overseas, generally claiming in those overseas countries the original priority (filing) date of the home country.

In relation to patents, that grace period is generally 12 months; in relation to registered trade marks, that grace period is generally six months.

Enforcing and protecting IPR

The IPR that we have described is of little use unless it acts as a barrier to entry to third parties. More often than not, in conducting due diligence and other pre-launch and pre-transaction enquiries, third-party latecomers will find the registered intellectual property rights of our imaginary start-up company, Dot.com Limited, and will adopt other names to avoid infringing registered trade marks or adopt other processes to avoid infringing patents.

However, if push comes to shove, enforcement action through the courts may well be required. Enforcement will generally be through the civil courts of whichever country is the chosen jurisdiction, although infringement of both copyright and registered trade mark can, in certain circumstances, be a criminal offence. Applications can also be mounted to invalidate earlier patents that were not novel or to remove prior registered trade works for non-use or invalidity.

A distinction needs to be made once again between the broadly common law systems of the United Kingdom and the United States and the so-called civil law systems of continental Europe and elsewhere. The civil law systems feature a greater emphasis on written pleadings rather than oral testimony and less disclosure or discovery of the opponent's documentation. The discovery system in the United States is particularly far reaching, enabling potential defendants' executives to be interviewed at length in what are called depositions, in order to seek out potentially incriminating documents. Accordingly, those in executive positions and, indeed, any employees should consider very carefully before committing pen to paper or sending emails, whether inside or outside the company. They should consider what view a court might subsequently take on any controversial subject they might choose to address.

Under whichever system any litigation is run, appeals will be available, perhaps only on points of law. In the United States, intellectual property matters are generally dealt with at the Federal Court level.

Since April 1998, there has been a comprehensive reform of the litigation process in England and Wales, these being generally known as the Woolf Reforms. Judges now practise case management. This has meant that much greater pre-proceedings preparation is needed and there are considerable penalties in costs for missing deadlines or failing to comply with court orders. All this has conspired to make litigation more expensive for the unprepared or the unwary.

Funding litigation

For approximately five years in the United Kingdom and for many years in the United States, innovative fee arrangements with lawyers have been available, in order to assist in the funding of litigation. Conditional fee arrangements in the United Kingdom enable the successful party's lawyer to recover a 100% uplift on the normal fees but nothing if unsuccessful. By contrast, there is in the United States a system of contingency fee litigation, which appears to work well and which is closely regulated by the courts, whereby a successful plaintiff's lawyers are able to recover as their fees something between 20% and 30% of the damages awarded to the plaintiff.

Remedies available in litigation will include the recovery of damages (or an account of the profit made by the defendant), injunctions and an award of costs. It is worth noting that the losing parties in American litigation generally do not have to pay the winning party's lawyer's costs. If this was funded on a contingency basis, the winning party's costs are of course paid out of the award of damages.

In all jurisdictions, urgent and even emergency applications can be made to the courts, even out of hours, for interlocutory (temporary) injunctions, in order to prevent an actionable event which would or could cause enormous damage to the claimant. The cost implications of such applications have to be thought about very carefully.

Case studies: registration and enforcement

Case study

Cola warfare – the Coca-Cola and Pepsi Cola trade marks

(*http://cyber.law.harvard.edu/property/respect/antibarbie.html*)

Coca-Cola was invented in 1886, Pepsi Cola in the 1890s, but it did not emerge as a challenger to Coca-Cola until the 1930s. In 1927, Coca-Cola was an early adopter of CRM (Customer Relationship Management), turning its salesmen into 'teachers'.

Coca-Cola was beset by US infringers from an early stage – these included Afri-Cola, Kos-Kola and Celery-Cola. By the early 1920s, there had been more than 7000 infringement actions. The most significant victory was over the Koke Company in the mid 1920s. Coca-Cola has at all times sought to tread the fine line between being generic (or descriptive) and distinctive as a trade mark.

Pepsi Cola re-emerged in 1931 out of insolvency and began to progress to the giant brand that it is today, driven by the vision of a strong man and a value platform. Coca-Cola brought a lawsuit for 'substitution' or passing off by substitution, where customers ask for Coca-Cola but are supplied with Pepsi Cola. Coca-Cola lost, and lost a subsequent trademark infringement case in the early 1940s. Despite Coca-Cola's legal and extra-legal efforts, Pepsi Cola grew to be a major competitor in the market through reinventing itself again and partnering with bottlers.

Coca-Cola erected barriers to entry, including legal ones, of which Pepsi Cola fought free, first, by competing on value and, then, by repositioning itself as a lifestyle product, where both now stand. By the time that Coca-Cola recognized the re-emergence of Pepsi Cola in the early 1930s, it was too late.

Case study

Virgin branding

Richard Branson started in the music area with Virgin. He was obviously looking for a powerful but different brand name. The name is in no way descriptive of any of the products or services in connection with which it is used. It nonetheless has some connotations which put it technically in the 'suggestive' category, suggesting innocence and freshness.

The use of the name has been extended to many products and services and to use by many companies, many of which are not wholly owned by Virgin. All the registered trade marks are owned by Virgin Enterprises Limited and will be licensed back to those many companies. The domain names are registered in the name of Virgin Enterprises Limited as well.

The use of the name has probably already been extended to more categories than any other brand name in history. Many have questioned whether the brand has been irretrievably diluted by association with, for example, trains but, so far, there is little sign of this. Virgin has been vigilant in protecting its IPR, including being a co-plaintiff in the *One in a Million* case.

Case study

Apple.com and Microsoft.com – a clash of copyright

The dispute between Apple and Microsoft over the Microsoft Windows operating system was over long before they adopted the above URLs. Apple and Microsoft were working together in the mid 1980s at a time when the DOS operating system ruled. The first round between them was settled.

Then, when Microsoft launched Windows 2, Apple sued for copyright infringement relating to the graphical user interface and ultimately lost. The court found that a GUI that consists mainly of uncopyrightable elements is not infringed unless the other side's work is virtually identical with the interface as a whole. Had Apple won, Windows and probably Microsoft would have been history.

More recently, Microsoft has hit the headlines as a result of the investigation by the US Department of Justice into alleged anti-competitive practices, with the private enforcement actions that move to follow. At the time of going to press, the Microsoft case remains unresolved but is closely watched by all industry players and their advisers and investors.

Great single-mindedness and resources are required to pursue the protection of IPR at this level and to square up to the competition regulators: not an endeavour for the faint hearted.

IPR considerations for e-commerce start-ups

It is important to draw up an action plan for creating and protecting your IPR in circumstances where this may be one of the only main assets of the business. At the same time, the expenditure on protection of IPR has to be proportionate to the total expenditure and resources of the business as it develops and matures.

The first step will almost certainly be to protect the confidentiality of the business concept, processes and business plan of the start-up. Non-disclosure agreements (NDAs) are discussed in Chapter 7. All documents prepared by and on behalf of the company should be clearly marked not only with the words 'Private and Confidential' but also with a statement claiming copyright, the so-called copyright notice, as for example: '© 2000 **Dot.com Limited**'.

Whilst intellectual property created by employees in the course of their duties will normally belong to the company, this needs to be reinforced by a specific assignment in the employee's terms and conditions of employment or service agreement. Even more important is to ensure that IPR created by third parties, such as technology consultants and marketing consultants, is assigned to the company in writing before it comes into existence.

The issues arising out of confidentiality and copyright can perhaps best be illustrated by the content of the business plan. This will disclose a name and chosen trade mark of the company, its business proposition and processes and probably some basic financial details. The measures outlined above should generally protect the IPR and the business plan. However, business is very much about people and, in the end, if there are those whom you do not trust, do not show them the business plan, even though they may be prepared to sign a non-disclosure agreement.

Selecting a name

In choosing the name of the company, its domain name or URL and the main trade mark, it is necessary to bear in mind the various categories of names. Often, those that are the most descriptive are the most favoured by marketing people. However, from the point of view of protection, it is those which are invented or distinctive which are much easier to work with. There is an in-between category which may well satisfy the desires and needs of the marketing people as well as the management and the lawyers: the so-called suggestive category. This is best illustrated by examples:

- descriptive – Travelstore for a travel portal (*www.travelstore.com*);
- invented or distinctive – Kodak for photographic products and services (*www.kodak.com*);
- suggestive – Iglu for a ski holiday portal (*www.iglu.co.uk*).

Domain names

Domain names or URLs (unique resource locators) are registered on a 'first come, first served' basis, which bears some resemblance to the first-to-register trade mark registration system. The crucial difference is that there is no requirement for any level of ability to distinguish. However, the most descriptive domain name could be the most valuable, an e-commerce paradox.

You should make sure that you cover off all the permutations and combinations of your own name. So, with our imaginary Dot.com Limited, this would involve *dot.com*, *dot.co.uk*, *dot.org*, as well as *ddot.com*, *dott.com*, and so on.

Registration of domain names is only part of the story. There are too many new businesses which have had unpleasant shocks, in that they have their domain name registered and are then blocked by a registered trade mark. 'Cybersquatting' is the other end of the problem, whereby unscrupulous third parties deliberately register well-known names as domain names. Fortunately, the courts in the UK and the legislature in the USA have been astute enough to deal with this. In the UK, the court in the *One in a Million* case took a severe view of cybersquatting (the transcript of the *One in a Million* judgment can be read at *www.io.io.news281197.html*, the transcript is reproduced on the WWW by permission of the Deputy Judge of the High Court of England and Wales); in the USA, the Anticybersquatting Consumer Protection Act 1999 strikes at deliberate (rather than innocent) cybersquatting and grants statutory damages.

Other businesses will have found that they have their name blocked by a prior registered trade mark. Pre-launch (and pre-final selection!) searches are, therefore, essential. The investment needs to be proportionate. There is little point in searching the US Federal Trade Mark Register for a trade mark to put into use in the United Kingdom purely domestically. Having said that, the Internet provides global access, so wider geographical searches than before are the order of the day.

Patenting software and business processes

Now that patenting of software that has a technical effect is almost certainly possible through the European patent system and in the United Kingdom, serious consideration should be given to this. Patenting of business processes is possible in the United States and this should be carefully considered as well.

The difficulty with e-commerce and patenting is that the timescales are not compatible. From application to grant for a patent may take two years, during which time an e-commerce start-up could have gone through several iterations and several technological changes.

In summarizing IPR considerations for Internet and e-commerce businesses, the single most important point is to ensure that the company actually owns the IPR that it thinks it owns. The assignment of IPR created by third parties, such as consultants and outside agencies, is absolutely crucial. Also, select a strong name, search and research it thoroughly and register it as a domain name and trade mark as soon as possible.

The cost of IPR

The cost of intellectual property can be considerable but the cost of not protecting IPR properly can be several orders of magnitude greater. This chapter has sought to give a basic understanding of the scope and value of IPR and, in order to complete the picture, it is necessary to look at the cost.

Copyright probably represents the best value, in that it does not require registration and is, therefore, largely free, subject to assignment considerations. The cost of getting an application on file for a registered trade mark in most jurisdictions is between £500 and £1000, although the cost of prosecuting the application to registration could well double that. The cost of a trade mark application at (European) Community level will be around £1500 to £2000. Costs in the United States will be in the same ballpark.

The cost of putting together a patent specification will be somewhere between £2000 and £5000 and thus, once drafted, subject to translation costs and the like, should be usable around the world. The cost of a global filing programme for a patent will be somewhere between £15 000 and £50 000, with prosecution costs which could easily more than double that. By comparison, registered design and similar less significant registered forms of IPR are fairly inexpensive.

Be selective

The important lesson in the protection of registered IPR is to *be selective*. Look at your major markets, examine their characteristics, balance the cost against the protection that will be afforded. For example, there is little point in applying for a patent for an alcoholic beverage in certain Middle Eastern countries!

6 Raising funds for a dotcom business venture

KPMG

Introduction

'Raising funds for a dotcom business venture has never been easier', according to Clive Hyman, partner in KPMG's European Private Equity team, 'but the number of people chasing after those funds is growing by the day'.

The first step in attempting to secure funding is to build an understanding of where the funds are coming from. Sources differ according to the stage the business venture has reached and the medium-term strategy adopted by the entrepreneur.

Raising seed-corn finance to develop an idea

One of the most common sources of £20 000–£100 000 of seed capital is private individuals using redundancy payments, maturing insurance policies and savings. Many entrepreneurs use their own funds or are able to convince friends and family to invest in their venture. It may also be possible to raise loan capital from a commercial bank. Some banks have special units to assist businesses with a focus on innovation and technology.

Other types of debt finance, such as factoring or leasing, are available from the appropriate trade association, such as the Factors and Discounters Association and the Finance and Leasing Association (*www.factors.org.uk*). There are also sources within the European Union for grants and other finance for Small and Medium-sized Enterprises (SMEs) (*http://europa.eu.int/comm/represent_en.htm*). The EU publishes a free guide to grants and loans entitled, *Funding from the European Union*. Business Link organizations are a good source of information about these and other finance sources available to companies in each region.

For larger amounts up to £250 000, it may be necessary to focus attention on traditional 'business angels'. These are private investors who tend to invest smaller amounts in earlier-stage businesses than most venture capital firms. These have become much more prevalent in recent years because of the perceived opportunities to get rich quick.

One of the difficulties faced by entrepreneurs in tracking down business angels is the fact they tend not to belong to a group, so there is no comprehensive directory. Some business angels can be reached via business angel networks, which act as introduction agencies. Some are listed in the free booklet *Sources of Business Angel Capital*, published by the British Venture Capital Association (BVCA) (*www.bvca.co.uk*).

Business angels tend to be locally or regionally oriented, so it is often possible to make contact through local business groups. These local business professionals are becoming an increasingly common source of funding for e-commerce start-ups. In early 2000 there are believed to be 'a few thousand' people who would actively be described in this way. Business angels usually add valuable management skills to a new enterprise and are unlikely to simply put money into a venture.

An increasing source of seed capital, according to Heather Bewers, Associate Director of KPMG Corporate Finance, is senior industry figures who do not necessarily describe themselves as business angels. Such people may not be known personally to the entrepreneur, but they are likely to be prominent in the industry at which they are aiming their venture.

'These are the chairmen and chief executives of quoted companies who put, say, £30 000–50 000 of their own money into a new venture and attract additional money from friends and contacts', says Bewers. 'The big plus of these people is that they will bring specific industry-sector knowledge. If you have somebody who has been chief executive of a major plc for a number of years they will bring their contacts, their knowledge of sector trends, their knowledge of technological difficulties for a specific industry and general management experience that can prove immensely valuable.'

Another potentially valuable source of contacts is that of 'generators' or 'incubators'. In addition to business contacts, these organizations offer management experience and some claim to have access to sources of funds. Generators offer to evaluate and develop business plans. They are often looking for equity, not just in return for funds, but also in return for providing these incubation-type services.

Raising funds when the venture has progressed beyond the 'good idea' phase

'Venture capital' is external finance exchanged for a shareholding in a company with high-growth prospects. Venture capital companies are professional organizations which invest sums ranging from a few thousand pounds to many millions in unquoted companies.

The companies are usually members of the BVCA, which means they are bound by the association's code of conduct and regulated by a self-regulatory authority. The BVCA produces *A Guide to Venture Capital*, and has a members' directory of venture capital companies.

Venture capital investors have traditionally worked on a timeframe of three to seven years. They will seek to make a return on their investment by selling the shares back to the management, selling the company to another, or listing the company on the Stock Exchange.

Venture capitalists never used to look at start-ups and were only prepared to consider businesses that were up and running, but traditional venture capitalists, such as 3i and Apax, are now looking at early-stage businesses in a way they never used to do.

Whilst they do not necessarily need a proven business model with existing revenues, venture capitalists will not generally consider a venture that is only at the 'ideas stage'. They will only talk with entrepreneurs who can demonstrate that they have thought through all aspects of their proposition, evaluated and analyzed business risks, identified potential competitors and, in short, understand what will drive the business forward rather than remaining as a concept.

Entrepreneurs need to show venture capitalists a genuine revenue model. They must also demonstrate how their pricing either replicates a traditional business model or is clearly distinct from it, and justify the choice.

American investment funds, such as GE Capital, are increasingly active in the UK market. Whilst they work on similar models to European investors, they have been typically much happier to invest in start-ups. 'They are genuine venture capitalists, rather than the type of private equity player we have conventionally seen in the UK', suggests Bewers. 'An increasing number are feeling the start-up field is becoming too expensive in the US and are looking to Europe to provide the next growth area. They regard the UK as the bridgehead.'

Another potential source is Internet investment funds that can be but are not necessarily quoted. 'They are not substantially different from the private equity players but come without the baggage of the venture capital houses', according to Bewers. 'They have a knowledge of the Internet arena and often have US tie-ups, such as an incubator service or another fund in the States, which they can tap into. These Internet investment funds can be academic institutions such as universities, they can be corporations such as Reuters, or quoted private funds which are prepared to incubate as well as invest.'

The first-round funding provided to new e-commerce enterprises by these investment funds is usually less than £5 million, though marketing budgets can sometimes push the total investment over the £5 million barrier.

Finding additional funds when the business is up and running

'Second-round' finance for a business that is already running is generally provided by the same or a similar group, or more and more by flotation. 'In the current market, people are increasingly feeling they will get a higher valuation by floating on AIM, Techmark, Nasdaq [*www.ft-se.co.uk*; *www.nasdaq.com* or *www.nasdaq.co.uk*] or one of the European markets', says Bewers. 'The whole financial decision is being influenced by the cost of the funds derived from the public arena.'

Additionally, people believe floating will give not only access to funds achieved through releasing a comparatively small proportion of equity (typically around 20%) but also a real benefit in terms of the PR that public status can give.

'At a time when there are literally thousands of dotcom propositions out there any kind of PR is perceived to be of value', Bewers observes. 'They also believe that when consolidation comes – and the most far-sighted recognize that it will happen sooner or later – then having highly visible paper will add to the value of their proposition.' Whether it will or not depends on the sustainability of the fundamental business model and, less controllably, on the status of the market.

It is currently difficult for traditional 'debt providers' to participate significantly in the funding of start-up dotcom enterprises. Not only is the risk level high, but also the business assets are minimal and cashflow meagre or non-existent. When the market begins to consolidate, however, it is entirely possible that some at least of the debt providers are likely to offer 'mezzanine finance'.

This is a high-cost debt instrument with repayment terms and interest. In order to increase the yield on mezzanine finance, an 'equity kicker' is usually involved. Mezzanine finance has traditionally been used on leveraged buyouts where there is a gap between what the equity provider is prepared to underwrite and what the senior debt provider is prepared to underwrite. The mezzanine finance provider fills the gap in the middle. When the business is subsequently sold, the 'equity kicker' is activated and the mezzanine financier is entitled to a percentage of the equity.

Entering into an alliance with an existing business

Another alternative for funding an e-commerce enterprise is corporate venturing. This is when a large company helps the formation and/or growth of a smaller business to their mutual advantage. In theory, it offers a chance to combine the entrepreneurial flair of a small business with the commercial and management skills of a large company.

It can be a formally structured arrangement with each partner given distinct areas of responsibility. Alternatively, it can be more informal with company executives being given the time and resources to explore and develop mutually beneficial business ideas.

A large company can set up corporate ventures through a direct minority equity investment in new or existing small independent businesses. In other cases, it can see business activities or technology from a large company being spun out into a new business in which it becomes a minority investor.

Corporate venturing is financially attractive for large companies because it keeps their options open. By attracting external venture funding, it allows large companies to spread their financial resources across a wider range of projects. They then have the flexibility to decide whether projects should be re-absorbed into the group structure, spun off into independent businesses or continue to operate as joint ventures.

Small businesses benefit not only through gaining financial support. They also gain credibility through the involvement of the large company, making it easier to attract finance. Corporate venturing can also allow the smaller business to use the large company's network of contacts, customers and suppliers or customers.

Problems can arise, however, because of cultural differences between bureaucratic bigger companies and more innovative smaller businesses with less formal decision-making processes. There can also be disputes about the strategic objectives, but corporate venturing is nevertheless worthy of serious consideration.

It should be noted that if the large company's profitability should start to fall, it is likely that it will focus its resources on its core business. Its commitment to a project can change rapidly as a result – unless the new venture can demonstrate rapid growth in profitability.

Corporate reorganizations can also undermine the stability of a business relationship between large and small companies. This may seriously restrict the chance for the venture to achieve its full potential. There is also a danger of the larger businesses stealing the intellectual property of the smaller ones.

Evidence from the USA proves that corporate venturing can be highly effective in achieving innovation and growth. It has been relatively uncommon in the UK, however, because many British companies concentrate on maximizing short-term performance. This may change as a result of tax incentives announced by Chancellor Gordon Brown. Corporate venturing is encouraged through corporation tax relief at a rate of 20% on equity investments in small higher-risk trading companies. (For further information visit *www.inlandrevenue.gov.uk*.)

Consolidation between bigger traditional companies and smaller dotcom enterprises is forecast to accelerate rapidly towards the end of 2000. Well established 'bricks and mortar' businesses are likely to move towards 'clicks and mortar' through purchasing existing e-commerce businesses in complementary business areas, rather than setting up greenfield operations.

It is important to distinguish between bigger corporates that have set aside a certain amount of their funds to invest in a number of e-com propositions', says Bewers, 'and those looking to invest in a number of businesses that are complementary to their existing businesses' – in other words potential competitors. The latter group often takes a minority stake as a means of monitoring developments and seeks to enhance its own share price by demonstrating to the market an understanding of e-businesses.

'Many of the existing corporates do not believe their culture is compatible with Internet companies, so they are looking to invest in separate companies and keep them separate', she says. 'Big companies generally have to be managed in a conventional hierarchical structure with a supporting bureaucracy. It is very difficult to run an Internet business in that sort of culture.'

The entrepreneurial culture of an Internet business does not necessarily fit comfortably inside a large corporation. Taking a minority stake in a separate company is recognition that it is not always easy to integrate the two, but it demonstrates that the large corporation wants to be involved.

Most investment proposals never make it past the first hurdle

Despite the wide variety of funding sources, only a very small number of dotcom propositions will ever attract investment. 'There are as many business ideas as there are people in a room', says Clive Hyman. 'What the entrepreneur needs to do is put himself in the shoes of the potential funder and understand what will make his proposition worthy of support.'

Heather Bewers agrees. 'There are several thousand propositions for "dotcom" businesses being presented every week', she observes. 'A lot will go nowhere because they are nothing more than an idea and many people are not prepared to put any further work into their ideas.' As a rough guide, only 25–40% actually move on to the next stage by actually doing something about it.

Another common area of naïvety is at the business planning stage when revenues are commonly built from a top-down perspective. 'Somebody takes a market size and glibly says they will take a 40 or even 55% share of that global market', says Bewers.

'Would-be dotcom entrepreneurs often make no attempt to justify their definition of market size', she adds. 'Nor do they define whether the market is on-line or off-line or seek to explain whether the same pricing model and volumes will apply in the future. As a result, it is impossible for any of them to justify their extravagant market share projections or demonstrate how they could be achievable.'

People need to pay more attention to the pricing model. 'The Internet commoditizes many products and services', Brewers observes. 'Therefore you have to justify why your prices won't fall. That should be the first thought in your mind. Many people have given no thought to the issue, so when they go to the market and say people will pay £30 for something they have no way of justifying that assertion. And simply being the first company to offer the service is not of itself the solution. It isn't a barrier to further entrants at all.'

Prerequisites of success

According to Clive Hyman, a successful Internet enterprise needs three things. 'First there must be a market opportunity. Secondly you need the right time to market', he says. 'Finally there must be the opportunity to exploit that market need without delay. It may be tempting to go for organic growth and retain 100% ownership, but the market is moving on at a tremendous pace and if you cannot attract the money to exploit it quickly the opportunity will probably pass you by.'

The dotcom propositions that are going to succeed, suggests Hyman, are those with experienced management teams. The marketplace is now beginning to mature. An increasing number of dotcom entrepreneurs are acknowledging that they lack the management skills to successfully implement their business concept.

'The successful entrepreneur is going to need to know when and how to step aside', says Hyman. 'He or she has got to have the maturity and vision to recognize the need for a strong management team.'

Developing the idea

A lot of hard work and preparation is essential before an entrepreneur can successfully present a funding proposal. The process is usually faster and almost certainly has a greater chance of success if the entrepreneur is prepared to take professional advice.

Advisers, such as KPMG, receive as many as 20 applications each day from entrepreneurs who have recognized the benefits which professional advisers can bring. Advising every applicant would be impossible, so KPMG operates a filtering process. The first stage of the filter is a questionnaire on the KPMG Web site (*www.kpmg.co.uk*). This asks entrepreneurs to answer all of the following questions:

- Does your proposition solve an existing market inefficiency?
- Is there fundamental market demand for this product or service?
- How big is that demand likely to be?
- What is the potential size of the opportunity in number of customers?
- Would customers pay for this service, product or system?
- What are they buying now?
- What is the potential revenue for your business?
- What are the revenue sources?
- Is there any way to protect the intellectual capital of your idea from imitators?
- Are there any firms providing this product or service now?
- What do they charge, or how do they generate revenue?
- Does your way of providing this product or service offer a superior ability to generate income or growth?

Demonstrating an ability to answer all of these questions shows that the entrepreneur has considered all the key elements of his or her business proposal. It allows KPMG to carry out a quasi-scientific evaluation of the business plans and to build up a picture of how the idea compares against other business propositions in different areas, how commercially the whole thing has been approached, and how it is matched to what the market is looking for.

An interdisciplinary group meets regularly to discuss the results of the screening. Most proposals are rejected at this second stage, but each month four or five entrepreneurs are then invited to present their proposal in further detail.

'The first trick of a successful presentation is to keep it to about 20 minutes', says Bewers. The entrepreneur needs to be able to say:

- what the proposition is – preferably in normal non-technical language;
- what the unique selling points are;
- what the market potential is;
- what share of the market is expected and how you, the entrepreneur, expect to achieve it;
- what risks could kill your business;
- what is going to keep you awake at night;
- what you are looking for.

'When you talk about it in detail you often find that the idea has not been thought through', says Bewers. 'We are looking for things we believe can generate sustainable businesses', she explains, 'and one of the key criteria is the management team. If they can't sell it to us, then they probably can't sell it to potential funders, and they certainly can't sell it to the market.'

Many of those presenting business proposals are sent away with instructions to carry out further work on specific aspects of their business plan. 'We are not telling them they are being rejected', explains Bewers. 'We explain that we cannot help them to approach potential funders until they are able to present more convincing answers to difficult questions.'

'If we are going to find a proposition that is fundable', adds Hyman, 'it has to be attractive for someone to invest – either in pure financial terms or in meeting a market need.

'If you are going to be making money from day one, then boy have you got a proposition', he continues. 'But if you have got to invest in a business infrastructure, spend large sums on building a brand, and you haven't got the right people or the right contracts in place, then investors will be justifiably edgy.'

There are growing numbers of people and institutions prepared to invest in dotcom ventures, but they are spoilt for choice. They are presented with a constant flow of business proposals and can afford to be very choosy.

A large proportion of proposals are never even read – let alone given serious consideration. The proposals that are likely to be studied in detail are those that have been thoroughly prepared and ideally come with the recommendation of a respected adviser, such as KPMG.

Incubating an idea

'If you really want to get rich and change your lifestyle', suggests Hyman, 'then take professional advice on how to take it into the marketplace, how to shape it and how to develop it.'

Incubation is about developing the business proposition. It often involves identifying and acquiring skills which are missing from the management team that has dreamt up the idea and put the first business plan together. 'Entrepreneurs often don't have a business infrastructure', says Bewers. 'The incubation process can help to find a chief financial officer, a commercial and technical director and other people required to build a complete management team.'

Evidence from the USA suggests that 90% of dotcom ideas that have been incubated will succeed, but many entrepreneurs dismiss the need for incubation. Clive Hyman is unimpressed by those who are determined to chart their own course. 'I consider it a sign of strength for somebody to be prepared to listen', he says. 'The person who is going to succeed is the person who has the maturity and the strength of personality to sit down, listen and learn.'

The incubation process, facilitated by companies such as KPMG, is designed to ensure that a business proposal is robust and well developed before it is presented to an appropriate investor. Without this professional assistance, even strong propositions can fail.

'Many entrepreneurs prefer to go direct to potential sources of finance', concedes Hyman. 'But because they aren't involving advisers in the incubation process, they are not getting the hints and tips about how to make it backable, how to get it lined up and how to gain the attention of the busy guy at the other end.'

Hyman believes that going direct to investors is the most common mistake made by dotcom entrepreneurs. 'They flood potential funders with raw, undeveloped business plans and they just get put on to the pile', he says.

If it is a proposal that has come through an adviser such as KPMG, there is going to be a stronger desire to look at it. 'The incubation adviser makes life easier for the investor', says Hyman. 'It's as simple as that.' Incubation advisers bridge the gap between busy investors and entrepreneurs.

'Our experience lets us know what they are looking for', claims Hyman. 'We know the critical success factors and how they differ between investors.'

For business angels, the 'hot button' may be a sense of belonging, a desire to contribute management skills and a participation in creating something. For the private equity community, however, it is more likely to be a confidence that the management team is going to be able to deliver on achieving the agreed business objectives.

'If my team gives a funder a call to say that a specific proposal is on its way, they know it's been through that first filter and they will give it serious consideration', says Hyman. It does not mean the proposal will always be accepted, but it greatly improves the odds.

'We deal closely with many investors', Hyman explains, 'and there is enough transparency in those relationships for them to tell us what is wrong with a proposal they don't like. The entrepreneur has got to be strong enough to take it on the chin.'

'It is a robust and brutal process, but successful business people are going to have to be prepared to take some hard feedback', he asserts. 'Quality entrepreneurs will take the feedback and won't be phased by it.'

Much of the reluctance to involve professional advisers in business incubation results from a belief that fees must be paid for the service. In reality, companies such as KPMG generally work on a contingent basis. Payment is made only if the entrepreneur is successful in raising investment funds.

'No-one should be taking out a triple mortgage to fund their dotcom concept', warns Hyman. 'If they find themselves having to do so, they are going to ruin themselves because it means their business idea is unbackable.'

Investors will certainly look for signs of commitment to the idea, Hyman explains. 'But if somebody is putting their own money in to get it running that's normally enough', he says. 'If you are investing your time and energy to set up a business and you are not expecting someone to pay for the effort you have already put in, that's usually sufficient commitment.'

Presenting the idea effectively

Potential investors expect proposals to be in a broadly consistent form, and contain the following:

- *executive summary* – this is an accurate and complete description of why your business should exist and win;
- *market analysis* – a description of the market serviced, customers and their purchasing criteria, and competition in both bricks-and-mortar and Internet arenas;
- *operational issues* – a description of existing supply-chain relationships and the position of your business within it. How will the required links be established?
- *management* – a description of roles and background of individuals to fill key management roles;
- *financials* – this should address the questions of: what are the revenue sources? What are the main costs? How much profit will this business generate, and when?

Constructing and writing a strong proposal is, however, just the first stage in making an effective presentation. Clive Hyman has been directly involved in hundreds of presentations and offers a valuable insight into the process. 'People think on three levels: rational, political and emotional. The rational is never normally the issue', he suggests. 'The issue is how to get inside the head of the person on the other side of the table who's going to give you the cheque. In order to do that, you need to tap into their emotions and deal with any political issues that he or she might be facing within the organization.'

The presentation must be well articulated and crystal clear. 'We have a ground rule here', says Hyman. 'If the entrepreneur can't articulate the proposition in less than half an hour, then forget it. The presentation is crucial. You have got to convince the funder of proof of concept and you have got to have signed contracts with some key alliance partners in place.'

Entrepreneurs are also being judged on the 'soft stuff', he says. 'How they react and deal with questions. They must display confidence to take the challenge on and be happy to admit they are not the best people to implement their idea.'

Reducing the risk of implementation

In listening to a proposal, suggests Hyman, the potential investor will be seeking to evaluate the risk of implementation. 'He will be asking himself, "Is the management team able to handle all of this? Have they done it before? What are the critical risks of getting the thing up and running?"'

If more people spent time 'de-risking', Hyman believes, there would be far fewer business failures. 'Your dotcom business plan should include an implementation plan that identifies the business risks and explains what you are going to do to deal with those risks', he says. 'You need to drill down through all the negatives, break down the big issues into manageable chunks and create an action plan.'

'To de-risk a proposition, you need to brainstorm constructively around the headline issues you are going to face', he advises. 'Then you can work out what practical steps you need to take to address the issues. "How do I go about it? Who is responsible?" An adviser can help by working through all the risks.

'Some of the best proposals have come from people who have said, "We're not the ones to do the techie bit, and we're not the guys to run this because our management skills aren't directly transferable to the proposition." The ability to demonstrate that you can make the business plan work is absolutely key.'

Useful contacts

The European Commission
8 Storey's Gate, London SW1P 3AT
or fax 0207 973 1900

Factors and Discounters Association
Tel: 0208 332 9955   Fax: 0208 332 2585   (*www.factors.org.uk*)

Finance and Leasing Association
Tel: 0207 836 6511   Fax: 0207 420 9600

British Venture Capital Association
Tel: 0207 240 3846   Fax: 0207 240 3849   (*www.bvca.co.uk*)

7 Legal aspects of setting up and running an Internet business

Andrew Millett, Mishcon de Reya

Introduction

The enthusiasm, optimism and sheer determination that feed the creative energies required to set up an Internet business, drive the business plan and seek investment are often dampened by the prospect of a visit to the lawyers (and their fees). Internet entrepreneurs can be forgiven for feeling daunted by the apparent minefield of legal obstacles to be overcome in order to achieve their ambitions. If, however, they remember that the law is there principally to protect rather than restrict them, their approach and that of their legal advisers will be that much more positive and often creative. The Internet revolution has itself brought changes to legislation, innovation to contractual relationships and changed the way many lawyers do business, including, of course, how they charge their clients.

This chapter is designed to alert entrepreneurs to the legal issues that face them as they begin the task of putting the business plan into reality. Entrepreneurs will no doubt be asking themselves the following questions:

How will my business be owned?

Where will the business be?

What is involved in setting up the company?

What does it mean to be a shareholder?

What does it mean to be a director?

What is involved in running company meetings?

How do I finance the company?

What do I need to consider when hiring and firing staff?

How do I incentivize the staff?

How are companies taxed?

What do I need to consider when acquiring premises?

What about insurance?

How do I make my agreements watertight?

What happens if the business goes bust?

How do I exit?

How will my business be owned?

How the business is structured will depend on the nature of the business, those collaborating in the business, the long-term goals for the business and how the business and those with an ownership interest in it will be taxed on the profits they make and the value created.

Unless the Internet entrepreneur is superhuman and able to run the business alone, from developing the software to providing all the finance, he will be relying on a team of people, most of whom will most likely expect part ownership of the business. It is not uncommon with Internet and other high-tech companies for the founder to give up to 70% of the business away on the basis that it is better to have a small percentage of a very large number (value) than a large percentage of a small number.

This chapter will assume that the business will be owned by the most common vehicle used for a continuing business – the limited liability company (or a number of limited liability companies) – but before we examine the limited liability company, let us consider a number of other possible legal vehicles.

A contractual venture

This is where the entrepreneur is going to be doing everything himself and will not be sharing ownership in the business. All his relationships will be entered into on the basis of independent contracts. He will be solely responsible (liable) for his actions. He will own all the property of and proprietary rights in his business. He will not be subject to any formal registration requirements as regards the business, and the profits and losses are his. If an entrepreneur could survive in this way, life would be simple.

However, it is unsuitable if others are to share in the ownership of the business, particularly when future finance is required and venture capital is sought. The contractual relationships themselves may inadvertently create a partnership in which the entrepreneur will be liable for the acts and omissions of his counterparty (see partnerships below). In addition, it is not tax efficient because any losses (e.g. due to initial start-up costs) arising in each such 'venture' may be kept separate from the profits of other ventures. If the entrepreneur has insufficient contemporaneous profits arising from other ventures immediately to absorb the losses of a venture, then those losses can only be carried forward against any profits eventually made in the same venture.

Partnerships

This is defined in law as *'the relation which subsists between persons carrying on a business in common with a view of profit'* (section 1, Partnership Act 1890). This is an objective test, if two or more people set up in business together, it is likely that they will be in partnership. The relationship is fairly simple: the partners each share directly in the profits and losses of the business, are each jointly and severally liable for the acts and omissions of the other partner(s). In other words, a third party can seek redress against any and all of the partners. As regards the outside world, this liability is unlimited.

A partnership deed is usually required by the partners in order to define their relationship so as to prescribe, for example, the percentage of profits which each is entitled to, the percentage ownership interest of each partner in the partnership property, the percentage by which each partner is required to fund the partnership and so on. There are no formal registration requirements.

A partnership has some tax advantages over a limited company because of its transparency. For Income Tax purposes, a partnership is not a legal entity and each partner is deemed to have directly incurred his proportion of the profits or losses of the partnership. Thus, dealings between an individual partner and the partnership do not give rise to Income Tax liabilities (compare the position of directors and limited companies) and any losses realized in the partnership business can be immediately set against a partner's contemporaneous other income (assuming the partner has any!).

However, the joint and several and unlimited liability of the partners for the debts of the business is often singularly unattractive to the entrepreneur (even though it is possible to form a limited liability partnership, see below). While he may commence business in partnership with his collaborators (often without actually knowing it), as it becomes a more serious financial venture, the entrepreneur will look to other ways to protect his interest. A partnership also has certain tax disadvantages. All the profits of a partnership are taxable on the partners at their marginal Income Tax rates as they arise, whether or not withdrawn from the business. This compares unfavourably with a limited company, where profits which are not drawn as directors' remuneration but are ploughed back into the business are taxed at Corporation Tax rates lower than the Income Tax rates suffered by partners.

Limited partnerships

This is somewhere between the limited liability company and the partnership. At least one partner must be a general partner who manages the partnership with unlimited liability (although the general partner can be a company); the others are limited partner(s) who may not manage the partnership, but will provide finance. This is useful where the collaborators are 'sleeping partners', only putting in finance. However, it will not necessarily be attractive to the entrepreneur who, as general partner, will remain with the burden of unlimited liability, nor will it necessarily be attractive to the limited partners who may want some control over the management of the business.

The limited liability partnership (LLP)

Initially, this was an American legal quirk. It is a hybrid between a limited liability company and a partnership to be created under the Limited Liability Partnership Act 2000, soon to come into force. An LLP has to be registered and is a separate legal person from that of its members or partners, but the liability of the members to contribute to the LLP's assets is limited. The main businesses to take advantage of this particular legal format have been the global professional service firms. The popularity of the LLP for smaller organizations remains to be seen.

The limited company

This is the most common vehicle. It is a body incorporated under the Companies Acts and it has directors and shareholders whose liability is limited (i.e. to pay for their shares and who cannot be liable for any debts incurred by the company, although all or some of the founders may have to guarantee the debts of the company). It is a separate legal entity. Contracts are entered into in its name and on its behalf and it is thus responsible for performing those contracts, and it can sue and be sued under them, without recourse to its shareholders or directors. Although there is a detailed body of law governing the operation of companies, it serves as a valuable framework within which the participants in the business and third parties dealing with the business can operate. It is relatively easy to accommodate those wishing to acquire an ownership, or equity interest, thus making the raising of finance that much easier. Monies can be borrowed by and secured over the assets of the company, including a charge over the ongoing performance of the company, known as a 'floating charge'. The company is, however, subject to certain publicity requirements, not only on establishment by filing its constitutional documents (the memorandum and articles of association, see below) but also during its lifetime, such as the requirements to file annual accounts and notices of any changes to its constitution and organization (including changes to its share capital).

Companies are also separate legal entities for tax purposes. Although this has the advantage of taxing profits remaining in the business at only Corporation Tax rates, problems can be caused if an entrepreneur blurs the distinction between himself and his company. Any benefit provided by the company to an entrepreneurial shareholder and/or director (e.g. an interest-free loan of money or the use of a material asset, such as a car) will give rise to Income Tax liabilities to the entrepreneur and must be recognized from the outset. Furthermore, if the business is sold at any time, the entrepreneur must usually sell the shares in the company, rather than the company sell the business, to avoid a 'double hit' of Capital Gains Tax.

In law, a company can be established as an unlimited company, in which case its shareholders will be liable without limit for all its debts, or it may be limited by guarantee, in which case its members are not shareholders (for there are usually no shares) but undertake each to find so much money to pay the liabilities of the company on winding up. These types of company are rare and the entrepreneur will mainly choose the limited company because of its limited liability status, its independent legal persona, its global recognition and its flexibility in bringing in investors as and when required. The remainder of this chapter will assume that a limited company will be used.

Where will the business be?

What makes the Internet and particularly e-commerce so attractive is their global reach. Customers do not know or need to know where the company which owns or runs the business is in order to make a purchase; they only need a Web site address (*www.xyz.com*). It is different if a customer wants to sue the company for he needs to know where it is incorporated and where its principal place of business is (and, of course, where it has its main assets). Even though for many years there have been plans within the European Commission to create a European company, apart from the European Economic Interest Grouping (unsuitable for the entrepreneur as it is designed as a non-profit-making entity), we are still obliged to set up our business structures within a particular chosen jurisdiction.

Although globally recognized, there is no such thing as a global company and cyberspace is not (yet) a separate jurisdiction! That is not to say that every element of the business needs to be owned by the same company in the same jurisdiction; it is possible to split up ownership of each of the elements. The shareholdings may be owned by individuals, trusts or through companies offshore, the intellectual property rights may be registered in the name of a separate offshore company, set up for the purpose, and the day-to-day operations may be conducted through different companies, each established in different jurisdictions. There are essentially two reasons for splitting the assets in this way:

(a) to make it more difficult (though not impossible) for a claimant or liquidator to enforce a claim against or realize the assets of the business; and

(b) for tax reasons, to attempt to shelter the profits and the growth in value of the shares of the companies from United Kingdom taxation. However, although this strategy may work for non-United Kingdom resident entrepreneurs or entrepreneurs who are tax resident, but not domiciled in the United Kingdom (essentially foreign nationals), it does not work for entrepreneurs who are tax resident and domiciled in the United Kingdom (essentially UK citizens). The Inland Revenue has copious and draconian powers to 'look through' foreign companies or trusts and to attribute their profits and gains to such persons for tax purposes.

Apart from the obvious costs (including legal fees) in setting up separate holding entities in different countries and putting in place the various licences and contracts between the companies so that the business can operate as one, the entrepreneur should keep in mind whether complex corporate structures are commensurate with his/her objectives as described in the business plan. How will it look to new investors? To what extent will it need to be reorganized in preparation for an IPO?

What is involved in setting up the company?

It takes time, from receipt of all the registration documents, for Companies House to issue a certificate of incorporation (the document validating the existence of the company, or the company's 'birth certificate'). Therefore, there are agencies which keep a stock of ready-to-use or 'off-the-shelf' companies, making it relatively easy to set up a company by simply purchasing one from a formation agent. (Web sites for formation agents for the UK include: *www.business-assist.co.uk* ; *www.creditman.co.uk* and *www.eden.co.uk* and *www.jordans.co.uk*.

On acquiring the company, the entrepreneur (or someone on his behalf) will have to take a transfer of the subscriber share(s) and put himself or someone else on the board of directors, in place of the formation agent's nominees named on the first registration documents. Once this is done, the company will effectively 'belong' to the entrepreneur. However, as it was 'off-the-shelf', the company will need to undergo further changes so as to tailor it to the entrepreneur's requirements, such as changing the constitution (i.e. the memorandum and articles of association), the share capital, the registered office, the accounting reference date, and by adding new directors and a company secretary. In addition, auditors will have to be appointed and bank accounts opened.

In order for the entrepreneur to be able to run the company effectively, he will need an understanding of the constitution of the company and the internal mechanisms by which it is owned, controlled and managed.

The two documents that govern the constitution are the memorandum of association and the articles of association.

The memorandum of association

The memorandum contains the following information.

The name of the company

Chapter 5 of this book deals with domain names and trade marks under which the business will operate. However, the company, as a separate legal person, requires a corporate name that is not the same as any other in the Company Registrar's index or which is otherwise prohibited (e.g. a name conveying the impression that the company is connected with government or local authorities or includes words and expressions prohibited by in regulation). The last word of the name must be 'limited' for a private company (and 'public limited company' for a public company). The abbreviations 'Ltd' (or 'Plc') are permissible. If the company is registered in Wales, then 'Cyfyngedig' ('cyf') should be used instead of 'Limited' (and 'Cwimni Cyfyngedig Cyhoeddus' ('ccc') should be used instead of 'Public Limited Company'). The full name is required to be affixed conspicuously outside every office or place of business of the company; it must appear on all business letters and notices, including invoices, receipts and letters of credit. To this end, emails should be considered no differently than letters or faxes. This is important because if, for example, a director or manager, or person acting on his behalf, signs a cheque which does not have the full name of the company clearly shown, he will be personally liable for payment under it.

Where the company's registered office is situated

The registered office shall be in the country in which the company is registered and, accordingly, that country will have jurisdiction governing the company's establishment (i.e. for the UK, England and Wales, or Scotland). Every company must have a registered office to which formal communications and notices can be addressed (and in the case of proceedings, validly served).

All official correspondence must contain details of the address of the registered office. Although not always strictly necessary, it is a good idea to include details of the registered office wherever the registered name is shown. The company's books are required to be kept at the registered office. In many cases, at least at the beginning of a company's life, particularly given the frequency of changes to the constitution, issuance of share capital, etc., the registered office and the books will be at the entrepreneur's solicitors' offices.

The company's 'objects' (i.e. the nature of and extent of its powers)

The company is simply not empowered to conduct an activity outside its objects and such activity would thus be void. This is designed to protect those who invest (or subscribe for shares) in the company and those who trade with the company. Although it is not appropriate here to explore this *ultra vires* rule, one should note that most objects clauses nowadays are drawn sufficiently wide so as to enable the company to undertake almost any type of trading activity. However, the entrepreneur should at least request from the formation agents a company with suitable objects, and a quick read will save the entrepreneur a great deal of trouble later.

A statement that the liability of its members is limited

'The liability of its members limited by the memorandum to the amount, if any, unpaid on the shares respectively held by them' (section 1(2)(a), Companies Act 1985). Therefore, the share capital clause must state the nominal amount (or par value) of the shares which determines the maximum liability of a shareholder (see below). This does not mean that the members will not be liable to put the company in funds by virtue of separate agreements, undertakings or guarantees, for example, as agreed under a separate shareholders' agreement, nor does it mean that members wishing to subscribe for a fresh issue of shares need only pay the par value. When new investment is sought, the investors will usually subscribe for the par value and a premium for the shares.

The amount of its registered share capital and the nominal amount of such shares

The capital clause must state the nominal amount of the share capital. This can be any amount that the founders think fit, depending on the relationship between the funding the company is going to require and the number of shares or percentage of 'ownership' of the company which will be held by each of the shareholders. In the early days, it is not easy to calculate this as a company may undergo several rounds of financing and (especially with Internet companies) in quick succession. One should note, however, that shares can be issued at a premium to their nominal value, therefore a £1 share can be issued for £1million. Also, one share can carry more than one vote at general meetings. Furthermore, the authorized share capital does not have to equate exactly to the amount of the issued share capital (although it cannot be less). It is usual to leave enough headroom in the amount of the authorized share capital to allow for all the anticipated share issues.

If the company is to be a public company (e.g. required for listing on the London Stock Exchange) the authorized share capital must exceed £50 000, which has to be fully issued (or subscribed). It is also possible to have a share capital expressed in different currencies, although if a plc, one class of share should be expressed in pounds sterling. In one case, it was held that a company could have four classes of shares, each denominated in different currencies (US$, £, SFr and Dm).

The articles of association

These contain the internal rules and regulations of the company. They contain rules governing the issuance of shares, the transfer of shares, the rights and restrictions of the shareholders, shareholders' meetings, appointment and removal of directors and the holding of directors' meetings, as well as various powers delegated to the directors such as borrowing powers. 'Off-the-shelf' companies usually have very short articles of association, instead cross-referring to a model set of articles contained in regulations in Table A of the Companies Act 1985 (see SI 1985/805). The articles require careful thought and, particularly when new investors take shares and join the company, often involve lengthy negotiation, as the rights of the shareholders will be governed by the articles (see below for shareholders' agreements).

The memorandum and articles are important documents, they form a contract between the shareholders and the company and between the shareholders themselves. Section 14(1) of the Companies Act 1985 states:

> . . . *the memorandum and articles, when registered, bind the company and its members to the same extent as if they respectively had been signed and sealed by each member, and contained covenants on the part of each member to observe all the provisions of the memorandum and of the articles.*

What does it mean to be a shareholder?

The definition of 'shareholder' is contained in section 22 of the Companies Act 1985:

1. *The subscribers of a company's memorandum are deemed to have agreed to become members of the company, and on its registration shall be entered as such in its register of members.*

2. *Every other person who agrees to become a member of a company, and whose name is entered in its register of members, is a member of the company.*

The key points to note are that (a) it is only upon entry in the register of members that a person is legally a shareholder. The share certificate itself is evidence of title to the shares but not definitive (except in the case of bearer shares), and (b) shares can be acquired either by subscription or by transfer.

Although the business and assets of the company will belong to the company itself, the shares in the company represent the proportion of the company owned by the holder of those shares.

Regulation 2 of Table A provides for shares to be issued *'with such rights or restrictions as the company may by ordinary resolution determine'* and unless otherwise provided, shares will usually carry the following principal rights:

- to dividends, if duly declared;
- to vote at meetings of the members;
- to receive a proportionate part of the capital or participate in the distribution of assets of the company on a winding-up, after payment of the debts;
- to receive copies of every balance sheet (and annexures thereto) laid before the general meeting;
- to receive copies of the memorandum and the articles;
- to inspect copies of directors' service contracts;
- to inspect the company's register;
- to subscribe for new shares of the same class on a fresh issue of shares, unless such right is expressly disapplied;
- to petition the court for winding-up in certain specified circumstances;
- to petition the court for remedies where the minority shareholder is subject to unfairly prejudicial conduct by the majority.

As mentioned earlier, the principal duty or liability of a shareholder *vis-à-vis* the company is to pay the nominal amount due on the shares.

If authorized by the company's articles of association, it is possible for the company to divide the share capital into different classes of shares, each with different rights. Each class of shares may carry preferred or deferred rights to dividends or capital, one class of share may carry more votes than other classes, or may carry more votes but only in specified circumstances (e.g. on a resolution to remove a director specifically appointed by the shareholder holding that class of shares). Shares may have restrictions on transferability (e.g. 'pre-emption rights' and 'lock-ins') and may be redeemable (i.e. they will be subject to buy-back by the company). It is also possible to provide for shares to be convertible from one class into another. This flexibility in creating the share capital structure is particularly useful when one considers the very different interests of those who seek part ownership of the business. For example, venture capitalists will invariably seek board participation by having the right (by virtue of their shareholdings) to appoint a director or a number of directors, whereas such a right would not be appropriate for shares issued to employees as part of a share option plan. In addition, in order to wrest some control from the majority and to protect the minority's interest, minority shareholdings usually carry specific rights to veto certain matters which may otherwise be carried out by resolution of the majority. These vetoes are often the subject of intense negotiation.

A class right is useful to 'ring fence' a shareholder's or class of shareholders' interest. Amendments to class rights usually require a 75% majority consent of the class in addition to the usual 75% majority of all shareholders required for amendments to the articles of association.

During the period from start-up to IPO, the company may issue shares a number of times, such as on each round of financing, on the exercise of share options and in order to capitalize dividends. Each time the shares are issued to new shareholders or to existing shareholders, but in different proportions to the existing shareholdings, one or a number of existing shareholders will suffer a dilution of their interest as a result. Therefore, it is not uncommon when issuing shares for all future share issues to be taken into account when setting the percentage each shareholder/investor is to receive (e.g. by reserving a fixed percentage for an employee share scheme). The resulting percentage and number of shares issued is commonly defined as the issuance of shares on a 'fully diluted basis'. However, as mentioned earlier, successful Internet entrepreneurs often accept dilution as they negotiate subsequent rounds of private financing, recognizing that it is better to have a smaller percentage of a bigger cake than a larger percentage of a smaller cake.

Shareholders owe no duties to the company; they can exercise their rights (i.e. to vote) as they wish. It is only when they are also directors that their duty as directors to act in the best interests of the company may be in conflict. It is, therefore, critical to understand fully in which capacity the shareholder-director is acting.

Initial investment and future investment rounds will usually involve entering into amended or new articles of association, especially if the share capital structure is to change. In addition, a separate shareholders' agreement (or corporate joint venture agreement) will be required, setting out the contractual rights and duties of the shareholders. There is obviously an overlap with the articles of association, but the shareholders' agreement is a private (non-registerable) document and therefore is often much more detailed and will contain more sensitive provisions many of which will be of a confidential nature (e.g. obligations in respect of future funding, exit strategies, management issues, the application of subscription monies, dividend policy, etc.). The company itself can be and in many cases is made a party to the agreement, though there may be circumstances at law where its obligations are not enforceable. It should be noted that shareholders' agreements are never standard documents; they will be prepared from scratch and will invariably be the focus of intense negotiation. Annexe A contains a pro forma Investment Term Sheet covering most of the issues that one would expect to be dealt with in the shareholders' agreement and the articles of a company seeking private equity investment.

What does it mean to be a director?

Responsibility for the management of a company falls upon its 'directors'. For a private company there only need be one director, but a public company must have at least two.

The shareholders delegate the management of the company to the board of directors in accordance with the articles of association. The directors of the company act collectively as a board, although the board itself can further delegate its powers or some of its powers to individual directors or committees of directors.

Although it is usual for the directors to be given (in the articles of association) extensive powers to manage the business, the law imposes specific duties and responsibilities on them. It is important to note that a director owes duties to the company which are similar to those imposed on an agent or a trustee. Although, as discussed, a company is a separate legal entity and the liability of the shareholders is usually limited, a director's position is different as a breach of one of his duties may attract personal liability for him. In addition, there are criminal sanctions for breaches of the Companies Acts. A director has a duty:

- to act in the best interests of the company as a whole;
- to carry out his duties as laid down by the articles of association;
- to exercise due care and skill in carrying out his duties;
- not to exceed his powers or instructions (but if he does, it does not follow that the company will not be bound);
- to exercise his powers for the proper purpose for which they were given (i.e. in accordance with the objects of the company as set out in the memorandum of association (see above));
- not to put himself in a position where his duty to the company and his own interests (e.g. as a shareholder) and/or the interests of other parties conflict, unless he has disclosed the conflict or potential conflict to the company in accordance with the articles of association and the legislation. The articles of association may provide specific provisions for this by restricting the director from either counting in the quorum for the board meeting or voting on the proposal;
- to notify the company of his interest in its shares or debentures;

■ to account to the company for any benefits he receives by virtue of his position as a director. This is not to say that a director cannot be remunerated for his services (this is normally by way of a service contract), simply that he may not receive 'secret profits';

■ to disclose for approval by shareholders at a general meeting any substantial non-cash transaction between him and the company; and

■ to have regard to the interests of employees.

Two of the most difficult duties to assess are the director's duty to perform with due skill and care, and the director's duty always to act in the best interests of the company.

■ *Skill and care.* A director is expected to exhibit in the performance of his duties no more skill and care than may be reasonably expected from a person with his knowledge and experience. In effect, a director will not be held liable for mere errors of judgement, nor is he required to have any special qualifications.

■ *In the best interests of the company.* It is common for entrepreneurs to be both directors and shareholders. It is, therefore, not surprising that the duty to act always in the best interests of the company can easily be confused with his own personal interests and is therefore considered to be one of a director's primary duties. It is sometimes referred to as the 'duty of loyalty'. In assessing whether or not the duty has been breached, the Courts will look to see whether the director acted in what he (the director) considered to be the best interests of the company.

If the company becomes insolvent, the director's performance will be under the spotlight. The general principle is that a director is free of liability for the unpaid debts of the company in the event of the company becoming insolvent. (However, see below ('What happens if a business goes bust?') for directors' and managers' responsibilities in the event of a company's insolvency.)

In addition (regardless of any insolvency), under the Company Directors Disqualification Act 1986, the Court has the power to make a disqualification order against any director where the director is found to be unfit to manage a company. A disqualification order can be based upon incompetence or dishonesty. The most serious category occurs where there is reckless or dishonest disregard of a director's duties to the detriment of creditors. Where directors exploit limited liability and disregard proper responsibility, a minimum period of disqualification of five years can be expected.

Directors of public limited companies will find themselves subject to additional, more onerous duties and responsibilities. Directors of Listed companies are also expected to follow the principles of good governance and best practice which are set out in a Code on Corporate Governance (Committee on Corporate Governance; The Combined Code, June 1998). Although not legally binding on directors, the Department of Trade and Industry (DTI) monitors compliance with the Code carefully.

It should be noted that a person who has not formally been appointed a director of the company may be deemed to be a 'shadow' director if he carries out duties associated with a director. In that event, he and, crucially, the company may incur liability as if he were a formally appointed director, by virtue of assuming that position.

There is no definitive list of duties to which a director can refer. However, the Law Commission (an independent body set up by Parliament to review the law and to recommend reform when it is needed) recently recommended in a report to the government that a statutory statement of the principal duties that a director owes to the company be introduced and that these duties be set out on the form of consent which a director signs on appointment. The DTI has produced a booklet explaining these duties, which is made available both to existing and prospective directors – (Law Commission Report No. 261 'Company Directors – Regulating Conflicts of Interests and Formulating a Statement of Duties', available at *www.lawcom.gov.uk*).

What is involved in running company meetings?

Formal decisions of a company are made in the meetings of either the directors or shareholders, depending on the nature of the decision to be made. Even where the directors and the shareholders are the same people, each type of meeting must be kept separate. The formalities to be observed and the considerations of the participants are very different at each.

Board meetings

Meetings of the board of directors are held to make decisions, known as resolutions, concerning the day-to-day running of the company. The articles of association will determine how regularly meetings are to be called, the notice to be given, the minimum number of directors to be present at the meeting in order for the meeting to be valid (the quorum), and the requisite percentage of votes needed for a resolution to be passed.

For example, it is common for articles of association to provide that any director can call a meeting on reasonable notice and that a majority of the directors present and voting will be sufficient to pass a resolution. Many articles of association provide for the chairman to have a casting vote where there is an equality of votes. It is also prudent for articles of association to allow for directors to hold or attend meetings by telephone.

It is good practice for there to be an agenda to enable directors to consider the issues in advance of the meeting. It is important that board meetings are carefully minuted, detailing who was present and what resolutions were passed. The minutes then should be kept in the company books as a permanent record.

Shareholder meetings

Certain fundamental decisions that affect the company's constitution, such as changing the memorandum or articles of association, will require the approval of the shareholders in general meeting. The procedural requirements of these meetings are governed largely by the Companies Act 1985.

An annual general meeting (or AGM) takes place normally once every calendar year. A newly formed company must hold its first AGM within 18 months of incorporation. Any other shareholder meeting is known as an extraordinary general meeting (or EGM). An EGM is usually called by the board of directors to pass resolutions that cannot wait until the next AGM. In limited circumstances, a shareholder may call an EGM. Shareholders must be given 21 days' clear notice of an AGM and (depending on the nature of the resolutions to be proposed) generally 14 days for an EGM. The notice must state the date and location of the meeting, together with an agenda giving the exact wording of the proposed resolutions.

Resolutions are classified into four different categories: ordinary; special; extraordinary; and elective, and different voting majorities are required for each. Additionally, 21 days' notice will be required for an EGM which has a proposed special resolution.

There are circumstances where shareholder meetings can be held on shorter notice (or where the written resolution procedure is used – no notice at all).

Shareholder meetings should also be minuted and for certain resolutions it is necessary to send a copy of the resolution to Companies House, for example, a resolution increasing the company's share capital.

A director should consider the following:

- Is it a decision which requires only board approval, or one that also requires shareholder approval?
- Who can call the meeting and what notice must be given and to whom?
- Prepare an agenda setting out the business to be conducted at the meeting.
- How many directors (for board meetings) and how many shareholders (for shareholders' meetings) will constitute a quorum?
- Where should the meeting be held, or is it possible to hold the meeting by telephone conference call?
- Who is entitled to vote and what majority is required to pass the resolution?
- Prepare a minute of the meeting.
- Assuming the passing of the resolutions, what procedures/requirements should then be followed?

How do I finance the company?

www.bvca.co.uk Unless the Internet entrepreneur manages an American-style start-up, whereby he or she might receive $4 million for 10% of the equity, the entrepreneur will need a fighting fund in the early days of several thousand pounds. This is what the French call, in their inimitable style, 'Love Money'! This will enable the Internet entrepreneur to do (or fund) the research needed to put together the business plan. Once he has a business plan (with an executive summary and demonstration site that will 'wow' his investors), he can start talking to potential investors and private equity houses. The British Venture Capital Association Web site contains details of a lot of venture capitalists available at *www.bvca.co.uk*. Private equity houses may look for anything up to 85% of the entrepreneur's equity; business angels may be useful for seed capital, say, up to £250 000. They tend to cluster around incubators, academic institutions, such as the London Business School, and professional intermediaries.

Further stages of finance, generally called round 1 and round 2, can follow, whereby (hopefully) increasing valuations are put on the business. The next stage is the IPO (initial public offering), which would require a chapter of its own to cover the legal issues.

The Internet entrepreneur will also need a bank, preferably one that includes a business `www.barclays.co.uk` team that understands the 'new economy'. Most banks have specialist teams in this area. See www.barclayscorporate.com for the Barclays Technology and Telecoms Team.

In the old economy, many businesses got started on debt finance. A start-up will not have much of a track record, so banks often look for personal guarantees from the directors. The Internet entrepreneur should seek to avoid these or at least limit them in some way.

In return for bank loans, banks will also seek a debenture over the company's assets (e.g. a floating charge over the ongoing performance of the business). It may call this in at any time.

There is a trade-off between debt and equity finance. For the moment, equity is in vogue but, sooner or later, equity investors will be looking for dividends, which many Internet company start-ups will not be able to produce for some time. There is a tension here. It is also worth remembering here that the more complicated the structure, the more expensive it will be to put together.

What do I need to consider when hiring and firing staff?

The value of an Internet business is in intellectual property, confidential information and the employment of individuals who can breathe life into the ideas behind the business. Whilst the law provides that all employees must have written terms of employment, for an Internet company it is vital that those contracts go beyond basic legal requirements and ensure that the company's intangible assets are protected from unscrupulous employees.

What written terms must be provided to an employee?

Employees must be given a written statement containing the following information:

- the name of the employer and the employee;
- the date the employee's employment started;

- the employee's rate of pay and when he is paid;

- hours of work, including a statement of normal hours of work;

- any terms relating to holiday pay. After 13 weeks' employment, employees are entitled to four weeks' holiday per year. This can include bank holidays. This means that the minimum holiday entitlement for an employee working five days per week is to bank holidays and a further 12 days of holiday per year;

- any terms relating to sick pay. If an employer does not intend to pay employees their salary for all or some time when they are absent due to illness, it should be specified. In any event, the employer will have to pay statutory sick pay. This is an amount set by the government (£60.20 per week as at April 2000) which becomes payable once the employee has been ill for four days. Employees must also tell the employer that they are ill and provide evidence of that illness in the form of a self-certification form or a doctor's sick note (depending on the length of the employee's absence);

- whether any pension benefits are offered;

- the length of notice (see below);

- the employee's job title *or* job description;

- if the employment is temporary or for a fixed term, that fact and when the employment is likely to end;

- the place of work.

If the employee will be required to work abroad for extended periods, other details are required.

What other issues should be addressed?

The details that are required to be given to employees are designed to protect employees' rights. They do nothing to protect an employer's rights. However, to prevent an employee from taking the employer's business ideas, contacts and even other employees and setting up in competition with the employer, the employer needs to have an express, written contract with the employee. This contract needs to be given careful thought and should be drafted carefully and specifically to ensure that it is enforceable. Some of the areas that should be covered are the following:

1. Confidential information should be expressly protected.

2. Intellectual property created by the employee that relates or could relate to the business should be assigned to the employer. Provision should be made to force the employee to assign intellectual property rights if he will not do it voluntarily.

3. The employee should be restricted from competing with the employer for a limited period (usually 6 to 12 months) after the termination of the employee's employment. This may include restricting his ability to work in a competing business, solicit or deal with customers or suppliers and work with or employ key employees of the employer.

4. Careful thought should be given to the notice period that should be applicable to the employee's contract. The law sets down minimum notice requirements. These are that, after one month, the employee is entitled to receive one week's notice up to two years of employment and, thereafter, one week's notice for each complete year of employment up to a maximum of 12 weeks. The employee is required to give one week's notice.

    However, with more senior employees there can be a tendency to give, and require to be given, longer notice periods. The employer should question very carefully if this is appropriate in every case. Once the employer has asked an employee to leave or the employee has resigned, does the employer want that employee to stay at work? Could the employee be disruptive, damage the business or try to steal confidential information? If it is unlikely that the employer would want the employee to work out his notice, why have a long notice period? It should also be remembered that the employer has to keep paying the employee whilst he works his notice period. Also, even if the employer does want the employee to work his notice, if the employee wants to leave, there is practically little that can be done to stop the employee from leaving. Even if the employee does not leave, he may not be very productive!

5. When an employee is on notice, the employer needs to have the right to exclude him from actually carrying out work. This is known as 'garden leave'. The employee continues to be paid throughout this period. He just does not do any work. If the employer does not have an express written agreement for this, the employee has a right to work during his notice. If the employer refuses him that right or tries to give him fewer responsibilities during his notice period, the employer will breach the employee's contract of employment. He would be entitled to leave and the employer would not be able to rely on the restrictive covenants referred to in paragraph (3) above. The employer may also have to pay the employee the rest of his salary for the remainder of the notice period.

Termination of employment

If the employer agrees a proper written contract of employment with his employees when they join, it will be far easier to deal with their departure.

If an employee is dismissed, the employer is usually required to let the employee work his notice, pay the employee in lieu of his notice (if there is a contractual right to do this) or put the employee on garden leave. The only exception to this rule is where the employee has committed an act of gross misconduct.

If the employee has one year's service with the employer, he may be entitled to bring a claim of unfair dismissal against the company if he does not believe he was treated fairly in being dismissed. In general terms, the employer can be liable for up to £50 000 in damages if the employee shows that he has been unfairly dismissed. The employee will be compensated for loss of income resulting from his dismissal, so how much compensation he is paid will depend on how much he has lost. If one includes the loss of the value of his share options then, in a successful Internet business, this may soon add up to £50 000.

If an employee believes that his dismissal is discriminatory on the grounds of race, sex or a disability, he can also pursue a claim against the employer. Damages can be awarded without limit. Whilst again, damages are predominantly related to any loss the employee has suffered as a result of dismissal, the value of any share options is relevant. If the employee has suffered a large loss of value in options or his options have lapsed as a result of his dismissal, he can claim for that loss. It should also be noted that discrimination claims can be brought if someone is not recruited for a discriminatory reason or is discriminated against whilst they are at work.

How do I incentivize the staff?

Good people will need to be attracted to work in the business at a time when cash is in short supply. A means of attracting and retaining them is to offer them a shareholding in the business itself. Two main alternatives are available:

- *The company issues shares to them at the outset for a nominal payment.* This causes an immediate Income Tax liability to arise to the employees based on the difference between the value of the shares at that time and the nominal payment made for them. However, if the shares are issued at a sufficiently early stage of development, the Income Tax liability will be minimal. The disadvantage of this alternative is that once a sale of the company or a flotation on a stock exchange ('an exit') occurs, the employees can sell their shares and the shares are no longer an incentive to remain with the company.

- *The company grants options to the employees to subscribe for shares in the company at a later date.* The employees usually can subscribe for the shares by paying only a nominal amount (e.g. £1 a share) but cannot exercise the option to subscribe until an exit is imminent *and* a set minimum period of service has been achieved. For example, if the right to exercise the option accrues evenly over four years, then on an exit occurring after two years, the employee can exercise immediately the option over 50% of his shares and an additional 25% on completing each of his third and fourth years of service.

The disadvantage of a share option is the tax treatment. Although some Inland Revenue approved share option schemes produce a tax liability only when an employee sells the shares obtained under option, these are restrictive. The maximum value of shares each employee can hold under option at any one time is at present limited to £30 000. A new form of Inland Revenue approved selective share option scheme (called the 'Enterprise Management Incentive Scheme') will be introduced by the Finance Bill 2000 (expected to become law by the end of July 2000). This scheme will permit the granting of options of up to £100 000 per employee for up to 15 employees per company. However, it will be restricted to smaller companies qualified to issue shares under the

Enterprise Investment Scheme and may cause difficulties to companies receiving substantial income from copyright royalties as they will qualify only if the intellectual property subject to copyright was created by the company.

Furthermore, as the options usually permit an exercise only when an exit is imminent, the shares are regarded as 'tradable' at the point of exercise. This means that the Income Tax liability is collected immediately under Pay As You Earn, and National Insurance Contributions are due on the 'profit'. The National Insurance contributions make little difference to the employees, who are normally paying the maximum annual contributions already, but they impose a substantial liability for secondary contributions on the company. This liability is 12.2% (11.7% from April 2001) of the 'profit', a figure almost impossible to control (especially on a flotation).

Many companies opt for a strategy involving two parallel share option schemes – a basic scheme (either Inland Revenue approved or unapproved) and then a more valuable unapproved scheme under which the employees also have to meet tough performance criteria before the options can be exercised on an exit.

How are companies taxed?

A company is subject to Corporation Tax on its worldwide profits including Capital Gains. The rate of Corporation Tax is set by Parliament annually and the current standard rate is 30%, reducing to 20% (or even 10%) for small companies. A small company is one with pre-tax profits of less than £300 000 per annum. Marginal rates apply over that limit until profits reach £1 500 000 per annum, when the full standard rate is levied. These profit limits are shared equally between the company and any companies associated with it by common shareholding control (*whether UK or foreign*). The greater the number of companies associated with it, the lower the profit at which the full standard rate of Corporation Tax is payable.

What do I need to consider when acquiring premises?

Businesses need premises from which to operate. The type and size of the premises depend on the nature of the business and the stage in its growth. Many Internet businesses have started in a bedroom, spare room or garage, but at some point almost every growing business needs to be run from an office. Businesses which take on fulfilment tasks may also need production, storage and/or distribution facilities.

Buying or renting

Almost all business premises in the UK are occupied by rent-paying tenants. Relatively few occupiers own their buildings. Start-up companies, especially, would be unwise to invest significant capital in real property in which to carry on their business operations. Ideally, the Internet entrepreneur should rent premises which will be suitable for the business in line with the short to medium-term business plan.

Lease terms

The terms on which landlords are prepared to let their premises vary considerably, depending usually on the type and location of the property and the state of the property market. There is no standard form of lease in widespread use and not much standardization of the main terms of lettings. Nevertheless, there is a distinct trend away from asking tenants to commit themselves to leases of 20 or 25 years' duration, and towards much shorter lettings – either for a short fixed duration or with the tenant's right to terminate early. Short or terminable leases relieve a tenant who wants to vacate from the burden of having to find a replacement tenant. However, short-term leases often preclude the tenant from claiming rights of renewal which might ordinarily arise at the end of the term under the Landlord and Tenant Act 1954.

Obligations imposed on the tenant by a lease usually reflect its duration. Longer leases are normally granted on a 'full repairing' basis; if the tenant is taking the whole building, he would have to carry out all repairs which are necessary during the term; if he rented just part of a building, he would have to pay his proportion of the cost of such works through a service charge. The rent payable under these leases is usually reviewable at intervals, commonly every five years, and normally increases to market-rent level, though occasionally some form of indexation may be applied; almost always, the reviews are 'upwards only', so that the rent will not reduce even if market rents have fallen. Short-term lettings, on the other hand, may be at fixed rents, with limits on the tenant's repairing obligations, and may have any service charge liability capped in amount or limited to routine expenditure.

Some property owners specifically aim at start-up businesses, offering small units (sometimes called 'incubator units'), short lettings and inclusive rents. In some cases, they provide 'serviced' offices with on-site facilities, such as furniture, reception, switchboards, copying, IT, conference facilities and even laundry and catering. Incubators and serviced offices offer a limitation of property risk and exposure, but may increase short-term cost. Occupiers are typically charged per person per month, anywhere between £400 and £1000. However, incubators may also offer seed capital, recruitment and other business services. Technology incubators are often found in the proximity of university campuses and on sites specifically zoned for start-up or enterprise initiatives.

Professional advice

The entrepreneur looking for premises should appoint a surveyor or estate agent to advise and assist him in negotiating with landlords or letting agents. An experienced agent can give worthwhile advice on the terms to negotiate, including the level of rent, and will take into account matters such as the level of business rates and other outgoings. Advice tendered by the landlord's letting agent should be viewed with caution – the agent will be acting for the landlord and may not have the prospective tenant's interests in mind.

If the entrepreneur has to take on significant repairing obligations, either directly or through a service charge, he should also instruct a building surveyor to survey the building and to advise whether costly repairs are likely to arise during the term of the lease.

A property solicitor should handle the taking of the lease. This requires expertise in the negotiation of letting documents, which often run to 60 or more pages, and checking matters such as town planning and title. Letting agents frequently negotiate only the main terms of a letting, leaving solicitors to deal with much of the detail.

Financial aspects

Just as the entrepreneur will need to assess the likely total cost of occupying the space, rent, service charges, insurance, business rates, etc., so the landlord will need to assess the tenant's ability to pay those costs, particularly the rent and any service charge.

Landlords usually require written references for prospective tenants from accountants, traders and any existing landlord, and will also want to see audited accounts for the tenant's last few years' trading. Where such information does not exist or it fails to show an adequate financial track record, the landlord may refuse to grant the letting unless he is given personal guarantees by financially viable guarantors, covering not only the rent, but also all other liabilities under the lease. The entrepreneur who is trying to arrange for his new company to be granted a lease may well be asked to give such guarantees. Alternatively, or sometimes in addition to guarantees, the landlord may require payment of a deposit, frequently equal to three or six months' rent or more.

Other lease terms

The duration, the level of rent and other outgoings, and the repairing liabilities are not the only factors which the entrepreneur will need to consider. Leases invariably impose various further positive obligations and also numerous restrictions.

Typical further obligations imposed on tenants include:

- compliance with planning law;
- compliance with health and safety regulations;
- observance of fire precautions;
- compliance with insurers' requirements;
- redecoration periodically and upon vacating.

Leases also typically require the landlord's permission if the tenant wishes:

- to change the use of the premises;
- to make alterations;
- to install machinery;
- to display external signs;
- to assign, sublet or share the premises.

The solicitor will advise the entrepreneur on how these issues are covered in the particular lease, and the entrepreneur should ensure that he and his company will be able to comply with the positive obligations and also that his business will not be unduly fettered by the restrictions.

What about insurance?

First priority – the office package policy

Before engaging the first employee, the employer must by law purchase *employer's liability insurance*. This policy indemnifies the employer for liability arising out of any accident that an employee may suffer during the course of his employment, and the certificate of this insurance must be displayed in a prominent position at each place of business.

In practice, the employer's liability insurance actually comes as part of a package of insurances for the office, which will include the following sections:

- *employer's liability insurance:* (as above);
- *public liability insurance:* as per employer's liability insurance, but for liability to the public, not employees;
- *office contents cover:* all risks of loss to the contents of the office, computers etc. (for e.g. fire, theft, etc.);
- *buildings cover:* all risks to the office buildings.

This package can be purchased directly from most insurance companies or through an insurance broker. In some circumstances, the insurers may insist on a survey of the premises, especially regarding the security aspects.

Second priority – before trading

This might include:

- *professional indemnity:* if the business is to give advice, professional indemnity insurance protects it from the consequences of rendering negligent advice;
- *esurance:* if a significant proportion of the business is carried out 'on-line', there are other risks which are not addressed by more traditional policies, such as the risks

associated with viruses, hackers, credit-card theft, etc. These areas are covered by a policy known as *esurance* or *cyber liability insurance*;

■ *Products liability*: if the business is to sell goods then products liability insurance protects the business from harm caused to the consumer, particularly for the negligence of manufacturers, for example, in respect of products aimed at children.

Third priority – before first-round financing

■ *Directors and officers insurance*: as the structure of the company becomes more complex, so do the responsibilities and duties of the directors. Directors and officers www.howdeninsurancebrokers.co.uk insurance covers the management's own liabilities towards shareholders, regulatory bodies, etc. Howden Insurance Brokers site is available at *www.howdeninsurance.co.uk*.

How do I make my agreements watertight?

The first contract that the Internet entrepreneur is likely to encounter and need is the non-disclosure agreement (NDA), to enable disclosure to be made to potential partners and investors in circumstances of confidentiality.

If we look at the pro forma short form NDA between Dotcom Limited and E-commerce Investments Limited in Annexe B, we can identify the essentials of a legally binding contract. In looking at these, we need to remember that, at least in the United Kingdom, a legally binding contract need not be in writing; it can just as well be created verbally. However, it is highly advisable to have all contracts in writing or at least in email form, as this is vital evidence of what is agreed.

The essentials of a legally binding contract are:

■ an offer, leading to . . .

■ acceptance by the person to whom the offer had been made, together with . . .

■ what is called consideration, which may take the form of a financial payment, but need not necessarily be financial, together with finally . . .

■ an intention to create legal relations.

Some contracts must be in writing, as, for example, a type of contract that many will have encountered before: a contract for the sale of land, i.e. real property.

If we look at the pro forma short form NDA in Annexe B we can identify an offer that is made in this letter-form agreement, together with acceptance on the part of E-commerce Investments Limited. The consideration is set out, that is, on the part of the disclosing party: the disclosure of the information; and, on the part of the party to which disclosure is made: various undertakings to keep the information confidential.

As far as the intention to create legal relations is concerned, this is more often than not expressed the other way around, so as to make it clear that a particular agreement is not intended to be legally binding.

A good way of proceeding is to draw up the commercial terms of any arrangement into a 'Heads of Agreement' or 'Memorandum of Understanding' (or Term Sheet; see Annexe A). There is no particular magic in any of these words and either can be legally binding or not, as suits the intentions of the parties. Quite often, such a heads or memorandum may be partially legally binding, in that the clauses dealing with confidentiality may well be legally binding but the rest, which will deal with the matters of principle relating to the management of a particular project, the taking of shareholdings in a new company and the like, will not be legally binding.

So, the first important tip in making contracts watertight is to make sure that the necessary essentials of a legally binding contract are set out, that the agreement is made in writing or otherwise is evidenced in permanent form, for example by email, and that both sides or all parties, as the case may be, have indicated their acceptance of the terms. In order to avoid a particular part of the contract being 'watertight' when that is not what is required, certain parts can be expressed to be not legally binding.

In looking again at the pro forma short form NDA in Annexe B, we will see that the last numbered clause is the so-called jurisdiction and proper law clause. In this instance, the agreement is to be interpreted according to English law (or, more precisely, the laws of England and Wales) and there is a submission to the jurisdiction of the English Courts (the Courts of England and Wales). Scotland and Northern Ireland are separate jurisdictions, which have different laws in various areas, including that relating to real property. The important point here is that e-commerce is a global business and the business should always seek to have agreements interpreted according to the laws of England and Wales if the business is an English company or other form of business entity established or carrying on its principal activities in England (and/or Wales), and that any dispute should be settled in the English Courts. Arbitration is another method of dispute resolution, the main advantage of which is confidentiality, in that disputes are resolved in private rather than in open court. It is often desirable to have an escalation process in dispute resolution and there are several ways of doing this, including mediation and the appointment of experts (not arbitrators), whose decisions are final. We look below at particular types of agreements.

Service agreements

These agreements will be with various kinds of service and technology providers and it is essential that the service or product that is to be delivered is clearly set out, together with milestones and above all cost. Penalties for missing deadlines may often be required, but it is essential that any such clause is a genuine pre-estimate of damages to be suffered rather than a penalty as such which is out of all proportion to the damages that would be suffered by the defaulting party in relation to, for example, late delivery.

Joint ventures

Two distinct types of agreement are encountered in this area. The first is the full corporate joint venture, which involves the establishment of a separate legal entity as the joint venture company. The considerations here are really no different from those which are set out elsewhere in this chapter on the establishment and the running of a company.

Non-corporate joint ventures or partnering arrangements are an alternative and will need to set out clearly what each of the contributors is bringing to the table. Strategic alliances and other forms of agreement are also in this general area, which may take the form of a long-term agreement between, for example, a content provider and a service provider or publisher. Once again, it is vital to set out clearly what is to be delivered by each side, against what milestones, and how much is to be paid.

e-commerce

The advent and growth of e-commerce has generated a number of completely new types of agreement, such as agreements relating to the development and design of Web sites and agreements for on-line trading. Any readers who consider that lawyers simply regurgitate old precedents will be heartened to know that most of the agreements under this category and the previous category have had to be drafted from scratch and that the lawyers have had much work to do, and much creative thinking has been required on the part of both clients and their lawyers. With on-line trading agreements, the crucial issues are what constitutes an offer and acceptance, making sure that the exclusions and liability are right, and that any remaining risk that is accepted by the parties is subject to appropriate limitations of liability. It is also important to make sure that what is called *force majeure* is covered, so that neither party is liable for non-performance of its obligations due to forces outside its control. A good example of *force majeure* would be a failure on the part of a third-party ISP.

Certain particular kinds of agreements will be subject to their own regulatory considerations. These will include those in the area of financial services and consumer credit and also data-protection considerations. In relation to data protection, in the United Kingdom, the Data Protection Act 1998 came into force on 1 March 2000 and similar updated laws will have been implemented in the rest of Europe. The new Act applies for the first time to certain kinds of manual records and also restricts the circumstances under which what is called 'sensitive personal data' can be processed.

Legal jargon

There are certain items of legal jargon which are worth understanding in this area, which we review below.

Boilerplate – the boilerplate refers to the general provisions at the back of most longer agreements. Besides important issues such as jurisdiction and proper law (see above), these specifically deal with provisions such as: an entire agreement clause, confirming that the agreement in question contains all the agreements between the parties relating to the subject matter; a severance clause, which allows any clause to be struck out which is found to be contrary to law, in order that the whole contract does not fall over; as well as provisions about effective service of documents. The boilerplate will not contain any of the commercial terms of the agreement, but this does not prevent parties and their lawyers from sometimes negotiating these provisions to the nth degree! This is generally not very productive.

Subject to contract – this is often seen, particularly on anything to do with real property transactions, and is designed to make it clear that a particular document is not open for acceptance to become legally binding. Strictly speaking, the words 'Subject to Contract' are probably inadequate and a phrase such as 'no agreement will be legally binding until a formal legally binding contract has been drawn up and executed by both parties' is more effective.

Without prejudice – this is seen mostly in relation to litigious matters, but is sometimes seen on pre-agreement drafts, where it is largely meaningless. The words 'Without Prejudice' are designed to indicate that a particular document or letter has been drafted and sent in a genuine attempt to achieve a settlement in a contentious matter and was not subsequently to be disclosed to a Court to 'prejudice' the legal position of the party that sent it.

Battle of the forms – most lawyers have war stories about the battle of the forms. The hypothesis is that the side that controls the drafting and production of the documentation tends to control the transaction, in that it is much more likely that this side's form or draft will be accepted. With the ability to receive drafts by email, amend them and send them back electronically, this is probably of less relevance nowadays. However, this does not mean that one should hesitate to amend a standard form document that is sent through by the other side and indeed amend it and sign it and send it back so that such offer is then open for acceptance by the original party. Any significant transaction or commercial arrangement will almost certainly merit the preparation of a bespoke document.

Any lawyer worth his salt will tell even a new client that the lawyer should never be brought in too late and, indeed, should be brought into a transaction or commercial negotiation as soon as possible. However, the parties themselves should endeavour to settle all the main commercial terms and to write those terms down in the form of a non-legally binding Heads of Terms or Memorandum of Understanding (or Term Sheet). If the main commercial terms have been agreed, the drafting of the subsequent agreement (or agreements) to document that commercial arrangement becomes a great deal easier.

What happens if the business goes bust?

When a company is unable to pay its debts, it is insolvent and should be liquidated. The relevant provisions can be found in the Insolvency Act 1986. There are two methods of liquidating a company – a voluntary liquidation, or a compulsory liquidation.

■ *Voluntary liquidation.* The directors can take the initiative by means of a voluntary winding-up. The directors make a statutory declaration of the company's insolvency and the company passes a resolution to wind up. A meeting of its creditors is then called to nominate a liquidator. The duty of a liquidator is to collect in assets and distribute this to the company's creditors in accordance with the order of priority. Preferential debts, including debts to the Inland Revenue and Customs & Excise, are paid before all other debts.

■ *Compulsory liquidation.* A company which is insolvent can also be wound up by the Court. A petition can be presented by a creditor on the basis that the company is unable to pay its debts. A company is deemed to be unable to pay its debts if a statutory demand is served for a claim of at least £750 requiring payment within 21 days. The petition is advertised and if a winding-up order is made, the Official Receiver is appointed as a provisional liquidator. The winding-up order has the effect of terminating the employment of all the employees of the company.

The liquidator in both methods of liquidation has extensive power to investigate the affairs of a company. The liquidator can apply for a person who has information concerning the affairs of the company to produce records and be examined on oath. The liquidator is also under a duty to investigate the conduct of the company prior to its liquidation. A transaction carried out previously by the company can be set aside where it has amounted to the giving of a preference or is a transaction at an undervalue.

Directors and managers can be subject to criminal liabilities. For example, if the business was carried out to defraud creditors, any person who was knowingly a party to the fraud may be required to make a contribution to the company's assets. A person may also be liable to contribute if the person knew or ought to have known that the company would go into liquidation. A director or shadow director could be liable for wrongful trading in circumstances where the company continues to trade and incurs liabilities when it was known that the insolvency was inevitable. In addition, see section above headed '*What does it mean to be a director?*' on directors' duties and the sanction of disqualification available under statute.

How do I exit?

Most shareholders' agreements (and see the Investment Term Sheet in Annexe A) provide for an 'exit' for the shareholders via a number of routes, for example, by the exercise of 'put' options requiring the other shareholders to buy the shares of the exiting shareholder or 'drag' and 'tag' provisions by which a shareholder is obliged to require that a third-party offer for his shares in the company is extended to the other shareholders ('tag right') and in certain circumstances (for example, where a controlling interest is proposed to be sold) the other shareholders can be required to accept such a third party's offer ('drag right'). The Companies Act 1985 includes provisions by which an offeror can compulsorily acquire minority holdings, provided that it has acceptances for an offer to acquire not less than nine-tenths in value of the shares to which the offer relates.

However, the Internet entrepreneur will often initially think of exiting (having made his fortune) either on the sale of the company or at an IPO (initial public offering). If the Internet entrepreneur himself is key to the business, such thinking may well itself jeopardize the success of any IPO and, depending on a purchaser's motives, may well put off a prospective purchaser.

From a legal point of view, it will be important to consider the various existing contractual relationships in the light of such a change in control of the company. Some of the contracts may terminate automatically, others may continue. In respect of the continuing contracts, it will be important to consider how they will operate and, particularly, their enforceability post-IPO or sale, when control of the company and ownership of the share capital will be in different hands.

Annexe

Investment term sheet

THIS TERM SHEET SUMMARIZES THE PRINCIPAL TERMS OF AN INVESTMENT IN XYZ.COM LIMITED (the 'Investment')

1. GENERAL

Issuer: xyz.com limited (the 'Company');

Securities to be issued: _ Investor Shares (*query class of share and rights*);

Financing: £_ million for a _% shareholding [*dilution*];

Pre-financing valuation: £_ million;

Subscription price: £_ per Share.

2. SHARE CAPITAL STRUCTURE

2.1 The authorized Share capital of the Company is proposed to be £ _ divided into _ Ordinary Shares of £ _ each and _ Investor Shares of £ _ each.

2.2 The issued Share capital of the Company prior to the Investment is proposed to be _ Ordinary Shares.

2.3 The issued Share capital of the Company following the Investment is proposed to be _ Ordinary Shares and _ Investor Shares.

3. INITIAL SHAREHOLDERS

	Ordinary Shares	%
3.1 Founder A	_	_ %
3.2 Founder B	_	_ %
3.3 Founder C	_	_ %

4. RIGHTS ATTACHING TO SHARES

4.1 Investor Shares

   4.1.1 Preference on a winding-up?

   4.1.2 Special weighted voting rights (e.g. on a resolution to remove a director appointed by the Investor)?

   4.1.3 Protective Provisions? If the Investor(s) are to be in a minority (see 4.2.2 below).

4.1.4   Anti-dilution mechanisms?

4.2   Ordinary Shares

4.2.1   Voting Rights. Presumably unchanged, although consider weighted voting on a resolution to remove a director appointed by the Founder(s).

4.2.2   Protective Provision, if the Founders are to be in a minority.

The consent of the holders of a [majority] [75%] [all] of the Ordinary Shares will be required to sanction the actions and events listed in paragraph 6.2 below. These are the minority protections, consider whether all or some only of the Founders require a veto. If the Founders can only exercise a veto when acting by majority, consider the consequences and the de facto control that this would give to the Investor as majority shareholder. The same issues arise where the Investor(s) are in a minority.

5.   DRAGALONG AND TAGALONG RIGHTS: *the following are indicative only; any combination or variation on the theme should be explored.*

5.1   If _ % of the total number of issued Shares are proposed to be sold then the transferor must procure that the transferee makes an offer to all the other shareholders. The offer, price and terms must be not less favourable than that first offered.

5.2   The offer having been made in 5.1 above, if _ % or 'control' is proposed to be sold then the transferor can require the other shareholders to accept the offer [provided that the offer is at the higher of the shareholder's entry price and fair market value].

6.   PROTECTIVE PROVISIONS

6.1   INFORMATION RIGHTS

The Company shall:

6.1.1   provide each Shareholder (including the Investor) within 30 days of the last day of each calendar quarter with unaudited management accounts for the previous quarter;

6.1.2   provide each Shareholder with copies of the audited accounts within 3 months of the financial year end;

6.1.3   deliver to each Shareholder (at its expense) as promptly as practicable such additional financial or other information as may be reasonably requested by such Shareholder upon giving reasonable prior written notice, not being less than 21 days.

6.2   SPECIAL CONSENT *The following are indicative only. The object is to prevent the majority using its majority position to prejudice the interests of the minority.*

6.3   Save with the prior written consent of: [all] [75%] [majority] of [Ordinary] [Investor] Shares, the [Founder's] [Investor's] [Board appointees] none of the actions or events listed below will be effected or permitted to occur whether in relation to the Company or any subsidiary of the Company:-

6.3.1   increase, alter or reduce its authorized or issued Share capital;

6.3.2   issue any Shares;

6.3.3   consolidate or sub-divide any Shares, create any new class of Shares, grant or agree to grant any option over Shares or any right to subscribe for Shares or other right to call for its Shares, issue or agree to issue any securities convertible into its Shares, alter any of the rights attached to any of its issued Shares, or otherwise reorganize or grant any rights in respect of its Share capital;

6.3.4   subscribe for, purchase or acquire in excess of £ _ any share or loan capital, debenture, mortgage or any interest therein;

6.3.5   acquire any subsidiary nor permit the disposal or dilution of its interest directly or indirectly in any subsidiary;

6.3.6   sell, transfer, lease, license, make any material alteration to or in any other way dispose of all or a substantial part of its business, undertaking or assets whether by a single transaction or series of transactions, related or not;

6.3.7   enter into or agree any variation or amendment or compromise in relation to any transaction or agreement with or for the benefit of any director or Shareholder of the Company or any connected person of such a director or Shareholder;

6.3.8   to effect a Listing or a Sale ('*Exit*');

6.3.9   enter into any transaction for an amount in excess of £ _ , or assume any liability or obligation otherwise than on an arm's length commercial basis or, in any event, outside the ordinary and proper course of its day-to-day business;

6.3.10   exercise the powers of the company to borrow any money or obtain any advance or credit in any form other than normal trade credit or on normal banking terms for sums borrowed in the ordinary and proper course of business of the Company or any of its subsidiaries;

6.3.11   lend any money to any person or grant any credit to any person (except to its customers in the normal course of business or any of its subsidiaries) in excess of £ _ ;

6.3.12   create or allow to subsist any encumbrance over any of its assets (other than a lien arising by operation of law or a retention of title agreement arising in the ordinary course of business) except for the purpose of securing any permitted indebtedness;

6.3.13   give any guarantee, indemnity or security in respect of the obligations of any other person (except one of its subsidiary companies);

6.3.14 appoint any new bankers or remove its bankers for the time being or make any material alteration in the terms agreed with its bankers for the borrowing of monies or for the operation of its bank accounts;

6.3.15 save in circumstances justifying summary dismissal, dismiss any senior employee;

6.3.16 subject to the Companies Act 1985, make any alteration to the Memorandum and Articles of Association of the Company.

7. TRANSFER OF SHARES

7.1 All Shareholders shall have a pro-rata right of first refusal with respect to the transfer of any Shares prior to such Shares being offered to any third party or any existing Shareholder. *Consider whether to include pre-emption within each class first.*

7.2 Notwithstanding 7.1 above, the following transfers shall be permitted: (a) if a company transfers intra-group, (b) if an individual transfers to his or her family or a trust on behalf of such family, (c) a transfer to a nominee holding on trust for the transferor.

7.3 No transfers to competitors of the Company. No transfers in respect of any shares for which any amount of the share capital (including premium) remains unpaid.

7.4 All transferees to enter into a deed of adherence to the Investment Agreement.

8. ISSUE OF SHARES TO NEW INVESTORS

8.1 All Shareholders shall have a pro-rata right of first refusal on any new issue of Shares. *Consider whether to include pre-emption within each class.*

8.2 No share issues to competitors of the Company.

8.3 All new shareholders to enter into a deed of adherence to the Investment Agreement.

9. EXIT

9.1 *Consider exit by way of Put and Call Options if a dispute arises between the Founders (acting collectively) and the Investors. Various 'Russian Roulette' provisions can be included. Note, however, that this is effectively a draconian measure and will force exit and the end of the Founder/Investor relationship.*

9.2 It is the present intention of the Founders and the Investor(s) to seek a listing of the Company's Shares on a recognized investment exchange or to dispose of the Company within the next three years, subject to favourable market conditions.

10. CHARGING OF SHARES

No Shareholder shall, except with the prior written consent of a majority of the Board of Directors, create or permit to subsist any pledge, lien, charge or any security interest over any or all of the Shares held by it.

11. COVENANTS

No Shareholder may, except with the prior written consent of a majority of the Board of Directors:-

11.1 be interested in any contract or proposed contract with the Company or any of its subsidiaries, whether directly or indirectly;

11.2 be involved in any matter which is competitive to the Company whilst a Shareholder and for a period of 12 months after ceasing to be a Shareholder. For the purposes of this paragraph 11.2 'competitive to the Company' shall relate to and mean competitive to any business [*describe the business*];

11.3 solicit any employee or customer of the Company whilst a Shareholder and for a period of 12 months after ceasing to be a Shareholder.

12. INTELLECTUAL PROPERTY RIGHTS

All Intellectual Property Rights in, developed by and relevant to the Company's business from time to time shall be the exclusive property of the Company.

13. CONFIDENTIALITY

All Shareholders will be under a duty of confidentiality in relation to the affairs of the Company and any of its subsidiaries as well as each other, which obligation will also extend indefinitely after such Shareholder ceases to be a Shareholder of the Company.

14. INSURANCE

The Company will obtain key man insurance on relevant employees and will obtain full directors and officers liability insurance on their behalf.

15. FUNDING AND FINANCING

15.1 Liability in respect of further funding requirements shall be borne pro rata to Shareholding.

15.2 *Consider Board powers to raise further finance by way of loan, bank facility or equity.*

16. APPLICATION OF MONIES

16.1 The investment funds shall be applied in accordance with terms of the Company's business plan from time to time.

17. DISTRIBUTIONS AND DIVIDEND POLICY

17.1 The Company shall distribute profits available to Shareholders subject only to 17.2 below.

17.2 The Company shall identify amounts that the Board of Directors reasonably consider (having regard to all other sources of funding available to the Company) should be retained from the distributable profits in order to meet foreseeable commitments and contingencies of the Company.

18. BOARD OF DIRECTORS

18.1 *How many (min. and max.)?*

18.2 *Names of those to be appointed at Completion?*

18.3 *Rights of which Shareholders (including share qualification, if any) to appoint (and remove)?*

18.4 *Chairman (but no casting vote)?*

18.5 *Quorum at Board meetings?*

18.6 *Frequency of meetings?*

18.7 *Telephone meetings?*

18.8 *Notice for meetings?*

19. MANAGEMENT CONTRACTS

[ ] and [ ] [*others?*] will enter into new service contracts with the Company, the terms of which are to be agreed to by the new Board of Directors.

20. EMPLOYEE SHARE OPTION SCHEME – APPROVED OR UNAPPROVED SCHEME OR BOTH

20.1 It is proposed that a Share Option Scheme be adopted for the benefit of and to incentivize executive management to be employed by the Company which shall represent a maximum of _ % of the total number of issued Shares in the Company (prior to the exercise of the options). [As the Share Option Scheme is to be approved by the Inland Revenue, the options will be granted over Ordinary Shares.] [As the Share Option Scheme will not be approved by the Inland Revenue, the options will be granted over 'C' Shares. This is a class of share specifically created for the purpose of the Share Option Scheme.]

20.2 The Share Options are intended to vest over a period of [4] years at the rate of [25%] per annum.

20.3 The Share Options shall be exercisable on an Exit (i.e. IPO or Sale).

20.4 The exercise price of the Share Options shall, unless otherwise agreed by [a 75% majority of the Board of Directors], not be less than the Subscription Price.

20.5 The Share Options will have a dilutative effect on [all Shareholders].

21. COMPANY SECRETARY, AUDITORS AND ACCOUNTS

21.1 The Company Secretary will be [ ].

21.2 The Company's Annual financial statements will be audited by [ ] or such other firm of reputable accountants approved by the Board of Directors from time to time.

21.3 The accounting reference period shall be determined by the Board of Directors from time to time.

22. All accounts and other financial information will be prepared using accounting bases, policies, practices and procedures (accounting principles) consistent (so far as practicable) in all material respects and in accordance with generally accepted accounting principles.

23. DEFINITIVE DOCUMENTATION AND TIMING

The parties to this Term Sheet hereby agree to negotiate in good faith the terms of an Investment Agreement, Articles of Association, Service Agreements and other ancillary documentation ('Definitive Documentation') in line with the Terms set out herein within [6] weeks of the signing of this Term Sheet.

24. LEGALLY BINDING

The Agreement contained in this Term Sheet is intended to be legally binding and enforceable by the parties hereto unless and until superseded by the execution of the Definitive Documentation.

25. GOVERNING LAW AND JURISDICTION

The Agreement contained in this Term Sheet shall be governed by and construed in accordance with the laws of England and the parties submit to the [non]-exclusive jurisdiction of the English Courts.

For and on behalf of   For and on behalf of

Founder   Founder

.... (Dated:)   .... (Dated:)

For and on behalf of   For and on behalf of

Founder   Founder

.... (Dated:)   .... (Dated:)

Pro forma short form NDA
Dotcom Limited

Dear Sirs,

PROJECT eX

We have certain information ('the Information') relating to an e-commerce business, provisionally called Project eX ('the Project'). The Information is absolutely secret and confidential. We wish to disclose the Information to you for the purpose of you evaluating the Project and, in consideration of our disclosing the Information to you, you undertake as follows:

1. to keep the Information absolutely secret and confidential and only to use the Information for the purpose of evaluating the Project;

2. only to disclose the Information on a need-to-know basis to such of your principals and employees as are directly involved in the Project and whose attention has been specifically drawn to the obligations of confidentiality in this letter;

3. to return to us the Information and all copies of the Information (on whatever medium) and to delete all copies of the Information from your electronic storage systems on completion of the Project or written request by us (whichever is the earlier);

4. these undertakings shall not apply to any of the Information which was already known to you at the date of this letter or which subsequently comes into your possession or comes into the public domain otherwise than in breach of the terms of this letter;

5. this letter shall be governed by and construed in accordance with English law and both of us submit to the non-exclusive jurisdiction of the English Courts.

Yours faithfully

For and on behalf of
Dotcom Limited

Signed . . . .

Accepted for and on behalf of
E-commerce Investments Limited

Signed . . . .

Dated . . . .

8 Downside protection

how to make sure you survive the bursting of the Internet bubble

Sebastian Nokes

Aim

The aim of this chapter is to stimulate your mind to think about a few important areas where you can take steps now to minimize the downside risk to your business, so that when the bad times hit you, your business stands the best possible chance of surviving. It also aims to give a few practical steps to take immediately if you are already in a problem market. It does not aim to be a comprehensive survey or discussion of the topic. It is a first-aid kit for a major accident, not a fully equipped hospital. However, the ideas in this chapter, had they been implemented, would have probably saved Boo.com from going bust.

All bubbles burst

Whoever it was who registered the domain name of Southseabubble.com had a sense of humour, a sense of history, and a commercial sense. Like all technology success stories before it, the Internet will also have ramps and relapses. The railroads of the nineteenth century could show investors and managers boom and bust within the same decade. In the last century, the technology industry was famous for continuing this see-saw: disk-drive manufacturers were one of the earliest IT sectors to show effects of modern tulipmania, and later the biotech industry did the same. It will be the same with the Internet and e-commerce. Your job as a manager is to weather the storm and steer your enterprise through the temporary turbulence of a market downturn, so that it survives and is ready to flourish when your market picks up.

It seems unfair to ask the reader to spend too much time considering an argument that all bubbles burst, so we will take that statement as a basic assumption. It may be worth spending a few sentences discussing whether the Internet sector in general is a bubble, which is a more complex issue. First, what is it that is bubbling? It is a widely held view that the stockmarket for Internet stocks is in a bubble phase, or at least it was in the first quarter of the year 2000. This may be so, though there are some arguments against that proposition. But as an Internet entrepreneur, you might also wish to consider the business bubble, which is related to but separate from the stock market bubble. In a stock market bubble it is investors who chase up the prices of stocks to unsustainable levels. In a business bubble, which, as we have said, is related to a stockmarket bubble, it is the business community – entrepreneurs, managers, customers, suppliers, analysts – who talk a business sector up to levels of unsustainable orders, or who invest to create unsustainable amounts of stock. Also be aware that within the Internet as a whole, different sectors such as B2B and B2C can behave quite differently.

Causes of business failure

In a downturn you want to avoid failure. The causes of business failure have been studied extensively and it may be useful to list what researchers have identified as the main causes of business failure. They are:

- inadequate financial control;
- poor management;
- inability to change;
- poor marketing;
- large projects;
- overtrading.

Inadequate financial control is one of the most common causes, and was the cause of Boo.com going bankrupt. Financial control systems need not be complex to be effective. The main requirement in a small business for a financial control system is that management should know the current state of finances, the projected state, the key risks to achieving the projected state, and that management should be in control of all expenditure. Poor management usually means that the management lacked the skills necessary to manage the business. In the entrepreneurial case, this means that the entrepreneur failed to hire someone or to take advice in a critical area where the entrepreneur himself/herself lacked the necessary skill. The inability to change and poor marketing are similar problems, as one of the main changes you must be able to identify and adapt to is change in your marketplace. How are customers wants and needs changing? How are you sure that you know? Marketing is a specific skill like law or finance. It is not a profession, at least not in the same way as law or medicine, but if your firm's revenue depends on marketing a product or service, then you need marketing expertise. This may sound obvious. It is obvious, but many technology firms run by technologists or financial people pay insufficient attention to marketing because marketing is perceived as being something that anyone can do. 'Large projects' as a cause of corporate failure is where a business bets more than it can afford to lose on a single large project. In high-technology and Internet ventures, large projects are risky. The world is littered with large IT projects and large Internet projects which consumed millions of pounds, dollars and euros and failed to deliver anything that worked. (By contrast, the film industry delivers something, a bad film, when it fails. The film industry is notoriously risky, but the IT and Internet industry is probably the only industry where it is almost *normal* to deliver nothing at all in a big project.) Many Internet entrepreneurs have made fortunes by betting the firm on a single large project and winning, but be aware that many more have failed and that after inadequate financial control it is probably the most popular way to go bust in the Internet. Finally, overtrading is as common a threat to solvency in the Internet business as it is in commerce generally.

Table 8.1 Action points to assess business risk or failure

Financial control	Are your accounts up to date?
	Do you know your main items of cost? What are they?
	What IT equipment and services are you buying and how are they financially justified?
Management	What are your areas of expertise?
	What management functions are critical to your business?
	Who manages the critical areas where you lack experience?
Inability to change	What is changing in your market?
	How is your firm responding?
	How are others responding? Do you know? Are you responding faster than the others? Why and how?
Poor marketing	What marketing does your firm need?
	Who owns marketing in your firm?
	How do you measure the effectiveness of marketing and feed back that measurement to the owner of the marketing function?
Large projects	What large projects do you have?
	Why not complete a chart like Table 8.2 (p.164)?
	Which projects should you focus on now?
Overtrading	What is your cashflow projection for the next three months?
	What are the risks in this cashflow?
	What is the risk to your cashflow from executing the business that you have in hand and on the books?

Three key activities to manage downside risk

There are three key activities that you should be able to do as a manager in relation to managing the downside risk in your business. These are to: reduce costs, plan for the next phase of the economic cycle (in this chapter this means a downturn) and thirdly, when that next phase comes, to implement your plans and modify them as you go to adapt to changing circumstances. Managing costs down is a core management skill and no doubt you would not be running your business or preparing to run it without already having a good understanding of this. Costs always tend to rise if no action is taken, and this soon leads to an uncompetitive business. But apart from day-to-day cost management, you will also need to have a plan for what to do when your market turns down.

Four key areas to consider in downside protection

We will look at four key areas for downside protection. These are:

■ assets;

■ liabilities;

■ revenue;

■ attitude.

The first three are also the main financial aspects of your business, and the fourth comes down to your own character and behaviour, which may need to be modified if you are to survive the coming storm. You may not read this chapter when you first buy the book, but you probably will read it when you see the first signs of a downturn in your business – revenues not quite what they should be perhaps, press articles forecasting blood on the streets in your industry, and staff becoming much easier to find than before. This chapter will help you to prepare well, but in addition to reading this chapter, we advise those readers who are first-time entrepreneurs and who also have not worked through a recession before to go out and find an entrepreneur who has and talk to him/her. That person is a survivor, and that is your primary aim in a downturn.

Assets

For the purposes of downside protection, your assets can be thought of in four classes: your tangible assets, intangible assets, your people and the goodwill that you have with your suppliers and customers.

Assets have costs and productive capability. Make a list of the assets that you have, with the highest cost assets first. Does each one justify its cost? If not, can this be changed by making it more productive? If not, what can be done to reduce the cost – for instance, equipment can be sold and staff can be made redundant.

Look for unused assets. Are there spare computers lying around? Do staff have company laptops at home as well as PCs at work? What rentals and subscriptions are being paid – property rent, telecoms, bandwidth, publications, training and so on? Is it all used? What if it were cut? Generally it is true that a free ISP (Internet service provider) offers an inferior quality of service compared with a paid ISP, but how much would your business save by moving to a free ISP? If you depreciate PCs over two years and then scrap them, could you extend the period by one year? What new equipment is on order and how much does it cost to cancel it? These all are the kinds of questions that you need to ask and, more importantly, act on to get costs under control and start making your assets sweat.

Liabilities

Current liabilities are sums of money that you owe now or, more generally, for the purposes of downside protection, activities that you are committed to that incur cost. Not all activities undertaken at one time cause current liabilities. Hiring someone, for example, causes a liability now, and future liabilities for pay. If the hire is granted options, then a further potential liability arises for National Insurance tax (payable by the firm) at the time those options are exercised. We will look at three ways to keep liabilities low: keeping general costs to a minimum, reviewing managers' spending and not hiring people.

Keep costs to a minimum

Besides staff, keep all costs to a minimum. Entrepreneurs have a habit of buying or leasing flashy cars at the first opportunity, and sometimes before the first opportunity. Office supplies are expensive – is scrap paper being used for rough notes and rough draft documents, or is new, heavy-weave linen-based paper that was bought especially for marketing letters being used? Are toner cartridges being refilled rather than replaced? Is new or second-hand furniture being used? There is nothing wrong necessarily with having filter coffee instead of instant, driving a 5-series BMW and working at a hand-made wooden desk with a top-of-the-range PC and a multi-function telephone system right from day one in your new venture, but just make sure that you really know what the minimum is that you need to spend, and that you are comfortable with every penny spent above that amount. It's your money, or at least partly your money, and all spending decisions boil down to nothing more than a choice of enjoy now or enjoy more later.

Two small businesses started in 1990 in west London. One had vast offices, a company Golf GTi, glossy brochures and a penchant for business breakfasts in one of London's smartest hotels. The other started in the flat of the entrepreneur, and even that was so small that when a second visitor came to see the entrepreneur, the first would have to leave. The second business hired out the use of its photocopier and fax machine to neighbouring residents and businesses, and used the bathroom as a stock room. The second entrepreneur now lives in a large mews house in west London, when not at his large estate in Suffolk. The other entrepreneur was last seen on guard duty at an embassy in Africa, working for a private security company. One understood the importance of managing costs, the other desired the high life. Which one are you going to be?

Review managers' spending

Some managers spend more than others. Review every manager and what they spend. Who is spending more than average – on expenses, on staff, on the cost of doing business? Why? Are they as individual managers worth the extra spend? Which manager can you do without? If you have a head of operations and a head of IT, can one of them take over the other's department?

Don't hire people

People cost money. Inexperienced entrepreneurs tend to hire people they like. Seasoned professional managers tend to hire skills that are needed to generate revenue. Inexperienced entrepreneurs often end up employing people whom they feel can grow to fit the job, or people who 'would be useful guys to have around'. Don't do it. Make a list of the critical skills needed to execute the work that your organization has to do, and then find the people who have those skills and demonstrable recent experience in getting results from using those skills. Staff selection and hiring processes are covered in full detail in Chapter 3, but one of the main areas of avoidable costs incurred by Internet start-ups is carrying too many people. This often starts at the idea stage. Another friend and another friend are pulled into the project until the board of directors is half a dozen people, of whom one had the idea and another has put in substantial effort, while the other four – who may be good people – have nothing specific to contribute and want substantial equity in the business. Don't have a board like that. By all means have very influential or well connected people on the board, but don't have people with no influence or contacts who do no work either.

After the bloated-board syndrome, the next area of avoidable staff costs is the lonely manager who hires an assistant without general skills. Hire people with specific skills and experience. Get the junior employees to do your administration until later on when your revenue shows that you really can afford a secretary, or alternatively, do your own administration.

It is right and proper to pay your staff a decent wage, but it is just as bad for the company to over-reward them as it is for them to be underpaid for the results they bring in. Find out what the market rate for each level of talent in each kind of job that you have is, and don't go too far above it. If you need to make special recognition of an outstanding employee or to find a rare person whom you want to hire, work out some performance-related equity-incentive scheme and try to avoid cash.

As well as the direct cash or cash and equity costs of employees, each additional employee adds cost to your organization in other ways. There is the cost of administering employee and state benefits through your payroll, as the government increasingly forces entrepreneurs to do the work of the DSS; there is the increased risk of employee litigation; there is the drain on your time to manage the employees; there is the increased risk of ideas being stolen. Of course, there are plenty of upsides to having more staff also – teamwork, sharing ideas, getting more work done – but be sure that you have revenue generating work to justify hiring new employees.

Finally, if you really do need another hire, can you use a contractor, a consultant, outsource the work to another firm, subcontract, or find a piece of software that will enable existing staff to take on the extra workload themselves? All these things should be considered and costed before taking on another staff member.

Revenue

Downside protection is not just about controlling costs and making assets sweat. Even in the worst recession people must eat, which means that people buy food, which means that food manufacturers buy packaging, which means that packaging companies buy packaging equipment and supplies, etc. There will still be orders out there. And the good thing about a market downturn is that if it gets bad, your competition starts to go out of business. Provided that you have not also, then a larger proportion of what's left is yours.

One danger that many Internet start-ups face is an over-reliance on advertising revenue. This risk can be identified and managed at the planning stage of the business.

Think revenue now – not advertising later

If every person alive in Europe today had the combined advertising budgets of the Fortune 500 companies to spend, there still wouldn't be enough to satisfy the expectations contained in all the business plans presented to Europe's venture capital houses. Advertising is not a reliable source of revenue for most Internet businesses launching today. Don't rely on it. Too many entrepreneurs are trying to rely on advertising revenue. Find other sources of revenue for your new Web-based business. If you get advertising revenue, great! Take it! But have a credible plan for extracting non-advertising revenue, and constantly adjust the revenue plan to reflect what your market is actually like. When Internet start-ups start going bust in droves in the coming Internet crash, the corporate pathologists will go in to dissect the corpses of the fallen businesses. In nearly every case the liquidators will find a massive gap between projected advertising revenue and actual advertising revenue. The over-reliance on advertising revenue that has no hope of ever arriving is the cancer of Internet start-ups today: dangerous and often fatal, but also often curable if recognized and treated in time. If you have not yet launched your business, re-plan it with advertising revenues set to zero. If you have launched, work out what you will do if advertising revenues fall by a half or a quarter from their current levels.

Business expansion

Focus is profit. One of the lowest-risk ways to grow business is to grow into overlapping businesses. So if you have a taxi company, consider setting up a garage to service taxis. If you have a garage, then think of buying a spare-parts business. In fact, the IT industry is generally quite good at this, and in the Internet it is a natural thing for businesses to expand in this way.

Business expansion connects liabilities to revenue. Business expansion requires investment in order to generate revenues. In a changing economic climate, such as in the run up to a recession, the risk/reward profile of projects can change very quickly, so that what looked like a good project that required a £50 000 investment last month may now look marginal or high risk. Table 8.2 shows a form that can be used for a quick emergency review of all projects under way that need investment. In a recession or a turbulent market, you may wish to refocus your firm's efforts on to those projects likely to create revenue soon with little extra investment, and away from projects with a longer payback or projects requiring significant further investment before any payback is likely.

Attitude

The biggest downside protection that your business can have comes from the attitude and character of you, the entrepreneur. There are reams that could be written, and have been, on the character of a successful entrepreneur, but here we will look at just three things that are important for controlling downside risk in Internet businesses.

Tell the bank what's happening

Bank managers have many businesses to look after and very little time. They also have considerable experience of customers hiding important information from them. Always remember that a bank manager is interested in seeing you succeed almost as much as you are. Bankrupt customers don't look good on a manager's annual appraisal, and, once bankrupt, they tend not to pay their bills in full. Wherever possible, banks generally try to help their customers survive. However, banks are also businesses, and have to apply business criteria to decisions just like the rest of the business sector. Always tell your bank manager what is going on, even if it is bad news. Don't overburden him with detail, but always immediately communicate any major changes to the plan last presented to him, e.g. a customer that hasn't paid, a significant shortfall in orders, or the loss of a key member of staff.

Table 8.2 Emergency review of projects under way in need of investment

(1) Name of Project	(2) Date first revenue due	(3) £K revenue due on date (2)	(4) £K project-specific spend prior to date (2) already committed to	(5) £K additional project-specific spend required prior to date (2)	(6) Rationale for (5)	(7) Greatest risk in the project	(8) £K project-specific spend after date (2) already committed to
(A) Toucan Blade	25/6/00	150	20	5	Major customers need/want modification	No major risks	5
(B) Mayan Sword	7/1/00	75	5	10	One customer wants design change	Project's 2 main customers rumoured to have trading problems	Nil
(C) Eternal Triangle	9/1/00	100	30	30	Required by new operating system version release	Complexity/project management	Nil
(D) Pole Position	14/9/00	NYK	Nil	30K	Feasibility study for the project and patent application	Feasibility	Nil

Plan ahead. When going into a business recession, as we all will when the Internet bubble bursts, revise your business plan to take account of revenue falls likely in the new economic climate. Determine what action to take to cut costs to match revenue falls. You might be able to:

- sell or rent out unused office space;
- terminate contracts for consultants, contractors, short-term staff;
- sell assets;
- hire out your own staff as contractors or consultants;
- sell equity to staff.

Write to your bank manager and set out all the options that are possible, and tell the bank manager which options you propose to follow, under what circumstances, and with what expected result.

OPM, always

In the offices of many successful entrepreneurs one sees a sign somewhere that says simply: 'OPM', which stands for 'Other People's Money'. The aspiring Internet entrepreneur should be aware of at least two aspects of OPM. First, if investors believe that you are using OPM when you could be using your own money, they may well conclude that you are taking risks with other people's money that you are not happy taking with your own money. This first point is a general rule of business, but in this chapter we are specifically concerned with downside protection and what you the entrepreneur should do when times get tough in your market – perhaps the Internet bubble bursts or perhaps just your sector collapses. Assuming that you have satisfied your investors and your business partners at large on the first point, there is a second aspect of OPM. If your company needs more money to survive but there is no more money in the company, you have no more money to invest, and the banks won't lend you more money, then your only source is OPM. This means that you must do three things. First, identify every possible source of OPM. Second, prioritize those sources according to your needs. Third, go and get OPM into your business.

There are many sources of OPM. Suppliers are one of the largest sources. Can the people who have given you 30 days' credit give you 45, 60, 90 or more? Will suppliers provide stock on a sale or return basis? If one supplier won't improve their credit, is there another who will offer better terms? Customers are another source of OPM. Can they be made to pay faster? Or will customers lend your business money? Will suppliers lend your business money? What development agencies, local government bureaucracies, EU funding agencies, research bodies or other organizations are there that might give your business grants, soft loans or loans? Will your landlords waive or roll up the rent?

Some of your competitors may be having as tough a time as you are. Who would suffer if they went bust; who would also suffer even more if you went bust? Try to get better terms from suppliers that you have in common with those competitors.

Are there assets that you have or future sales that you expect that can be sold forward, mortgaged, or on which options for future delivery can be sold? Any one of these ideas can save a business that is in trouble.

In the 1980s a well known fabric manufacturer in the UK faced financial difficulties. They had bought and paid for a new computer system a few months before – the Aesthedes system had cost over £100 000. The fabric manufacturer contacted Aesthedes NV, the original equipment manufacturer of the system, and asked to return it on the basis that the computer performed poorly, and threatened to spread negative publicity about the computer system if the manufacturer did not take the machine back and give a full refund. The computer had not been supplied by the Aesthedes company, but by an independent distributor. Nonetheless, Aesthedes NV took back the machine and provided a full refund, though subsequent tests showed that the system had worked productively and as specified. Days later the fabric manufacturer declared bankruptcy: they had never been dissatisfied with the Aesthedes computer at all, they simply saw a ploy to get OPM. They succeeded in getting their £100 000, but that was not nearly enough to save them. Some people are brutal in their pursuit of OPM, and sometimes it pays off.

Use time well

Time is money. It is unusual for entrepreneurs to use their time badly, for of all people the typical entrepreneur understands very well that time is money. But what about your staff and your customers? Are your staff managing their time well? If they travel on business, are they working on their laptops while on the train? What about your customers – are they using your time well?

Alter the capital structure

Except in companies facing financial distress, equity is high-risk capital and debt is low-risk capital. But if you are facing financial distress, it may be time to alter the financial structure of the company. What assets are not mortgaged that could be mortgaged? For instance, are there mortgages or other charges over property, plant and equipment? What scope remains for a floating charge? What intellectual property is there that could be sold or leased or mortgaged? If the business or part of the business is run by a manager or a group of managers, can they be persuaded to invest more? Can they be persuaded to give personal guarantees?

Consider paying in equity instead of cash. What equity is there that can be used for this purpose? What employees, suppliers and others would take equity instead of cash? Should equity be straight equity, or equity with restrictive covenants, or equity options or some form of hybridized equity such as preference shares?

Conclusion

In good times it is vital to manage costs and to plan for the bad times. When the bad times arrive, you will have to make tough decisions based on hard and careful thinking about your business. This chapter has covered some of the main areas that successful entrepreneurs have said they found valuable in surviving previous downturns. It is not a comprehensive checklist, and the relative importance of each activity will depend on what particular business you are in. But if your business has been based on a good idea and you have a sensible plan for when the downturn comes, and you have the right attitude to managing in the downturn, you will probably survive. Good luck.

9 Dotcom enterprises

realizing value on exit

KPMG

Aim

It is essential that dotcom entrepreneurs consider their exit strategy at an early stage of business development. It not only can have a major influence on the type of funding that will be required for business development, but also potential investors will demand clarity of thought on this issue. It is all very well to create a business that carries a high value, but if the value cannot be realized at least over time, the market valuation is merely academic.

Extraordinary valuations of dotcom companies are creating a new breed of paper millionaires. Actually realizing the value of a substantial proportion of these holdings could be more of a headache for the founders of Internet propositions than is generally assumed. They currently find themselves in the uneasy position of sitting on an enormous theoretical sum of money, which the market demands that they continue to hold by way of equity, for the sake of credibility.

Funders of dotcom companies are backing the vision of the founders to create new business models. They are, therefore, against managers selling down stock before the proposition has been fully developed and launched. Opportunities for realization by dotcom entrepreneurs are thus extremely limited, not least because at two traditional exit points, new rounds of financing and flotation, the immature businesses are still in need of development capital.

For the original external investors, such as business angels and venture capitalists, there are fewer constraints on selling down stock at these stages. Effervescent markets, often driven higher by the enthusiasm of private investors either to hold or to take quick gains, are still chasing comparatively little stock, sending prices higher still.

These dizzy costs of entry cannot necessarily be taken as a benchmark for an exit price. An acquirer of a significant block of shares would be more likely to make a more rigorous assessment of the underlying business than in a market currently driven by speculative demand.

As the supply of dotcom offerings increases, more conventional investment techniques will start to apply – particularly as better performance benchmarks become available.

Although flotation is likely to remain the dream for many dotcom entrepreneurs, another well-established exit route will emerge from the shadows: trade sales.

Many established corporates are specifically raising funds to strengthen their Internet presence. Although no major deals have been concluded in the UK to date, acquisitions are likely to be made as corporates realize the necessity of increasing their dotcom appeal to justify traditional ratings. More mature Internet businesses will also be looking to buy up promising ideas to strengthen their market position. The merger between AOL and Time Warner marks the first material step in the convergence between the old and the new economies.

For dotcom entrepreneurs, trade sales represent much the cleanest exit route. Many will start to appreciate their logic, as they grapple with the realities of running a publicly quoted company.

Nor should a less happy exit route be entirely discounted. Although investors are currently happy to tolerate cash burn – or losses – in developing Internet models, their forbearance cannot be expected to last indefinitely. In the normal course of events, receiverships or fire sales can be expected to provide a route for realizing at least some value in brilliant dotcom ideas that have been poorly managed.

In current market conditions, however, dotcom entrepreneurs are likely to experience more discomfort from two specific tax problems: Capital Gains at a level quite unforeseen in most business plans and the potentially severe disruption to cashflow caused by the exercise of share options.

This chapter is designed to give initial guidance on realizing the value of a significant stake in dotcom enterprises at three traditional exit points – refinancing, flotation, trade sale – and to at least raise the possibility of receivership.

Refinancing

A fresh round of funding usually offers founders simply dilution but it may offer an early opportunity to realize a potential gain. It represents a particularly effective mechanism for replacing one set of funds with another without major publicity and without interfering with the structure of the business.

Under normal conditions, business angels and seed capital would exit to be replaced by more mainstream sources of funding. The value uplift in the market has been so strong in dotcoms, however, that some investors have indicated a preference to stay in for the ride. For second-round funding onwards, the primary sources of funds are the traditional venture capital houses, Internet investment funds (quoted and unquoted) and corporates. From the founder's perspective, the key issue is frequently how to minimize dilution rather than necessarily realizing value.

As the market stabilizes, early-stage investors will be more prone to exit and invest in emerging or more fashionable areas of technology. However, any new investor coming in will be particularly keen to keep the management team in place.

To date, the emotional attachment among founders of dotcom enterprises to taking ideas through to long-term development is significantly stronger than in previous cycles. Previously, entrepreneurs have tended to be replaced by 'developers' who have more interest in growing and maintaining a sustainable business. There have been few signs of a willingness to relinquish control to another management team to take the business on to a new phase. In structuring dotcom business models, however, it is important for founders to take an early view about how many rounds of funding they foresee, how much dilution they are prepared to tolerate, and when they expect to realize cash.

For managers concerned at losing control, there may be more support forthcoming from one notable absentee so far in the dotcom market: commercial debt providers. Although security is difficult in an environment where the principal assets are intangible, in the form of IPR, know-how or customer-based content, lenders are aggressively looking to enter the market, as earnings streams become more reliable, particularly those underpinned by contractual arrangements with corporate or trade partners. Inevitably, initial moves are likely to come from the more creative end of debt, such as convertibles and mezzanine. Debt offers cheaper funds and the ability for founders to hold more equity; however, it is dependent on a number of criteria, which are frequently absent from the current round of e-ventures – including security and cashflows.

Flotations

Flotations have been a highly effective method for dotcom companies to capitalize on the excitement surrounding Internet propositions and secure relatively cheap money in the long term. For first movers, offerings have arguably been even more valuable in raising awareness of the brand through the PR and news attention they have received.

Flotations may allow financial backers to exit, but for the creators of the idea it is principally a fund-raising exercise for the company. In many ways, flotations cut down the realization options for founders. Given that flotations are occurring at such an early stage of dotcom companies' development, founders are generally required to stay in and create the business. For most Internet entrepreneurs who are passionately committed to their business model, this is a satisfactory condition. However, it does have the effect of potentially restricting exit options to either being bought by a trade buyer or by an investment house or by another quoted vehicle.

Appraisal

In assessing offerings from dotcom companies, sponsors and brokers on behalf of investors will be looking to satisfy several points. A genuine business plan that is going to be followed through is the first requirement. Although there is no suggestion of any intended fraud, regulators are increasingly pointing out that it is the role of advisers to ensure that false markets are not being created through false expectations of success being made – however genuinely believed.

The credibility of the management team is, therefore, an important determinant. Does it have the breadth of skills, the relevant experience and the network of contacts to capitalize on the company's business model?

In the world of e-commerce, success of failure often depends on alliances. Does the management team have the stature to argue with major industry players? Or is it just going to get swamped?

In the dotcom world, despite all the benefits of share option schemes, there appears to be a dearth of senior talent able to fulfil the demands of managing an Internet proposition and to assume a public face. Successful teams will, therefore, be applauded – but expected to stay and capitalize on that success rather than take cash to 'sit on a beach'.

Valuation

At present, it appears that there may be three distinct values applying with particular force to dotcom floats: conventional underlying business value, the entry price and the exit price. Each may be different – and each will be reflected in the potential value available to realizing investors.

Business value

A number of studies have attempted to justify previous market values by reference to the CAGR (compound annual growth rate) required to support the current price, usually on a discounted cashflow (DCF) basis. For many businesses two significant stumbling blocks arise from such methods: the CAGR required appears to be unsustainably high (150–250%) and the cash outlays in the early years are too high.

A key issue with the approach is that it is based on an expectation that businesses will have a fairly steady growth rate – varying by perhaps 25% on a year-to-year basis. Reality for Internet businesses can be very different: in 1996 Yahoo!'s market capitalization required a long-term growth rate of 250% p.a. to justify it, which many said was unachievable. In reality, from 1996–1998 its growth rate was close to 2500% p.a. This had two consequences for valuation modellers: the longer-term growth rate to sustain a very high value was significantly reduced, and cashflows were very different from those expected. With hindsight, therefore, the 1996 value looked undercooked!

One of the other key issues in business valuation lies in the difficulty of applying many of the conventional multiple-based value techniques – price/EBITDA (earnings before interest, tax, depreciation and amortization) or price/earnings ratios – for two reasons. There is frequently no peer group from which to create benchmarks and, perhaps more importantly, there are no earnings. As a result, a number of other multiple-based methods are being applied – for example, revenue per user, which has historically shown perhaps the best correlation to the market price.

One key trouble lies in defining users. Too many sites have subscribers who do not pay anything: no great loyalty can be claimed if it does not cost anything to stay on. Also, subscribers and active users can be two very different things.

As with the parameters of any valuation model, it is important to understand the benchmark group. Is your user base comparable to others quoted? There can be huge differences between corporate and personal user groups, both in terms of loyalty rates, as well as in their ability to pay and their credit rating.

The difficulty with the business valuation (whichever model is used) from an investor's or founder's perspective is that it does not take account of market sentiment, which may be related to matters outside of the specific business – demand and supply of stock, alternative investment, stage of business development etc. For this reason, whilst it may be the most justifiable basis for valuation, it may well not be the value realized.

Entry price

Conventional valuation methods have been to little avail in dotcom public offerings. Offers have been ten, 20, 30 or even 40 times oversubscribed, resulting in substantial price rises on the first day, which in most conventional markets would be seen as a clear indication of underpricing.

As a result, dotcom valuations are becoming increasingly demand-led. Without sector benchmarks, brokers are relying more on the extent of oversubscription and other trading histories including an expectation of how far the price should rise on the first day of trading. From spring 2000, pricing is likely to be more aggressive, as brokers learn by experience. There are now enough comparatives in the marketplace, showing initial rises and how the price settled, to enable more realistic pricings to market to be made, particularly as prices are adjusted (upwards by c.70% in the case of lastminute.com in March) during the grey market as demand is recognized.

In other industry sectors, investment houses make a selection of stocks. As yet, they are not yet in a position to choose Internet stocks with any great degree of certainty. So many are taking a portfolio approach, purchasing all or most which are available, rather than the two or three they would normally home in on.

Market conditions are also driving prices up. There are comparatively few genuine Internet stocks, perhaps 50 as of March 2000. Of these, very few have more than 20% of their shares available on the market. As the supply of floated dotcom companies increases, that part of the value driven by excess demand is likely to experience a significant fall. In early 2000 in the UK, more than ten floats a month were taking place with plenty still in the pipeline from brokers.

As those flotations come through, a clearer set of benchmarks will start to develop. Two or three propositions will occupy the same space, rather than just one. Similarly, clearer performance patterns will start to emerge, as six months' worth of figures are pub-lished by companies floated earlier. As the market settles down, the attention of investors, as has happened in the USA, will focus more on the underlying business valuations – these may still be high in some cases for reasons given above, but they are unlikely to be ubiq-uitously high.

Exit price

When management or founders of Internet businesses wish to sell their shareholdings in the business, the exit price is not necessarily the same as the cost of entry. (Exit price means the value at which a significant holding could be sold. Freeserve and Dixons are a case in point. Freeserve was valued at £7.7bn in February 2000, with Dixons owning 80%. If the value of that holding is taken from Dixons' current market capitalization, it implies that Dixons itself is worth less than £400m. The suggestion is, therefore, that the entry price, i.e. the current share price, for Freeserve is clearly not what Dixons would get if it liquidated its entire holding, or indeed any substantial portion of it.

It is likely, therefore, that any significant realizations by founding shareholders still closely allied to the business either commercially or by way of management would have a detrimental impact on the share price and could only be realized at a significant discount to current values.

Markets

In selecting on which market to list, it is as important as with a conventional business to match the expectations of the investor base with the business. As well as an under-standing of the proposition, investors' aspirations on holding and realizing their stakes should ideally coincide with the founder's perspective on the development needs of the company.

Given this perspective, it is perhaps surprising how many companies automatically per-ceive NASDAQ to be the first and most logical float target. If the objective is to run a European business, then there may not be a great deal of point in floating on NASDAQ. Management will find itself disappearing to the USA every quarter to keep investors informed, creating a distraction from its operations in Europe and the performance of the shares will relate to market sentiment about e-business in the USA, which may or may not be reflective of the UK general market position or the state of the business itself.

The question then perhaps should be: the UK or Europe? The London Stock Exchange (LSE) brings credibility and an international audience. Although TechMark, the new cat-egory for technology companies on the LSE, is designed to be a growth market (where you do not necessarily need a trading record), there are still rules and regulations to be fol-lowed – but it does give you a full London listing.

Companies in high-tech, high-growth markets, which can tolerate a high degree of volatility and whose shares may be of more interest to private rather than public investors, may find AIM or Ofex in London to be more appealing.

Alternatively, Europe has a huge range of markets (and it seems to be ever increasing). There are several common features to all these high-growth markets – liquidity is a real issue on them all. Limited stock and few active sellers of substantial holdings mean that if an institution buys a stake, it ends up with a large chunk, leading to enormous volatility. Even relatively small trades can trigger large swings in prices.

Post-flotation management

The PR profile established has a plus and a negative side. On the one hand, it is 'free' publicity which can be invaluable for young businesses seeking to establish a high-profile brand or deep-market awareness. On the other hand, mistakes, surprises and lack of performance will be glaringly exposed.

Once a company has been listed, the culture of dotcom companies may be opportunistic, but the expectations of investors have to be carefully managed. Any surprises, particularly over timing of break-even or swings in performance, are likely to be received poorly.

Reviewing the composition of the board may make life easier. Ideally an appointment of an experienced candidate can help to deal with an investment audience. Such individuals should understand the business, but are not necessarily to be involved in it day to day. Their background may well be in the City of London, but they must understand what investors need to hear and the frequency with which they need to hear it.

Unless prepared and properly resourced, management teams will find the quarterly reporting schedule on TechMark quite onerous. For some, this may encourage an early exit. While the advantages of raising initial funding of the market are obvious, the longer-term benefits of remaining in the public arena may be less so.

Trade sales

To date, trade sales have been a relatively neglected exit route for dotcoms. Unlike conventional ventures, flotation is plausibly taken to be the most desirable option: an assumption which venture capitalists and other early funders have been happy to accept in a market as buoyant as tech stocks. As the market settles down, however, trade sales will become an increasingly important factor.

Trade buyers come in one of two guises, the traditional player looking to establish itself in the Internet economy, and quoted Internet companies, sitting on a huge value in paper, which believe that it is worth paying to acquire a business that is generating revenue now rather than in the future, or one which complements its own Internet model.

The AOL and Time Warner merger is likely to represent a watershed in the market, illustrating the importance for both traditional corporates and major Internet stocks in occupying new space in the market and demonstrating the real synergy to be achieved by combining both models.

Trade sales will also be driven by the founders of dotcom companies who have grasped the fact that they may be good innovators, but that they are not people to stay with the business longer term. Trade sales offer much the cleanest exit route for both them and their backers. A high exit price may also be achievable, especially if a buyer has a strong strategic and commercial rationale for buying the business or indeed if it represents a threat to its own business model.

For corporate buyers, the most attractive targets are generally those where the owners have disassociated themselves from the development of the business or have reached a platform in development which requires further alliances or partnerships – perhaps for content, or reach (customer base) or distribution.

Corporates

An increasing number of traditional corporates are already entering the market as investors. The next phase is likely to be outright acquisitions, either of companies in the public arena or private businesses.

Established businesses, particularly in the media and the telecoms sector, have already begun moving up the value chain from distribution and infrastructure to encompass content and technology Internet and e-business as a natural fit. In particular, they will be looking for propositions which enable them to build on their own customer loyalty.

Many utilities, for example, currently have high rates of customer retention but they do not necessarily command high levels of loyalty, particularly when the bill pops through the door. If customers are able to buy something rather more palatable from them, then that reinforces the relationship. Centrica, for example, has thus developed Goldfish.

An important part of corporate strategies in buying dotcom assets will be an objective of reinforcing and dominating customer groups, whose demand for access and content would then be met from a common platform. Pearson, for instance, is making it clear that its strategy is to dominate entire market spaces, such as the deal it has set up *vis-à-vis* the education market with AOL.

It can, therefore, be safely assumed that on the back of a dotcom war-chest of £500m raised by Pearson specifically to pursue Internet opportunities, a number of educational propositions will be bought up to provide a skills base for the AOL venture, not least because Pearson will be approached by entrepreneurs for funding, and has the option of taking substantial stakes early on.

Internet majors

Major Internet groups are emerging as a significant category of trade buyers in their own right, particularly those whose initial business model is under threat.

Challenges to Freeserve's telecoms-based proposition, for instance, is encouraging it to pick up other business and diversify into related areas, piggybacking on the value of its Internet paper. As in the case of AOL, acquisitions of traditional companies as well as dotcoms, give such companies the opportunity to underpin high valuations with genuine streams of revenue. For content companies, one of the attractions of selling out is that while they can see value in the e-space, they cannot necessarily realize it themselves.

Funding structures

Acquisitions driven by an Internet company will generally want to use highly rated paper. At present, this can be attractive to targets. Merging the cultures of the old and new economies is likely to be a much stiffer test.

With established business looking to buy an Internet company, an entirely different structure will apply. The entrepreneur will probably be hoping to realize, so a deal could be expected to involve a hefty cash element funded either by debt or a placing.

Receivership

Among all the Internet propositions coming to the market, there is likely be a significant sub-group of brilliant, but poorly managed propositions. Should cashflow dry up, they could face receivership, once the honeymoon period is over and the present high loss levels are no longer acceptable. Such businesses are a likely target for venture capitalists or other investors seeking to acquire under-performing businesses at an early stage to then put in management teams to exploit what remain good Internet propositions. They might also be expected to put companies together within their portfolio.

Capital gains

The sheer scale of some capital gains makes it hard to factor into the original business plan. Significant gains on exit or realization are clearly the objective of entrepreneurs in both new and established businesses. If, however, these individuals wish to avoid or reduce the substantial tax charge they would otherwise face, then planning in advance can assist. The gamble of tax planning in advance is to what extent tax law will be changed in the intervening period before exit – less of an issue perhaps for the new businesses where growth and realization may occur more rapidly than for traditional manufacturing or service industries.

However, recent legislation has focused on 'taper relief' to encourage retention of shareholdings over a longer period. Taper relief reduces the Capital Gains Tax (CGT) rate over time, with CGT minimized after (currently) ten years. It is, therefore, difficult to reconcile optimum taper relief with start-up businesses where the present speed of development suggests a much shorter period of ownership for the entrepreneurs concerned.

Some other options for reducing CGT have traditionally focused on retirement-type benefits – for example, FURBs (funded, unapproved retirement benefits scheme) which are designed as a pension provision. Again, for entrepreneurs in their twenties, such schemes, whilst prudent, do not necessarily have immediate relevance.

Reinvestment relief, a long-standing method of deferring tax on gains, under which the gain is 'rolled over' into newly subscribed shares, has been replaced by EIS deferral relief. To qualify, shares must fit into certain categories – they must be unquoted (although this classification does include some AIM companies), have gross assets of less than £15 million and they must carry on a qualifying trade – characteristics which fit some but not all businesses.

Trades which fail to qualify include (broadly) leasing, certain financial activities, accounting and legal activities and (in some cases) trades which generate licence fees. To further complicate the issue, if the acquired shares cease to qualify after reinvestment, then the tax mitigated will fall due.

There are, however, more sophisticated schemes for reducing the tax which can be tailored for individuals or companies in particular circumstances. It is critical with any tax planning that professional advice is sought early – not least because this is an area liable to change as the Chancellor addresses his twin incentives of encouraging new businesses whilst nurturing tax revenues.

National Insurance contributions

In retaining and recruiting the best talent, share options are common currency in dotcom enterprises. However, soaring valuations are creating potentially heavy liabilities on National Insurance contributions (NICs), which in many cases could severely disrupt cashflow.

Options exercised under Inland Revenue approved schemes are not subject to NICs, but clearly the scheme itself will be constrained by the rules and guidelines on approved schemes. Both employers' (i.e. paid by the company) and, where relevant, employees' NICs are payable on the profit on exercise (i.e. the difference between the exercise price and the market value on the exercise date) of options granted under unapproved schemes after 5 April 1999.

This is in contrast to unapproved options granted between 5 December 1996 and 6 April 1999, where NICs were applicable on the grant of the option – calculated on the discount between the lowest exercise price payable per share and the market value per share at the time of grant. For options granted in this period no NIC is payable on exercise.

In either case, once the options are either granted or exercised, the NICs become payable – a cash outlay which may be both unplanned and unwelcome to a fledgling company.

Conclusion

There is a real distinction to be made between **valuization** (for example, on a flotation where the market ascribes a value to the business share capital) and **realization** which for an entrepreneur means selling (his shares in return for cash).

The ability to ascribe value is currently widely available with significant numbers of propositions coming to market at early stages. To achieve cash returns will require realization of these values – which probably means developing the business to the next stage.

Entrepreneurs need to recognize the distinction and to ensure that their expectations are those of the market. As yet, there is insufficient evidence of how long it will take or at what stage those recently quoted companies will be deemed mature enough to effect genuine realizations for their founders.

10 How Investors see the entrepreneur

Edmond Jackson

Editor's introduction

Edmond Jackson is an experienced private investor who shares his insights via *Taking Stock*, a diary column in *The Sunday Telegraph*, also a daily notepad on Citywire, the specialist Web site for investors. He has worked in investment and corporate finance in London merchant banks, but enjoys the challenge of start-ups. Presently he is involved with a range of Internet companies as a proactive investor. He sees plenty of risks in the sector and a few major opportunities ahead. In your quest to convince investors, Edmond can help you understand their perspective. (See also *www.telegraph.co.uk* and *www.citywire.co.uk*.)

An investor's perspective to aid the entrepreneur

Risk capital for the Internet revolution is being provided by equity investors. I do not want to dissuade you from approaching banks for loan capital – but many Internet ventures hardly amount to a bankable proposition! So you need to understand what makes investors tick, our hopes and fears, to be able to engage our interest.

Many entrepreneurs harbour suspicions about venture capitalists – yet, the financial community is diverse, so you should not lapse into prejudice. In fact, you are in the best position of all. Such has been the growth of 'incubator funds' for Internet and e-commerce related investment, that the best projects are encountering competition for their equity.

Durlacher Corporation is regarded as the grand-daddy of this burgeoning family. Its own recent development has been remarkable, helping to found, not simply finance, ventures. There is now a host of funds, many listed on the Alternative Investment Market of the London Stock Exchange (LSE), chasing the best opportunities.

One advantage of seeking out a specialist fund is that you are likely to be offered useful support at all stages of your venture: compared with a bank's worry about the security of its loan, a fund wants to see its investment flourish. The classic Internet fund is being managed by a thirty-something who has assembled a board and network of people who can help Internet ventures succeed. A great deal of support is on offer and this should influence your choice of financial partner. The funds are receptive, so 'get in there' and make your pitch – which is why this chapter is structured around the key issues which you should address in a business plan.

Certain funds are moving to develop their own investor communities around Web sites that enable private investors to invest alongside the fund, in unquoted companies. However, this trend is involved with pre-flotation financing rather than start-ups.

Consider the role of private investors too, not that we are a softer touch – but there is similar scope to network and locate financial partners who can assist the company's development. Time can be critical when going through financing rounds, and the quoted funds are increasingly swamped with propositions, so be ready to find your own share-holders. Make approaches directly to businesspeople whom you would like to be involved, whose contacts could help.

One has to be careful of investment regulations when effectively soliciting for funds – for example, a company cannot itself place an advertisement to sell shares. But that has never stopped word of mouth from putting entrepreneurs and investors together – witness the £2000 stumped up in a Soho wine bar for Mike Lynch to develop Autonomy Corporation (*www.autonomy.com*), after bankers turned down his business plan. Revolutionizing Internet search engines, Autonomy is now seen as Britain's answer to Microsoft.

Investor associations are moving to enable their members to participate in unquoted companies. Again, this is more likely at the pre-flotation than start-up stage, though there is a firm trend to empower private investors – watch for developments! The Guild of Shareholders (*www.guild.org.uk*) is one such group taking regular initiatives.

A DIY approach via private investors has its logical outcome via flotation on the Ofex market (*www.ofex.co.uk*). Outside the London Stock Exchange, this is managed by J.P. Jenkins as both regulator and market maker; this has sometimes led to criticism, however Ofex has aided successful companies, such as *www.icollector.com* and *www.cityjobs.com*. In time, most companies tend to graduate to AIM or the main market, enjoying a re-rating in the process. Managers often find that Ofex proves a highly cost-effective means to raise a company's profile, introduce liquidity for early-stage investors and share option schemes.

Autonomy's experience did not show the LSE in a good light: Lynch decided to list his company on Easdaq, the European exchange for emerging technology companies (*www.easdaq.com*). Amid the rush of LSE flotations, complaints continue from companies and advisers about the delays involved.

You should not assume that a listing on any exchange automatically confers benefits – indeed the reverse is possible. Amid the March flotation of lastminute.com, its advisers made the error of raising the offer price amid public enthusiasm and allocated each applicant 35 shares – turning exuberance to anger and resulting in a price slump and a media backlash. After being cast as heroes, lastminute.com's founders learned the sharp lesson that markets can tend both ways. Do not push your luck.

This event was seen by many as a defining moment in the Internet share boom, the easy days of companies raising money and investors making a fast mint, being over. Yet, it is healthy that much of the froth surrounding the Internet investment theme has been wiped away. True, investors are set to be more discriminating; that is, again, to your advantage if you are presenting a quality proposition.

Of course, it may be in the company's development interests that you ally financially with a commercial partner. In which case, you need to consider carefully that organization's objectives before drafting a proposal, and recognize yours too. Collaboration is not easy in a rapidly changing Internet world, as new opportunities arise all the time.

Essentials of a business plan

Whether your enterprise is business-to-business, or consumer, infrastructural support, etc., there are key questions at the back of investors' minds. Ironically, even managements of quoted Internet/technology businesses, fully trained in PR, fail to address these concerns effectively.

They tend to make their presentations too detailed – even for analysts and specialist fund-managers. Realize that in today's busy markets, these professionals are constantly being propositioned; you must make your pitch succinct, to elicit interest. Once generated, specifics can be resolved in later discussion. By all means, show that you have thoroughly researched and planned your venture, but ensure that its rationale for investors is crystal clear.

As a matter of style, appreciate that even fund managers may not have been in the Internet game for long; many investors have entered in the last year, so don't assume detailed technology understanding. This is not to imply dumb money: along the bridge you need to cross, you will encounter classic questions.

The following overview is no final solution – stay flexible to evolve a plan that best suits your project. But it will give you a sense of investors' priorities.

This is what we are thinking:

Management

1. Do these people genuinely want – and have the ability – to build a sustainable Internet business? Or is their real goal to generate paper wealth amid a stockmarket boom, and then jump to another project?

Investors need assurance that they are not simply a means for an entrepreneur to keep moving on, taking a turn at each project, before it is properly established.

2. Can they work effectively as a team? Is the business dependent on one or how many key individuals? How committed are these individuals to the enterprise?

Investors want to see a culture of employment/freelance contracts that will attract and retain the right talent. A balance between tying in key individuals – yet not making them feel restricted to an extent that they will move on after, say, a year's initial commitment. The Internet culture is recognized as creative and freewheeling; if good people don't like the atmosphere, they will move on. Are the founders demonstrating an awareness of this, as they build and manage a team?

3.   If the business is one person's idea and principal ownership, is this founder able to cede control steadily as the venture progresses? Is a realistic portion of shares and/or options available for key individuals? A strength of Internet companies is ability to poach individuals from traditional employment – also rival Internet companies – by offers of serious equity. This depends on whether competitive equity is made available by the founders. Otherwise, the business risks empowering bright people with commercial nous – who later move on to set up a rival enterprise with proper equity for themselves. Despite the best efforts at non-competition agreements and imposing 'gardening leave', it happens.

4.   Can the founders evolve a management structure to cope with anticipated growth? The venture may be stronger on creative than managerial talent. What kind of help might 'ideas people' need?

Do not feel coy at asking potential investors what they might be able to offer via their networks. Incubator funds are competing between themselves on this strength; private investors, too, may be businesspeople with useful contacts and experience.

The concept

5.   Can this enterprise succeed when it comes to market?

What research and evaluation has been done to test the likely response? Much money may need to be invested, simply to get the Web site or service established. You need to provide a realistic sense of the market opportunity and how your business is going to succeed. What budget for what kind of marketing strategy? Are operational/marketing partners required, with appropriate equity?

You cannot be expected to give a definitive answer ahead of a market launch, but you can show possible scenarios. Over-hype and the proposition will be binned.

6.   What is known about actual/potential competition?

Investors like a sense of 'first-mover advantage'; however, we are generally cautious about markets that may attract so much competition no one ends up making any money!

Several Internet themes, such as last-minute goods/services and financial information/advice, look vulnerable to this dilemma. Of course, one can never know all the plans that might be hatched over six months alone – but you will earn respect by disclosing what you do know and anticipate.

Has the Internet been scoured for likely competition – also domain name registration?

If this enterprise registers domain names, might other Web sites sue? Include such a report in the business plan.

Remember, investors will appreciate a diligent approach to assessing the risks – but you will lose all credibility if you knowingly sweep them under the carpet.

7.   How is the enterprise going to generate revenues?

A plethora of dotcom sites may be successful in terms of hits – but generating revenues and profits may be quite a different challenge.

What is this project's business model? If it is e-commerce – advertising and services – have key companies been approached? What interest and level of commitment have been generated?

Certain content can always command a subscription; however, there is no doubting that people are accustomed to free access. New sites often launch with free access as a teaser, before trying to exact a subscription. Yet, some managements have back-tracked, realizing they cannot lose vital hits if people are resistant to subscriptions. While every business must stay flexible to the market opportunity, some don't seem to have a realistic revenue plan. Investors tend not to back mere billboards.

Finance

8.   Is sufficient capital being raised?

Early-stage ventures frequently underestimate what is needed and the time required to meet key objectives. Very few projections are correct – but investors are wary that against anticipated revenue prospects, timescales for achieving them are usually underestimated.

Outline several scenarios in your spreadsheet.

9.   On what terms are outside investors being invited?

A concern is that we may not be participating on as favourable a basis as certain founder shareholders. Start-ups frequently evolve through several rounds of equity, raising the company's value as certain stages are achieved. An element of auctioneering may be introduced, among potential investors. The suspicion at the back of our minds is that some investors are more equal than others.

Ensure as equitable terms as possible.

10.   Will an exit route be prepared?

It is not 'short-termist' but good practice for an investor to want to identify an ultimate exit – via sale of the business, flotation or by being personally bought out.

Clarify this as far as possible.

11.   Are private investors being offered a tax-efficient deal?

The Enterprise Investment Scheme was amended in the March 2000 Budget, making it an even more attractive tool for entrepreneurs to raise capital from individuals. Shares now need holding for three years instead of five to be exempt from Capital Gains Tax. The amount invested can also be offset against one's Income Tax liability for the year in which the investment is made: ideal for higher-rate taxpayers who prefer to fund businesses rather than the Inland Revenue.

Top tips

- Be as realistic as you can.
- Keep your investors informed.
- Avoid nasty surprises, wherever possible.
- Foster a sense of partnership.
- Create a route to exit.
- Go with people with whom you are most comfortable.

Sample business plan for Meringue.com

The business plan that follows, for the project named 'Meringue'[1], was used for real in late 1999. It resulted in seed funding of £50 000 that was used for a further analysis of the market. It also generated many useful contacts and work for the small organization that wrote the plan. As you read it, you will see that it does not conform to every aspect of the advice given in Chapter 2, but it does follow Chapter 2's advice to set out clearly and in detail the idea behind the proposed business. The plan itself admits that there are critical gaps in the plan in four areas – marketing, IT, legal, actuarial. The business that wrote the plan was working under time pressure – Internet time pressure – and felt that there was a trade-off between all the suggestions in Chapter 2 and getting the plan at least partially complete but in a very short time. The plan achieved its objective, which was to secure seed funding and strong links to a large organization. The plan has not been edited in any way, and is included as an example of the sort of thing that works in real life. The biggest omission from this plan is any spreadsheet showing projected revenues and projected expenditure.

Meringue.com – A proposal to set up a new mutually owned on-line insurance and retail financial services provider for Great Britain and Europe

Table of contents

Introduction

The purpose of this business plan is to convey an idea as the basis for further discussion and analysis, with a view to forming a small consortium to evaluate the idea and, if the evaluation is positive, execute it. Please treat the ideas and information as confidential.

The working name for the project is Meringue.com. We believe that Meringue.com may change the European life insurance market in the way that Amazon has changed the world's book market and Schwab has changed the world's retail stockbroking market, but only if we act at Internet speed and launch in March 2000.

Meringue.com – summary

A mutual life company to sell over the Internet

The key idea in Meringue.com is to sell life insurance by exploiting three strong trends: first, cost reduction by new technology, such as the Internet; second, the growth in consumer acceptance of direct sales channels for retail financial products, including insurance; and third, the greed of the carpetbagger.

Meringue.com will be a mutual life insurance company that sells life insurance policies over the Internet. Life insurance can be a very profitable business because the customer signs up for a long period, typically at least ten years. A life company that used the Internet for all sales, operations and customer servicing should be able to achieve massive cost reductions: 90% cost reductions compared with a traditionally managed business are often cited in banking and stockbroking as being achievable through the use of advanced IT, particularly the Internet.

The two greatest problems facing a start-up in the UK life insurance industry are the industry's image and the customer's lack of interest in the product. The image of the industry as a whole is recovering as memories of the endowment-linked mortgage scandals of the 1980s fade and better regulation of salesforces is taking effect and the market has started expanding again. Meringue.com will overcome the consumer's lack of interest in life insurance by appealing to the carpetbagging instinct. Instead of actively selling life insurance to customers, Meringue.com will attract customers by a promise to demutualize. It will be the leading demutualization target for carpetbaggers because it will be run by a management keen on demutualization. Carpetbagging is such a strong effect that financial institutions rumoured to be likely to demutualize often close to new business or adopt other non-price rationing tactics, so great is the flood of new deposits. The implicit promise of demutualization has already been used in the Internet Service Provider market, and we believe it will work for life insurance.

The other benefits of a mutual structure are, first, in lowering the cost of capital; which capital is then used, second, to build a major Internet financial products distribution channel in the UK and elsewhere, for which, third, the customers (carpetbaggers) will be in good supply, which means that as a distribution channel, Meringue.com should have a high valuation.

Speed is a vital

Speed is a vital. The opportunity is so great that others will be working on the same idea already. Why hasn't it been done before? There may be regulatory issues that need to be resolved, and one of the first things to do is to get expert legal advice on how to proceed, and whether there are insuperable regulatory obstacles to Meringue.com. However, we note that life insurance is sold over the Internet in the USA, and secondly that although anyone could have started an Internet banking operation in the UK from about 1994 onwards, it was not until about 1998/99 that Norwich & Peterborough, Prudential/Egg and others actually executed. Conservatism and inertia in the established market players therefore seem to be the main reasons why nothing like Meringue.com has been tried before.

Key value drivers in Meringue.com

Meringue.com's strategy is to exploit three powerful trends, and to position itself in the intersection of all three:

- IT and the Internet's ability to lower costs in financial services;
- rising direct sales of insurance products;
- carpetbagging and demutualization.

What these trends mean and why there is value in exploiting them are explained next.

The Internet's low cost will enable Meringue to achieve a cost advantage

When used well, IT can make an order of magnitude's difference to costs. The Internet is an extreme case of this power of IT. The following are examples of how IT or the Internet, when used well, can reduce costs:

- Jim Spowart, MD of Standard Life Bank – 'The savings volume of one of our telephone operators is equivalent to that of 11 building society branches.'
- Egg believes that its Internet-based service operates at one-third of the cost of its telephone-based service.
- 'Life policies sold by direct means can be up to 50% cheaper than those sold through traditional channels such as agents.' (*Life Insurance International*, 3/99)
- In the banking sector in 1996 leaders had an expense ratio of 50%–55%, against a projected expense ratio of 15%–20% for Internet banks, and the estimated unit transaction cost for a non-cash payment was $1.08 for a bank branch, $0.54 for a telephone call centre and $0.13 for the Internet. (Booze, Allen and Hamilton, *Internet Banking in Europe: A Survey of Current Use and Future Prospects*, 1996)

Management and acquisition expenses in the life insurance industry fell from a peak of over 25% of total premia in 1988 to 16% in 1995 and are still falling (see Table 1 – Acquisition and management expenses of UK life insurance firms, p. 212). Legacy organizations in the insurance industry find it almost impossible to operate as efficiently as the occasional entrepreneur who takes a smarter approach to a niche: Mark Weinburg's Abbey Life is one example in the life insurance sector, and Direct Line is an example in the motor sector. (The insurance sector is no worse than any other sector for bureaucracy and inertia – in the IT sector IBM and others gave up massive economic rents to newer, nimbler firms that understood the PC.)

Meringue.com will beat competition on management and acquisition costs not just by using technology well but also by not employing legacy people; in fact, the plan is to employ as few people as possible. Meringue.com aims to have management and acquisition expenses of below 5% of premia, with a target of below 3% within six years.

Direct selling is effective in both life and other forms of insurance. In the UK 25% of motor policies are sold direct, and the life industry believes that the same can be done for direct sales of life policies. Meringue.com's rationale presumes that the Internet is just the lowest cost direct channel.

Direct sales of retail financial services over the Internet are rising

In 1990 it was feasible to sell financial services over the Internet but no one did because few people with any money had access to the Internet. In 1995, many people had access to the Internet, but most stockbrokers, insurance salesmen and investment bankers were confident that the Internet would never amount to much. Today these same people lie awake at night sweating because the Internet may well drive them into early retirement from firms too poor to give them a tin handshake, let alone a golden one.

In 1Q97 (first quarter of 1997) US investors made 95 500 on-line securities trades per day, and this had grown to 252 600 by 3Q98, a 165% increase. The US retail Internet stockbroking leaders such as Schwab, E*Trade, DLJ Direct and Ameritrade have grown on the back of this trend. Growth in Internet delivery of other retail financial services is also strong, although retail stockbroking is the strongest.

In insurance the trend towards direct sales over the Internet lags the stockbroking trend, but what little data is available is consistent with the trend in stockbroking, and industry opinion is that the trend in insurance will be as great as in stockbroking.

A mutual that promises to demutualize will bring in customers

In the last ten years the UK and European experiences are that customers will open building society accounts, join Internet service providers and buy products from life insurance companies (including life policies) in order to carpetbag the institution suspected of being about to demutualize. This feature of customer behaviour can be exploited by Meringue.com to sell policies at low cost.

Potential demutualization candidates have tended to receive large extra inflows of deposits at times when they were the subject of demutualization speculation:

- in 1997 the Britannia Building Society stopped opening new Instant Access accounts; these accounts required a minimum balance of £500. 7000 people tried to become members of Britannia by opening these accounts (i.e. over £3.5m of would-be new deposits), which was ten times normal levels;[2]

- at the Woolwich Building Society 40 000 new accounts were opened in the expectation of carpetbagging in January 1996;[3]

- also in January 1996, Bristol & West and Bradford & Bingley said that they had experienced very high numbers of new account openings because of speculation on demutualization;

- in 1999 the Chelsea Building Society raised the minimum deposit required to open an account to £1000 and paid minimal interest, all in response to speculation about demutualization, but queues to open new accounts still formed outside its branches;

- the Portman, Nationwide, Norwich & Peterborough and all but the smallest other building societies have experienced similar demand associated with carpetbagging.

One enterprise that has taken the mutual-now-promise-to-demutualize-later approach is TheMutual.Net. This is not a financial services company, but a portal and ISP. More details of this venture are given in the section on competition, below.

Value is created by building high-value relationships with many customers

The traditional mutual life company offers windfall profits on demutualization because it has accumulated a surplus of profit over the years that has not been distributed to previous policyholders. This source of value will not be available to the policyholders of Meringue.com on demutualization, because being a new enterprise there will be no accumulated retained profit. If Meringue.com is to be able to attract customers with the lure of a demutualization windfall, then there must be some other source of value, and there is. Internet businesses are valued according to the number and quality of customers they have. In this sense quality is determined by the propensity of a customer to go on visiting the site and to go on spending money there. As long-term contracts, life insurance policies should be a uniquely good way to ensure that customers of Meringue.com maintain a long-term relationship. Equitable Life offers immediate valuations of its products to individual policyholders through a secure Web site; this is to encourage regular contact by policyholders. (Poor execution means that this site is useful to only those policyholders with nothing better to do in working hours.) Meringue.com will use this and other tactics to build strong customer relationships by creating a reason for customers to use the Meringue.com Web site.

Meringue.com will be valuable because of the value of its portfolio of long-term relationships with financial services customers. From the policyholder's point of view, Meringue.com will crystallize such value and hand it to the policyholder. From the point of view of an acquirer (e.g. on demutualization) the value will be justified for four reasons: access to a customer base with a proven desire to buy retail financial products over the Internet; ownership of leading-edge Internet-based financial service technology; brand name; and first-mover advantage.

What value does the market place on each customer of an Internet business?

One of the most widely used methods of valuing Internet companies at present is by means of per-customer based ratios. We believe that while these may be superseded by other valuation techniques in the long term, right now this approach is one of the very few viable valuation techniques for Internet businesses.[4]

Non-financial Internet companies have been valued in the UK at between about £1400 and £2000 per customer. Internet financial service firms, however, attract higher valuations. For instance, comdirect is a telephone bank and Internet broker, which Commerzbank reportedly believes might be worth €8.7bn to €9.2bn (£5.5bn to £5.8bn) if listed. This implies market value per customer of the order of €46 000 (£29 000). However, in the USA Internet brokers are valued in the region of $12 500 (£7700) per customer. The existing listed German Internet broker ConSors Discount Broker has a market cap./customer value of over €33 000, which is remarkably high compared to its US peers, but still far below €46 000.

At this early stage, assuming a reasonable uptake of customers, we will use a value per customer of £5000.

First movers can build barriers to entry: brand, technology

What is to stop someone else from implementing the idea behind Meringue.com first? Very little, but whoever is first will be well positioned to stay ahead of the second entrant. Amazon.com, Direct Line, Standard Life Bank and others have demonstrated this effect in their own markets. For the first mover to erect barriers to entry it must obey three rules:

1. To *maintain leadership in the application and development of technology to serve its customer base.* For example, in 1995 anyone could have built an Internet brokerage from scratch. But by 1999 the level of technological expertise in this market is such that building the technology from scratch is much harder. For instance, the leaders (E*Trade, Schwab, Datek, Ameritrade, DLJ Direct) have had to develop techniques for dealing with larger numbers of simultaneous real-time transactions than anyone else has previously needed. This technical leadership has proved a most effective barrier to entry in the Internet stockbroking market recently.

2. To *build its brand.* It is easier for the first in a market to build its brand, other things equal, than for the number two.

3. To *build the right alliances.* The first into a new market similarly has an advantage in choosing with whom to build alliances.

The first-mover advantages are not guaranteed, but by being first in, Meringue will be more valuable than the followers.

Life insurance can be very profitable

Life insurance can be a very profitable business. It has two special characteristics. First, customers commit to providing a long-term stream of revenue. For tax reasons, the shortest endowment policy sold in the UK is usually a ten-year policy, and 25-year policies are not unusual. Few other businesses have such long-term contracts with customers. Second, capital spending can be funded out of revenue streams. In order to make the most of these features of life insurance, policies need to be sold and the operations and investments of the firm need to be well managed.

One of the biggest brakes on profitability in the life insurance business is cost. In life insurance the two greatest areas of cost are sales costs and operations and technology costs (we believe that operations and technology are best regarded as a single cost category, as in modern financial services operations is utterly dependent on technology). A mutual life office that is generally considered to be among the best managed of UK life insurers charges policyholders 41.67% of the first year's premium to meet the cost of setting up the policy, and 4.8% annually thereafter.[5] Meringue will operate at much lower cost by using the Internet for all sales and policy maintenance. Egg has shown that an Internet-only retail financial service is feasible. Like Egg, Meringue.com will also offer only one product initially, which will increase economies of scale in all operations by eliminating variety. (This was Henry Ford's rationale for offering only black paintwork on the Model T.)

Sell only 'plain vanilla' life policies at first, then other products

Meringue.com will start with a simple product with few options aimed at only the majority of consumers. This will enable business processes to be kept as simple as possible, thereby minimizing costs and maximizing returns; similarly, this will also enable marketing to be highly focused. As competition increases, it will be necessary to add products, and as the customer base grows, so there will be greater opportunity to cross-sell other products to policyholders. The term 'life insurance product' covers a variety of particular possible products, and at this stage it has not been resolved exactly which product should be used as the 'plain vanilla' launch product. The exact product will be determined by consultation with insurance industry experts and further market research, but something like a whole of life with profits endowment policy might be a candidate product. It might also be helpful if the risk of investment performance could be passed on entirely to the policyholder, perhaps by investing 100% of the investment element in an index-tracker fund.

In selling life insurance policies, its first of many retail financial products, to customers Meringue.com will use advanced database technology and marketing techniques to learn as much as possible about what other products to sell next. The retail financial services industry is good at talking about cross-selling of financial products, but the poor results of attempts at cross-selling so far suggest that either the implementation has been poor or customers just do not want as much cross-selling as the industry plans to offer. (Just two of many examples of how unsuccessful cross-selling has been in the UK are provided by NatWest. First, it bought Gartmore, the fund manager, in order to cross-sell Gartmore products to NatWest customers. This has been so unsuccessful that NatWest is now trying to sell Gartmore. Second, when NatWest tried to use the cross-selling argument as justification for its bid for Legal & General, its shareholders revolted, the CEO was dismissed, and one of the Scottish banks made a takeover bid that was very well received by everyone except the NatWest management and unions.) Meringue.com must plan carefully to make cross-selling a success. This will mean executing well, and identifying and matching potential cross-selling customers and products precisely.

Good retail financial brands are rare, Meringue is a way to build one

Financial institutions generally have a poor image with the UK consumer; a survey around 1996 showed that the average consumer would trust a well known non-bank retail brand with his money more than he would trust his own bank. The supermarkets have exploited exactly this fact in setting up their own banks to the detriment of the established high street banks. Meringue.com has an opportunity to build a better brand than its competitors by justifying the trust that the consumer wants to put in a financial services organization but is reluctant to put in his bank or traditional insurance company.

The life insurance industry discloses very little about its costs structure to clients. Yet almost two-thirds of the UK population believe that insurance advisers should not be paid commission.[6] The owners of mutual life companies, the with-profits policyholders, cannot tell from the report and accounts whether poor returns now are a result of poor management, a bad market, poor investment strategy or sound investment for the future.[7] However, it seems that customers would like to know much more about the cost structure of the industry, especially as it affects their policies' values.[8] The US technology company Cisco has management systems that report P&L daily. Meringue.com might disclose monthly, weekly, or even a daily P&L and balance sheet, or other financial information, in order to be as transparent as possible, thereby building a brand reputation for transparency and openness in an industry where neither is normal.

Further information required

The general idea for Meringue.com as set out in this document has lacunae in four places – marketing, IT, legal, actuarial. In two of these areas, IT and marketing, most of the specialist advice needed during the feasibility study stage can be obtained at no cost. In the other two areas, legal and actuarial opinion, one would normally expect to incur substantial costs in feasibility studies, but as recently many professional firms have been prepared to take equity in proposed ventures in lieu of fees, it may be possible to avoid excessive costs in these areas also.

Legal opinion on regulatory and legal feasibility

Life insurance is heavily regulated in most states, and the life insurance industry's lobbying power has historically been so strong as to be able to bring about changes to government decisions. (This is nothing new. In 1864 Gladstone 'horrified by the low morals and high prices of the commercial insurance industry, passed legislation allowing the Post Office to sell life insurance. The life companies . . . lobbied successfully for its remit to be limited to assurances worth between £20 and £100. This was high enough to prevent its damaging life companies, and ensured the long-term failure of the Post Office scheme.' Dominic Hobson, *The National Wealth*, 1999.)

Key questions for expert legal opinion are:

- What rules govern setting up a mutual life company? How explicit can the promise to demutualize be?

- EU law: What is the best jurisdiction in which to set up Meringue.com within the EU? How common is the Common Market for selling life insurance – if based in the UK, would Meringue.com have the right to sell throughout the EU or EEA (European Economic Area)?

- What is the best corporate structure? E.g. mutual life insurance company, Italian community bank, friendly society?

- What opportunities and problems are posed by the two European directives on liberalizing the insurance market?

- What are the options for investors who have invested in a mutual to harvest their investment? Options for the policyholder-investor and for the early-stage financial backers?

- Given existing legislation, how can life policies be sold direct to investors on the Internet? (In particular, what are the legal constraints on business processes, what records must be kept, and will digital signatures be valid for policy sales and direct debit bank mandates?)

- What are the rules concerning demutualization as they affect the Meringue.com idea? In the UK and the other EU countries?

Actuarial consulting so that the model will be profitable

Life insurance is more complex than an ordinary business undertaking for a number of reasons, listed below. Expert advice from an experienced life insurance actuary will be needed to ensure a proper business appreciation is made and such advice should cover, *inter alia*:

- life insurance companies in the UK must retain an Appointed Actuary. He is responsible for reporting liabilities to the UK regulator, and must certify the adequacy of the long-term assets against long-term liabilities, and that the business sold in the previous year was sold on adequate terms;

- the sound management of a life company depends on accurate modelling of mortality rates. Any difference between the mortality assumed by the life industry's standard mortality rates and the actual mortality rates in the Internet user population must be identified and adjustments made;

- investment funds such as life and pension funds can draw cash for investment from deposit or premium income. The desirability of taking this approach to funding compared to alternatives such as borrowing or issuing debt depends on the details of each situation. To what extent can Meringue.com be self-funding?

- the regulations governing capital adequacy for running a life company, especially for asset and liability matching over the long term, are complex.

Expert opinion on technology feasibility and requirements

We have been in touch with two small technology firms and asked the following questions:

- In general, how feasible is it to build from scratch a life insurance site and database that is scalable to avoid performance problems caused by 100 times as many hits as planned?

- What are the options for buy/build/outsource, etc.? What are the major advantages/disadvantages of each?

- What are the high-level planning steps, with costs, required to get to a point at which the IT and Web site can start to be built? What would the approximate cost of something like this be? How many IT people, doing what, would be needed?

We told the technologists to assume that the main business processes are:

1. Customer visits site and can (a) browse/download product information; (b) get on-line quote; (c) buy life insurance.

2. Proposal based on quote is emailed to potential customer for them to print out. Can also be snail-mailed at potential customer's request.

3. Completed proposal received from customer by post (email only if digital signatures are legal by then). Wherever possible check boxes are used to speed automatic data entry, but assume 25% of forms need manual keying of data.

4. Decision point: accept/reject the policy proposal. (From rules + data from completed proposal.)

5. Standard form letter to potential customer's doctor sent out snail mail.

6. Doctor's reply received, same data entry approach as per (3).

7. Decision point: accept/reject.

8. Direct debit initiated, individual client sub a/c set up.

9. Normal fund management procedures from here onwards, and clients can log on to Web site whenever they wish to check performance. Regular emails to inform customers of value of fund.

10. Servicing. Customers must be able to notify changes of address, and request cancellations or sales of policies by logging on to the Web site.

Both technology firms believe that building the right site is entirely feasible. One suggests hiring programmers who have worked in a traditional life company for a few days to be interrogated on low-level programming issues specific to the life insurance industry. This up-front cost should result in cost savings and improved service quality later on in the project.

Some miscellaneous points to be remembered when considering the technology issues:

■ it took Direct Line 18 months to plan its Web site (*Insurance Times*, 2/4/99);

■ scalability is vital;

■ a delay of greater than one second is undesirable in human–computer interactions, and a delay of more than ten seconds will lose many Web site visitors.

A high-level 'strawman' marketing plan

Marketing is vital in any consumer retail venture. However, it is also expensive and in the UK Internet sales channel, marketing is far from an exact science. There is thus a great risk of spending money ineffectively on marketing. However, the novelty of the idea together with the stir that it will cause in the general and financial press, the insurance industry, government and regulators can be used to ensure that Meringue.com gets a high profile in the consumer's mind, provided that the PR is sensitively handled. Meringue.com will also exploit technology to log the email address and salient details of visitors to the site in order to keep their awareness of Meringue.com's products and value proposition by subsequent regular email shots.

Risks

The product – 'Life insurance is sold, not bought'

It is an old life insurance industry saying that 'Life insurance is sold, not bought', meaning that unless put under some sort of marketing pressure, people do not buy life insurance. People buy motor insurance because they have to by law; they buy building insurance because they are required to by the terms of their mortgages; and they buy household contents insurance because they are willing to face the risk that their house will be burgled. But, in general, people are not willing to face the risk that they will die before what they consider to be their appointed time. Added to this, in theory, today's consumer has no need for endowment life policies at all: a more transparent and cheaper substitute is a package of 'death-only' life insurance and pure savings product (such as index tracking or other collective savings products).

However, we believe that the carpetbagger is a special consumer who will ignore these reasons not to buy life insurance from Meringue.com. The evidence is that a large number of carpetbaggers exist, and that they will buy savings products with poor returns in exchange for the chance of a demutualization windfall. Secondly, although the argument that traditional life insurance is obsolete as a product is theoretically sound, there are two major reasons why life insurance is expected to persist as a significant retail financial product. First, it is arguable that the pricing and return on life investment is so opaque that it is all but impossible for ordinary consumers to realize what bad value these policies are. Opaque means that the NPV (Net Present Value) of an investment is not readily discernible by the customer. (And opacity is a feature of long-term savings products in general, not just life insurance. For example, were UK pensions less opaque the average customer would have seen so much value eroded by recent changes to the treatment of ACT (Advance Corporation Tax) and FID (Foreign Income/Dividends) that there would have been a mass protest, but in the event the consumer smiled on in blissful ignorance as the UK government ram-raided his pension before his eyes.) Meringue.com will be different and will actually provide good value and totally transparent costs and return calculations. Second, despite recent image problems in the UK, life insurance is still assumed by many consumers to be a good savings vehicle. And considering that the average consumer will say that they buy lottery tickets as an investment, it is probably not misguided to think of life insurance as a good investment for the average consumer.

Implementation – the 'Egg risk'

Successful Internet companies face a particularly hard kind of technology implementation risk, which we call the 'Egg risk'. If an Internet-based service takes off in the mind of the consumer, the Web sites and systems behind it can face demand from user numbers far greater than the best case plan allowed for. Egg is an example of a company that suffered this problem not once, but twice, and one assumes that at least on the second occasion they had had some experience of the problem. Egg was overwhelmed by the number of people trying to open an account when it was launched at the beginning of 1999, but was again overwhelmed with the numbers trying to apply for its credit card when launched in September 1999. On both occasions the Internet site failed, the telephone call centre failed, and the database failed to cope with the volume of demand. At first Egg looked as if it had managed to create the best financial services brand in the UK; now there may be some that in the minds of the most valuable consumers it is just another British retail bank with ordinary managers and staff who, if they care about the customer are powerless to override systems. For instance, some transactions vanish without trace; the systems have been set up so that all existing customers who have chosen certain passwords for their Egg bank accounts are automatically rejected for Egg credit cards; and Egg advertises itself as a 24-hour bank, but in one recent survey Egg's systems were unavailable to customers 75% of the time. Cash takes eight working days to clear in Egg, and staff agree this is too long but seem powerless to change the system. The point is that Meringue.com faces a serious risk that if it is successful much beyond the best case for which planning is done, then its systems may be unable to cope, with disastrous consequences for Meringue's reputation and franchise. If Egg has these kinds of problems, then such problems are likely to be non-trivial. In other words, the problems of unanticipated success cannot be left unanalyzed as 'problems it would be nice to have' but rather must be part of the business planning *ab initio*.

Meringue can manage the risk of these problems in several ways. From the very beginning, the technical architecture should have massive scalability as the first principle. The products and processes should be kept very simple with a minimum of variety, in order to keep the IT as simple and scalable as possible. Thorough testing should be conducted at every stage – especially stress/volume testing, and performance testing. Partnership with a major IT supplier experienced in managing ultra-high capacity retail Web sites should be explored, to see if their size or expertise could be the basis of managing the Egg risk. Possible partners might include Cisco, HP, IBM, Oracle or Sun.

Capital adequacy and investment performance risk

One of the problems faced by a number of life companies has been underperformance of investment funds. There will be ways in which Meringue.com can avoid this risk. For instance, suppose that the product selected for Meringue.com's launch was something like an index tracking with profit life policy where the investment content was explicitly advertised as accruing in a collective investment vehicle; this means that after deduction of fees, all money will be invested in unit trusts or other collective schemes. Then the investment performance risk is passed on to the customer and not retained by the society. This leaves the risk to the with-profits fund that the mortality of policyholders does not match the mortality rate projected by Meringue.com for policyholders. However, this mortality model risk will be laid off by reinsurance.

Difficulties building an insurance or retail financial services brand

Financial institutions generally have a poor image with the consumer. This is particularly so after the pension and mortgage mis-selling of the 1980s, although the effects of that on the reputations of life companies are now beginning to wear off. In the UK, the average consumer trusts their supermarket more in matters of personal finance than they trust their bank or building society, and Bank of Scotland research shows that 'the traditional insurance moniker [doesn't] create a positive impression on the typical customer'.

Competition. There is no shortage of attempts to build new retail financial service brands, many backed by substantial capital. In the US, Schwab is a notable success, and in the UK, Egg, Virgin and Direct Line have succeeded. The section on competition, below, looks at some of these firms in more detail.

Anti-demutualization regulation

The present socialist government in the UK is instinctively against demutualization and has introduced new legislation making it harder to demutualize. The most significant change is that the quorum for a vote on demutualization has been raised from 20% of membership to 50%. While government interference in an industry should never be completely discounted, we believe that the risk to Meringue.com from anti-demutualization legislation will be minimal because the whole membership of the enterprise will have been recruited in a marketing campaign in which demutualization will feature prominently.

The product and the market

Size of the market

Market facts

In Egg's first year it attracted 15m new customers. The UK's population is 58m, so more than one person in four opened an Egg account.

In the UK in 1997, 3 931 000 new life policies were written, totalling £1.3 bn of premia for the year. The UK life insurance market has been growing since 1995.

In 1997 the average annual premium for new yearly premium policies was £343; the average over the five years to 1999 was £327.[9] (For many life companies, the minimum contribution to a life policy is £35 p.c.m., or £420 p.a.)

The Britannia and the Woolwich Building Societies believe that an additional 7000 and 40 000 potential customers respectively were attracted by the potential for demutualization.

In October 1999 the Norwich & Peterborough Building Society had so many applications to open Internet banking accounts that there had built up a three-week backlog of applications. A spokesman declined to estimate the volume of Internet accounts being opened (personal research).

In June 1997 the Nationwide Building Society, then Britain's largest still-mutual building society, was receiving 25 000 applications per day from carpetbaggers. It responded by closing to new business (*Independent*, 17 October 1997). However, before it closed to new business it raised the minimum amount required to open a new account, first to £500 then to £1000.

In May 1999 Scottish Widows reported that it had extra staff in over a weekend to cope with a surge in applicants for savings products from carpetbaggers, but it refused to say how many extra applicants beyond normal it had had on the grounds of commercial confidentiality (*Independent*, 18 May 1999).

Having to pledge away demutualization windfalls in advance of opening a new account does not stop large numbers of carpetbaggers (*Telegraph*, 7 August 1998). In the year from November 1997, when it required all new members to assign any future windfall to charity, the Nationwide still received 300 000 new savers (*Independent*, 6 November 1998).

In April 1996 the Birmingham Midshires Building Society was taking about 1500 new applications for membership per day, most of which it believed were carpetbaggers (*Retail Banker International*, 24 April 1996).

In 1998 Standard Life raised the minimum monthly premium for its standard with profits life insurance policy to £50 per month in response to the large numbers of carpetbaggers taking out these policies (*Irish Times*, 20 August 1999).

UK savers are opening accounts in large numbers with the remaining Irish mutual building societies in the hope of carpetbagging (personal research, August 1999).

Half the UK population has less than £750 in liquid savings (i.e. cash, bank and building society accounts, equities, bonds, investment trusts, PEPs and TESSAs). In 1996 10% of households were classed as having no wealth. The average liquid savings is £7136. The bottom 30% have less than £100 saved. The average savings among the richest 10% of the UK's population is £22 139, but half of this top 10% have only £6500 in easily liquidisable savings ('Household Savings in the UK', Institute of Fiscal Studies).

The Meringue.com financial model and cashflow model assumes that 20 000 people will buy Meringue.com life policies in the first year of operation, paying an average of £180 in annual premia. We believe that this is feasible given the combination of a suspected demutualization and a good Internet play, because both of these ideas have proved to have significant momentum recently. This would give a half percent market share.

We believe that £180 in annual premia is a reasonable planning figure for the following reasons:

- in 1997 the average annual premium for new yearly premium policies was £343; in the five years to 1997 the figure was £327;

- £180 is an easily manageable sum for the richest 70% of the UK population to save (the mean liquid wealth of the 7th richest decile of the UK is £5140);

- £180 should be a manageable sum for most of the population over the age of 21. The mean financial wealth of the 22–29 age group in the UK is £1746. A £180 saving means using just over a tenth of this figure.

20 000 customers would be only half the number of people as tried to carpetbag the Woolwich Building Society, and less than tried to carpetbag the Nationwide each day at the peak of the Nationwide carpetbagging fashion. It would be almost three times as many as the Britannia says tried to carpetbag the Britannia. We believe that 20 000 is a good planning figure rather than a number closer to 7000 for four reasons.

1. We believe that as Woolwich was a larger building society operating in a wealthier area than the Britannia and had more branches, it was more accessible to carpetbaggers. Meringue.com will be accessible to anyone with the Internet. (While many people in the UK still do not have the Internet, we believe that the Internet usage among carpetbaggers is high.) The Woolwich had 97% more branches than the Britannia (394 to 200). The Woolwich's home territory of London and the South East is richer and probably also more densely populated by carpetbaggers than the Britannia's home territory of Staffordshire. The Woolwich had 2.57m members prior to its flotation in 1997, 133% more than the Britannia's 1.1m in the same year.

2. Woolwich's management supported the idea of demutualization, whereas Britannia's has always opposed the idea.

3. All other building societies for whom data is available report a far stronger carpetbagging effect than Britannia, and it may well be that for its own reasons Britannia has chosen to play down the number of carpetbaggers.

4. The Egg experience suggests that large numbers of new customers will sign up to a well designed Internet financial service.

What is the product?

The traditional, or endowment, life insurance policy is a hybrid product offering protection (insurance against death) and savings (annual and terminal bonuses, i.e. a lump sum at the end of the policy even if the holder does not die). However, modern retail finance offers both these elementary products separately: term insurance for insurance against death without any savings element, and a unit trust or other collective investment vehicle as a low-risk savings vehicle. There thus might appear to be little benefit for consumers in continuing to buy traditional endowment life policies. But the fact is that consumers do buy the product, and overall the life insurance market is a growing market (we have not yet found data that splits out sales trends of endowment policies from other kinds of life policy). Part of the explanation probably lies in the financial ignorance of consumers and the inertia of their preferences, and part in the opacity of the product's financial performance. However, there are several other features of the product in addition to savings and protection that may be influencing consumer behaviour:

■ an option on demutualization – i.e. carpetbagging;

■ a recognized product – consumers have had many generations to become familiar with the product, whereas alternatives to the savings element of life insurance policies such as unit trusts, investment trusts, OEICs, PEPs, TESSAs, ISAs, etc. have been ephemeral in comparison. This means that as a class of product life insurance may be more trusted than many other kinds of savings product;

■ recognized brands – life insurance brands may have traditionally been stronger than competing savings product brands;

■ loan collateral – life policies are assets which their owners can pledge as security, and which have a less volatile value than most competing savings products.

In the USA, life insurance is the fourth biggest sector of the insurance market. Motor insurance is the biggest, then health, then home, then life. We believe that the ranking in the UK and Europe is similar. However, endowment life insurance is a hybrid product, because it has many characteristics of an investment rather than being purely an insurance product. In this way it is different from motor, health and home insurance. It is probably best categorized as a long-term savings product, along with pensions, and school fees plans.

Channels

In 1997 a survey (FMS, Ireland) found that 62% of UK insurance companies plan to investigate the Internet as a life insurance distribution channel. One must assume that by now the figure is 100%.

Potential customers are ripe for the picking, but the insurance industry is still ambivalent about conflicts between the Internet and broker/agent distribution structure.
                                    Forrester Research, *Making Open Finance Pay.*

Traditional channels in the UK life industry and their 1995 share of new life premia:

■ independent intermediaries/IFAs – 35%

■ appointed representatives – 62%

■ direct – 3%

The channels in Germany reveal similar statistics, although in Germany channels are not categorized by market researchers in exactly the same way as in the UK. In Germany direct channels also account for 3% of business.

The term 'direct' includes telephone, direct mail and the Internet. By contrast with the 3% share of life policies sold direct in 1995, about 25% of motor policies were sold direct. This indicates that massive growth in the direct sale of life policies should be possible, and indeed the direct sales are in fact growing.

The broker distribution channel is already under severe pressure. This is attributed to three sources: increased regulatory costs; competition from low-cost, direct channels; and a poor public perception of IFAs and retail insurance brokers. This presents an opportunity for a new entrant with lower costs to win more market share by forcing a significant part of the IFA channel out of business. This is not the sort of thing that a new entrant on the small scale of Meringue.com could expect to achieve early on, but the demise of IFAs as a mainstream distribution channel for retail financial products is a probable scenario given the high costs of the IFA channel and the low cost of an Internet channel. In the short term the complexity of retail financial services products and the naïvety of the average customer will probably ensure the survival of the IFA channel, but the potential for future Internet and IT developments to educate the average customer about finance should not be underestimated, nor should the potential for Internet to evolve to a level where it can match the quality of service offered by IFAs.

Evidence that the Internet may be capable of delivering a complex service better than IFAs and also of providing the educational or quasi-educational function of IFAs comes from two areas. First, sites such as Clearstation in the USA and Interactive Investor in the UK show that the Internet can be used to deliver effective education to retail investors, and Quicken has already shown that a software package can change spending behaviour in large numbers of individuals. Second, many traditional stockbrokers felt that the Internet would be unable to match the quality of service of traditional brokers, but E*Trade and others have proved the traditional stockbrokers mistaken. If the Internet-delivered financial services can destroy the IFA channel, or at least decimate it, then a very large number of relationships with retail financial service customers will be up for grabs, and Meringue.com should be poised to claim the most attractive of these relationships for itself.

> *The Insurance Times* (2/9/99) stated that a third of [insurance] brokers are close to bankruptcy, and the lagging third of brokerage firms generate 24p of sales per £1 invested, against an average of 73p.

Now if one assumes that the profit margin for a broker is one third (comments from experts in this area are welcome), and if the bottom third of UK insurance brokers generate 24p of sales for every £1 invested, then this implies an 8% return on capital for those brokers. In 1997 the life insurance sector of the London stock exchange gave a return of 14% above the market's average return.[10] Further assume that the average return on the market is 8%, and the lagging third of brokers would need 92% profit margins on sales to compete with the average return for the life industry. Although this argument conflates 1997 and 1999 data, and ignores the differences between a broker's business and the life industry as a whole because the data required to do otherwise is unavailable, the data nonetheless is highly likely to be indicative of the precariousness of the insurance broker as a channel. The point is that with lower costs and higher margins, Meringue.com should be able to compete successfully against at least one third of all UK insurance brokers.

In the USA AnnuityNet.com has demonstrated the feasibility of using the Internet as a channel in the annuity market, which is a business closely related to life insurance. AnnuityNet.com is a new entrant to the annuity business in the USA. Although annuities are different from life insurance, they are similar in that they are long-term financial products and have opaque payoff structures more complex than the average customer really understands. Also, like life insurance in the UK, but for different reasons, the annuity business in the USA has suffered an image problem recently. The success of AnnuityNet.com in the USA suggests that a direct channel strategy using the Internet is a viable way to sell and distribute long-term financial products.

AnnuityNet.com was set up to focus on a channel strategy, and specifically on the assumption that the Internet is the ideal distribution channel for annuity products in the USA. The company intends to use the Internet as a sales and service channel, particularly to cut costs and the opaqueness of costs, and thereby make annuities as attractive and accessible as mutual funds.

Market concentration

In the UK the life insurance industry is one of the least concentrated. The market share of the top five companies in the UK in 1995 was 2.9% compared with 3.9% in the USA, 5.7% in France and 4.1% in Germany. (Moody's)

It is generally held that for a newcomer a fragmented market is easier to enter than a concentrated market. If this applies to the life insurance business, then the UK is one of the most attractive Western G7 markets for a new entrant.

Regulation of the market

The life insurance industry is heavily regulated. Expert advice will be required to understand properly the regulatory issues facing Meringue.com. For this reason we propose that one of the next things to do is to get such advice from solicitors.

The regulator for the industry used to be the UK Department of Trade and Industry. However, life products and life offices are now regulated by the Personal Investment Authority. EC law means that it may soon be possible for new entrants to choose their regulatory jurisdiction, although at this stage we think it is unlikely that there would be much advantage to Meringue.com in an EC regulatory domicile other than the UK.

Who buys life insurance, and why?

A US survey found that the following factors affect the image of the life insurance industry. Anecdotal evidence suggests that the UK is little different, and if so, it is easy to see why the industry has the poor reputation it currently suffers. US customers say that they want:

- no high-pressure sales tactics;
- policies that match needs;
- regular, informative communication;
- sensitive handling of transactions;
- clear advice and information;
- clear, easily understood policies.

Why hasn't this been done before?

If Meringue.com is the goldmine it appears to be, then why hasn't it been done before? This is the classic question to pose to any new idea. It may be that traditional life offices have not acted along the lines of Meringue for a combination of natural inertia and fear of channel cannibalization.

> Major insurance carriers have, generally, not embraced the Internet because they do not want to alienate their agents, the most important insurance sales channel. In addition, many policy types are simply too complex for Internet-based selling.
>
> *Meridian Research, Internet-Based Insurance*

Competition

In this section we list life insurance and related companies that either pose an immediate competitive threat to Meringue.com or have demonstrated in the market a strategy that has significant lessons for Meringue.com.

Standard Life Bank – probably the biggest risk to Meringue

Standard Life is not yet selling life insurance direct over the Internet, but it must be assumed that it is investigating the idea. It is likely that the sales over the Internet of other products, such as mortgages, savings accounts, ISAs and PHI over the Internet will be more attractive to Standard Life than selling life insurance because these represent larger and faster growing markets than life insurance. However, if Standard Life did sell life insurance over the Internet, any rumour or suspicion among retail investors that Standard Life might demutualize would probably cause it to dominate Meringue.com's franchise at least in the short term. This is probably the biggest risk facing Meringue.com. Were Standard Life to sell policies over the Internet and at the same time to become known as a hot carpetbagging bet, then it would be likely that Standard Life would take most sales away from Meringue.com, although in so doing it would also prove that being a carpetbaggers' target sells life policies over the Internet. Standard Life has already admitted that being a carpetbaggers' target sells more policies through ordinary channels, because in 1998 it raised its minimum premium to £50 per month for ordinary with profits life insurance policies in direct response to increased demand from carpetbaggers. A number of responses would be open to Meringue.com if Standard Life competed directly with Meringue.com and made itself a demutualization target. Meringue.com could:

- wait out the demutualization of Standard Life, after which Meringue.com would be the number one demutualization target once more;
- sell itself through a trade sale to a Standard Life competitor lagging in Internet distribution capability;
- leverage off the interest generated by the Standard Life demutualization, and try to demutualize faster and better.

Prudential/Egg

In Egg's first year it attracted 15m new customers. Industry opinion is that there are a number of reasons for the enormous success that Egg has had in attracting new business:

- Egg has offered loss-leading rates of interest on deposits;
- the public knows that Egg has the full backing of Prudential;
- Egg's launch was heavily promoted by advertising.

While Egg/Prudential cannot offer the incentive of potential demutualization to prospective customers, they have the capital, the management and the experience in Internet-delivered financial services to pose a serious threat to Meringue.com, if they thought Meringue.com posed a serious threat to Egg's franchise.

Egg has experienced problems maintaining its quality of service to customers in the face of far greater success than was anticipated or planned for. This may be damaging the Egg brand. Whereas Egg offers services that are likely to cause complex relationships with customers, Meringue's launch products will be far simpler to manage from the point of view of financial and risk management, operations and technology.

Comparison of complexity of products – finance, risk, operations and technology points of view

Egg	Meringue.com
Manual processing for setting up accounts.	Manual processing for setting up policies.
Customer can make deposits at any time.	Premia are paid by direct debit (DD) at predetermined times.
Deposits can be made by DD, by paying in at a third party branch, or by post.	No other deposits accepted.
Customers can withdraw money to one of two named accounts.	Payment to customer is a rarer event than for Egg – death, early cancellation and maturity are the only events triggering a payment.
In practice, Egg accounts are demand accounts.	No demand accounts.
Customers can elect to have an Internet-only service instead of also using the call centre.	From the start the service will be Internet only. (However, a small call centre will probably be necessary.)

Direct Line

Direct Line pioneered the telephone call centre as a direct channel for motor insurance policies, and successfully expanded into other insurance markets. At present industry opinion is that it suffers from having old technology compared with newer competitors such as Standard Life Bank and Virgin Direct, but Direct Line still has significant first-mover advantages, the most important of which is that it has a good brand. Direct Line shows that innovation in technology is as reliable a way to create new value in insurance as innovation in sales and product was for Mark Weinberg.

AnnuityNet.com (USA)

AnnuityNet.com was set up on the assumption that the Internet is the ideal distribution channel for annuity products in the USA. Shane Chalke is president and CEO. The company intends to use the Internet as a sales and service channel, particularly to cut costs and the opaqueness of costs, and thereby make annuities as attractive and accessible as mutual funds. Part of AnnuityNet's strategy is to simplify the product, avoid jargon, and allow informed customers to self-select. AnnuityNet's typical customer is a mid-career professional whose net worth has just turned positive but is relatively low, and who has a high annual income in the $100K–$125K range.

The propensity to buy without being sold is probably greater for annuities than for life policies. There are often legal requirements or lifecycle imperatives that drive customers to buy annuities, but these forces are usually absent in the life insurance business.

German direct insurers

After a late start, the German retail financial services industry is embracing the Internet. There is no indication yet that any of these are planning to concentrate on selling life insurance over the Internet, but it must be assumed that they are researching the idea.

The leading German direct insurers are:

- Cosmos Direkt;
- Hannoversche;
- Lebensverischerung;
- Ontos;
- Quelle Lebensversicherung;
- Leben Direkt.

TheMutual.Net (www.themutual.net)

TheMutual.Net is a UK-based Internet portal that uses the bait of 'demutualization' windfalls to attract new subscribers. TheMutual.Net is not in fact a mutual, but has structured its customer benefits so that when the company goes public, and the management have promised that it will, the benefits to customers will resemble those of a mutual company on demutualization. TheMutual.Net is owned by Hague Ltd, and the conversion of units into shares is decided by Hague Ltd, which promises to give away 50% of its equity to registered users on flotation. It allocates 1000 units to new members on signing up, and a further 100 units for each member joining as a result of a referral from the existing member. It intends to issue 2.1 billion units on a first-come first-served basis, each unit to be convertible into a share.

All of TheMutual's services are free to users. According to TheMutual's Web site, 'The value of an Internet portal lies in its active user base . . . The Dresdner Kleinwort Benson report (April 1999) suggests that each user will add £1400 to the value of the company. This analysis has been supported by the market valuation of Freeserve which implies a per customer value in excess of £2000.' The recent drop in Freeserve's price may raise a question of the accuracy of this valuation, but the principle of valuing an Internet business according to the number of users probably needs to be refined only by considering also the quality of the users and the strength of their relationship with the site to remain a valid valuation model.

TheMutual.Net has formed marketing alliances with Lycos, Guardian-Observer newspapers, and Scrum.com, a football news service. As at 30 June 1999, TheMutual.Net expects new user registrations to exceed the current 1500 per week mark.

TheMutual.Net took 115 000 applications for subscription in its first two weeks of service.[11] However, applications to TheMutual.Net cost nothing, whereas life insurance has a monthly premium. Another significant difference between TheMutual.Net and Meringue.com is that TheMutual.Net is not in fact a mutual company, whereas it is proposed that Meringue.com should be. Consequently, the success of TheMutual.Net may not be a reliable indicator of the likely success of the marketing strategy of Meringue.com. However, Meringue.com should be able to watch TheMutual.Net and learn from its progress enough to identify critical marketing issues.

Although it is not currently a financial service provider, TheMutual.Net is likely to be considering financial services as a possible product because this is an obvious move. However, we think it unlikely that life insurance is high on its list of things to do for the next few years, because for an Internet business that already has a large number of customers there are many retail financial products that are more attractive than life insurance to use for entry into that market.

InsWeb

According to *RedHerring* magazine (8 March 1999), InsWeb is the current market leader in on-line insurance. InsWeb is a Silicon Valley-based company, and operates an on-line insurance in the four biggest insurance market categories – health, motor, home and life.

InsWeb was backed by private and institutional capital, but has gone public (INSW). Hussein A Enan is CEO. For the six months to June 1999 revenues were $8.4m, giving a net loss of $15m. Market capitalization is $560m. The shares were launched at just over $30 in July 1999, and stood down at $17 in mid October. Start-up backers include Softbank ($30m), the leading Japanese Internet investor, Nationwide Insurance, one of America's biggest insurance carriers, AMS Services, a consortium of leading insurance companies led by CNA (CNA), Century Capital, the oldest investment fund specializing in insurance, and Marsh & McLennan (MMC), the largest insurance broker in the world.

The company recently bought Benelytics, an on-line health services and information provider, as part of its health insurance strategy.

It currently has an exclusive relationship with Yahoo! and deals with 60 Web sites that are tied to events that trigger insurance policy purchases, such as buying a car or a home.

InsWeb sends consumers the policy by snail mail and they must complete the transaction off-line.

HealthAxis

Until it merged with its parent in 1999, HealthAxis was a subsidiary of the Provident American Corporation (Nasdaq PAMC). Provident's advisers for the merger were Advest

(NYSE, ADV), and HealthAxis' were BancBoston Robertson Stephens (BKB). Intel was one of the investors in HealthAxis.

HealthAxis is an 'electronic provider of health insurance for individuals', based in the USA. At HealthAxis consumers can buy healthcare insurance policies directly over the Internet. It claims to be the only site offering end-to-end health insurance shopping on-line.

HealthAxis seems to have a marketing alliance with the insurance company Fortis Health (as well as with Provident), and with the administrator Plan Services. It has Internet marketing alliances with Lycos, AOL (America Online), Snap.com and CINET. It also has alliances with Insurance.com, IBM, WellPoint, Ceres, and Ameritas Life Insurance.

Insurance.Com

Insurance.com is a US site that provides the consumer with decision support information about the life insurance industry. It provides all the usual information that one would expect from this kind of site, such as links to vendors, but it also provides a library of lawsuits against insurance companies and advice on selecting policies. We believe that this site illustrates the growth potential for educational sites specific to insurance products, in the way that Clearstation (USA) and Interactive Investor (UK) have shown the potential for Internet sites that provide education about equity investment.

Totalise

Totalise plc is another 'mutual' ISP that uses the lure of 'demutualization' to attract customers. It has a two-tier structure of ordinary and convertible deferred shares. The intention is that 67% of the ordinary shares shall be transferred to the users of Totalise's service. It is intended that Totalise's ordinary shares shall be traded on OFEX.

TradeHall.Com

TradeHall.Com is another quasi-mutual Internet company, also based in the USA. It describes itself as a 'global trading network' and offers loyalty points to customers.

High-level project plan

- Test high-level idea against a range of 'experts' – potential backers, technologists, Internet marketers, life and pensions managers.
- Develop business plan and first cut cashflow forecast.
- Get first legal opinion on feasibility and choice of jurisdiction.
- Get opinion on feasibility from consulting actuary.
- Revise business plan.

- Review strategies and revise plans for: technology, marketing, financing.
- Design, build and test technology.
- Develop marketing.
- Launch.
- Continuous improvement.

Glossary

Endowment	An endowment policy is one which pays out a lump sum in the first of either event: that the person whose life is insured dies or on the expiration of a specified period. These are hybrid products, combining investment plans with life cover.
Non-profit	The sum assured remains fixed throughout the life of the policy.
Sum assured	The lump sum guaranteed by the policy, usually in the event of death, and sometimes irrespective of death.
Term insurance	Guarantees a *sum assured* if the person whose life is insured dies within the period specified. If the person survives, nothing is paid.
Unit-linked	In unit-linked policies, the policyholder can choose the apportionment of the premium between life cover and investment.
Whole-of-life assurance	Pays out a lump sum whether the person whose life is insured dies or not. Such policies can be non-profit, with-profits or unit-linked.
With-profits	An irrevocable bonus is added to the sum assured from time to time during the life of the policy. The bonus originated in surplus profits of life companies, but now there is some expectation of a bonus. Bonuses are usually declared annually.

Endnotes

1 The project name 'Meringue.com' is unrelated to the IT business of the same name in Scandinavia. It is a pure coincidence that the same name was chosen.
2 *Independent*, 22 January 1997, 'Britannia Closes Doors on Carpetbaggers', John Willcock.
3 *Independent*, 16 January 1996, 'Societies Move to Shut Out Speculators', Nic Cicutti.
4 One of the most popular means to value an Internet business to have emerged in the last few years has been valuations derived from customer-based ratios. Rather than accepting this

approach without qualification, we believe that it is worth reflecting on two reasons why this approach to valuation is so popular for Internet firms. Traditionally the financial analyst's valuation tools have required reasonable amounts of historic data. Secondly, many of the valuation techniques used by finance professionals today evolved from the heyday of the physical goods economy, when world trade derived from things that would hurt if they dropped on one's foot. But in the Internet economy, there is still little historical data. Most Internet businesses have not been in existence over a complete economic cycle yet. And much of the value in Internet businesses, even those such as Amazon that trade in the physical goods of the legacy economy, derives from intellectual rather than physical property. It is thus hard to apply many conventional valuation tools to Internet businesses. (Indeed, when the author was in his final year of an MSc in Finance at London Business School in 1998, there was not a single class on how to tackle Internet valuations, so new was the problem to the financial analyst community.) It seems to us that per-customer valuations are used because no better valuation methodologies have yet been discovered, and that is in turn probably the case because there is not yet sufficient historical data.

5 Personal communication from the life office concerned, 9/99.
6 Life Insurance Industry 11/93.
7 This problem was covered in 'Number Crunch', *Financial Times*, 25/9/99, which prompted an above average number of readers to write to its author.
8 E.g. *Money Management*, 4/99.
9 This number differs from the implied average premium in the previous statistic because the two statistics are taken from different insurance industry reports.
10 London Business School, Risk Measurement Service, January–March 1997.
11 Newsbytes News Networks, LLC, 30 July 1999.

Table 1 Acquisition and management expenses of UK life insurance firms

Acquisition expenses (as % of total premia)

	Acquisition expense			Management expense			Acquisition + Management expenses		
	Mutuals	Non-mutuals	Top 50	Mutuals	Non-mutuals	Top 50	Mutuals	Non-mutuals	Top 50
1985	14.9%	12.8%	13.3%	7.9%	9.4%	8.9%	22.8%	22.2%	22.2%
1986	14.8%	12.5%	13.1%	7.6%	8.9%	8.5%	22.4%	21.4%	21.6%
1987	13.2%	12.6%	12.8%	7.0%	9.2%	8.6%	20.2%	21.8%	21.4%
1988	15.5%	15.5%	15.5%	8.1%	9.9%	9.4%	23.6%	25.4%	24.9%
1989	13.2%	13.2%	13.1%	7.6%	8.2%	8.0%	20.8%	21.4%	21.1%
1990	13.1%	13.1%	12.9%	7.2%	8.1%	7.9%	20.3%	21.2%	20.8%
1991	12.6%	12.1%	12.2%	6.7%	8.2%	7.9%	19.3%	20.3%	20.1%
1992	12.2%	10.9%	11.1%	6.0%	7.0%	6.7%	18.2%	17.9%	17.8%
1993	11.9%	10.4%	10.8%	5.9%	8.0%	7.4%	17.8%	18.4%	18.2%
1994	11.4%	10.1%	10.5%	6.8%	8.1%	7.8%	18.2%	18.2%	18.3%
1995	9.4%	9.2%	9.2%	6.9%	8.6%	8.0%	16.3%	17.8%	17.2%

Source: Moody's Special Comment: Consolidation in the UK Life Insurance Industry, 1 June 1997 (© Moody's)

Index